To: Elliston with [handwritten inscription] best wishes

DO IT RIGHT: DO IT NOW!

People - the essential ingredient for success

JOHN A. DEMBITZ

Do It Right: Do It Now!

Published by The Conrad Press in the United Kingdom 2021

Tel: +44(0)1227 472 874
www.theconradpress.com
info@theconradpress.com

ISBN 978-1-913567-71-2

Typesetting and Cover Design by: Charlotte Mouncey, www.bookstyle.co.uk

The Conrad Press logo was designed by Maria Priestley.

Printed and bound in Great Britain by Clays Ltd, Elcograf S.p.A.

CONTENTS

ACKNOWLEDGEMENTS   7

INTRODUCTION   11

1. THE HUMAN CAPITAL EQUATION   16
    PERSONNEL TO HR TO HC   17
    PEOPLE AS ASSETS   20
    THE WHYS   24

2. PASSIONATE ABOUT PASSION   27
    PASSION IN CAREER CHOICE   28
    THE WHYS   30
    PASSION IN WORK   32
    ENTREPRENEURS AND PASSION   35
    AS A 'STRAP LINE'   41

3. FINDING GREAT PEOPLE   46
    PERSONAL NETWORK   46
    KNOW YOUR EXISTING RESOURCE   51
    SUCCESSION PLANNING   54
    THE WHYS   57
    REACHING OUTSIDE   62
    THE NED NONESENSE   65
    MORE WHYS   70
    HELP AVAILABLE   71
      SEARCH   71
      SELECTION   76
      INTERIM   78
      INTERNAL   81

4. KEEPING TALENTED PEOPLE   85
        DAYS OF SLAVERY ARE OVER   85
        WHAT EFFECTS RETENTION?   87
        THE WHYS   90
        LOGIC NOT WORKING   93
        BIRDS OF A FEATHER   94
        CASH   97
        OTHER FACTORS   99
        WHO CARES?   102
        A FINAL RANT-ABUSE OF THE YOUNG   106

5. THE FEEL GOOD INTERVIEW   109
        LISTENING   109
        THE JOB INTERVIEW   110
        APPRAISALS   112
        INTERVIEW ENIRONMENT   114
        STAYING FRESH   116

6: DAY ONE   120
        POSITIVE   120
        NEGATIVE   123
        THE WHYS   128
        HELLO-GOODBYE!   131

7: INSPIRING FROM THE START   132
        'YOUNGISM'   132
        STUCK IN BOREDOM   135
        THE WHYS   138
        RE-REVVING   139

8: THE POSITIVE EXIT   142
        EXs ARE INFLUENCERS   142
        TO DEMONISE OR NOT TO DEMONISE?   143
        BY THE BOOK   146

RESPECT AND COURTESY 148
THE WHYS 148
VALUE-ADDED ON EXIT 153

9: PURSUIT OF Y 156
CHALLENGING THE STATUS QUO 156
SHEEP MENTALITY 157
OUTSIDERS REQUIRED 158
THE WHYS 160
THEORY vs. PRACTICAL 161
CSR IN PRACTICE 165

10: *DO IT RIGHT: DO IT NOW!* 168
INACTIVITY IS NO-ACTIVITY 168
THINK IT, DO IT 171
THE WHYS & DO IT RIGHT: DO IT NOW! 175

11. THE 3 'CS' - COMMUNICATE, COMMUNICATE, COMMUNICATE!
179
THE WHYS 179
PHONE INERTIA 180
WALKING AROUND 181
NO COST 186

12: THE POSITIVE 'NO'! 187
TINY WORD BIG IMPACT 187
CHILDREN NO 187
ADULT NO 189
THE WHYS 190
LEARN EARLY TO SAY NO 191

13: THE NO PAY GAIN 203
DON'T COMPLICATE 205
THE WHYS 206

REAL REWARD 207
THE INVISIBLE LEADER 209

14:. 'PEOPLE - THE ESSENTIAL INGREDIENT FOR SUCCESS.'...
MY CONCLUDING 'BITZ & PIECES! 215
LISTENING 215
LEADING FROM THE FRONT 217
BORED BOARD 220
BUILDING LOYALTY/EXCEEDING EXPECTATIONS 222
RESPECT 224
COMMON SENSE 228
CREATING AN OPEN AND RISK-FREE CULTURE 232
ALIGNING ASPIRATIONS WITH REALITY 233
PURSUIT OF THE BEST, 'NO' TO MEDIOCRITY 235
TRAINING 238
AGEISM AND OTHER 'ISMS'! 245
REVIEW/FEEDBACK 248
PROMOTING EARLY TO CREATE STRETCH 251
FIRING 254
RETAINING REALITY 257
INTERNAL COMMUNICATION 260
TRUST 263

AUTHOR'S BACKGROUND... IN GREATER DETAIL 264

SUMMARY OF *DO IT RIGHT: DO IT NOW!* CHAPTER BY CHAPTER
281

ACKNOWLEDGEMENTS

I am indebted to a vast number of people.

A significant majority are not aware of the important contributions they have made to this book. A significant number will remain nameless, unacknowledged without a corporate identity, in that they have provided me with a wealth of experience of what not to do.

But, there are many to whom I do owe a real debt of gratitude for their support, tolerance, encouragement, and understanding.

I want to start by thanking my partner-in-life, my wife, Alexandra. She was not only always encouraging, was not only always ready to be supportive, but also undertook a lot of the early proof reading and correcting the English of an émigré!

I would like to give special thanks and acknowledgement to Max Landsberg for being amazingly encouraging and pushing me to pursue my writing of *It's the People! What really drives great management and leadership*, the original edition of this re-write. Max read early drafts and provided valuable advice for a novice author. A number of other people helped with the original edition including Belden Menkus for reading drafts and sharing his honest views with me; my amazing mother-in-law, Helen Barnett, who proofread the original manuscript and picked up numerous errors in punctuation and spelling.

In addition I would like to thank very specifically the good guys in my life, the guys from whom I have learnt an awful lot... Charles Handy, and in particular for giving me the opportunity to gain an MBA from London Business School; Brigadier Harry Langstaff, and in particular for opening the door to McKinsey

& Co. Inc. and thereafter for his long ongoing wise council and friendship; Rudolph Agnew; Bruce Fireman; Reg Valin; my brother Alexander Dembitz and the whole team at IDOM; Leo Noé, Carl Whayman, Ian Jones, Simon Harding and the team and Lee Baron; Nick Naismith, Tim Newberry, Charles Trace and the team and Coffee Point; Eric Pillinger, Louise Gulliver and the team at TACK International; Esther Dyson, an incredibly wise, knowledgeable and supportive co-director, Norrie Sinclair, Stephen Kerkow and the team at CVO Group; Robert Appleby, Joe Appleby, Tom Appleby and the team at Titus International; Peter Johnson, Chris Houghton and the team at Park Group; Nick Robeson and Lisa Farmer and the team at Boyden; Neil Hedges, Andrew Boys and the team at Valin Pollen; Daniel Spinath; Patrick Flockhart; my clients all over the world and in particular at Rolls-Royce who provided me with the opportunity to work with them as a sole trader; Dirk Schavemaker, Bernard Meyer and all the advisory board members of Marriott Vacation Club International; and to all the companies I have had the privilege of working with over the past 20+ years in a non-executive capacity including the above and Anstey Horne, Cripps, Confirm, FHO, Winmark and Future Thinking: they have contributed untold volumes to the creation of this book.

I offer my gratitude also for the many excellent articles, in particular in the *Financial Times* and the *Director* magazine, *The Economist*, and numerous other public or private journals, periodicals, and publications from around the world, from which I have gained insights, ideas, quotations and other reference material.

I wish to express my gratitude to my publisher James Essinger, founder and principal, The Conrad Press, for making the re-publication of this book under its new title, *Do it Right: Do it Now! - People the essential ingredient of success,* a reality.

I would like to make special reference to my children, Robert and Sarah, for furnishing some invaluable experiences and for recounting anecdotes of experiences of their friends, many of which have found their way into the pages that follow. And equally my daughter-in-law, Heather, and my son-in-law, Laurent, both of whom have also contributed with valuable anecdotes from their own experiences.

But the most important acknowledgement, the acknowledgement left to the last, goes to my parents, Marianne and Leslie Dembitz, who took the enormously difficult and wrenching decision to emigrate to the UK and start afresh in 1957, to give my brother and myself the opportunity to grow up in a free society. - You Did it Right; You Did it Then! and for that I, my brother and all of our families are eternally grateful!

INTRODUCTION

'Of all the decisions an executive makes, none are as important as the decision about people because they ultimately determine the performance capacity of the organization.'

PETER DRUCKER

This book is aimed at leaders. Actual, and potential leaders. All leaders in all forms of organisations: large corporations or small businesses, entrepreneurial businesses or professionally owned and managed businesses, not for profit entities including charitable organisations, public sector and massive supranational organisations, or any form of endeavour where people come together and work together.

This is a book based on my experiences, and the experiences of others with whom I have worked and interacted, observed or just been aware of through the media, notoriety, literature, anecdotes and case studies.

THIS IS NOT A THEORETICAL BOOK! IT HAS NO AMBITION TO LECTURE, TO SUGGEST THAT THERE IS A RIGHT WAY OF PROVIDING LEADERSHIP... THERE ISN'T. IT'S A BOOK BASED ENTIRELY ON EMPIRICAL EVIDENCE/EXPERIENCE!

I have deliberately endeavoured to make this book pithy. Why? Because I have a real belief in the value of brevity! Because I'm in total harmony with what pithy means – 'Precisely meaningful; forceful and brief'.

From the very beginning, right the way through all the various stages of my career, I have asked 'why?' Throughout this book I shall frequently ask 'why' and attempt to provide a few 'hows'. How to deal with people, how to recruit, how to interview, how to deliver difficult messages, how to motivate and inspire, how to create extraordinary loyalty.

This book is about actions and behaviours to pursue, and actions and behaviours to avoid, based on what, in my experience, seems to have worked, and equally, based on my experience, what definitely did not work and caused pain and anguish!

Within each chapter there are a number of 'whys' always aimed at asking the simple questions that so often get overlooked. Equally, within each chapter, there is a section devoted to *Do it Right: Do it Now!*, very much with the intention of underlining simple steps that can be taken immediately. Steps that just may make sense to you, and that just may have a positive impact in your business environment too. Steps that can materially impact on the motivation and drive of your employees and hence their productivity, initiative, creativity, and potential genius!

The first and most frequently repeated *Do it Right: Do it Now!* is that doing things right is not difficult; often it is just an attitude of the mind. Equally it is not difficult to do them wrong, but the benefit of a little forethought can be substantial.

This is not an A-Z of management concepts and buzz words. Instead I have tried to use ordinary language and wherever possible anecdotes, vignettes, mini cases and real-life examples to help dramatise different situations. I hope I have kept it relevant to everyday life.

There may or there may not be a body of research behind my assertions, assertions that I have based on personal, empirical evidence. Evidence from my some 49 years of working and from putting into practice all of the recommendations whenever and wherever it was possible to do so, from having had the privilege of working with some of the most outstanding organisations in the world, and from having experienced working life in less remarkable organisations too. From having experienced creating a business from scratch with my brother and seeing it grow to over 350 people and $40m of revenue; to working with one of the world's largest and most reputable management consultancies; to being chairman/non-executive director/advisor to hedge fund owned, Private Equity owned, family owned, partnerships, AiM listed businesses; and lots more along the way.

Each chapter will deal with a specific topic. As the chapters progress there will be a gentle transition from the 'why' to the 'how'… although I will continue to ask the 'why' right to the end. You can either cherry pick your way through the pages, or read it cover to cover, front to back, or back to front! You can dip in and out at your leisure.

The chapters commence with the general ('The Human Capital Equation'), get increasingly more specific, and conclude with a series of rapid bite sized sections, my concluding 'bitz and pieces': a veritable potpourri, which when taken together covers many aspects of leadership and management that can have a material impact on the destiny of a business, and the people within it.

What I very much wish to achieve is to touch a nerve within you. A nerve that sparks a shared experience, a nerve that leads to some recognition of behaviour patterns, a nerve that elicits some response.

I would like to believe that I will be able to see people reading this book and nodding in agreement or disagreement, smiling, even laughing at the recognition of a scenario. I would like to believe that people reading this book will say, 'Yes, that's exactly what happened to me,' 'Oh great, so I wasn't alone in having that experience,' 'OMG this is so real, it's exactly what happened to me!'

But above all I hope that it will help to bring about change. Change, in what to me is without doubt the single most important, and probably the most abused, resource within all companies, PEOPLE, and the way people are dealt with. Change by recognising the very fact that getting it right is really not that difficult. Change by those who are today in positions of authority, leadership, and have the power to get change implemented, recognising the pain they went through when they started their careers and when they were building their careers.

The ultimate objective is to stimulate actions. Actions that will improve people's working environment and their working lives, actions that will release energies and creativity that in turn will add value to society and in a very real sense help to build 'value,' however defined.

Jack Welch, the retired Chairman and CEO of GE described himself as 'the world's best paid human-resource director' given that he believed in, and practised, being very close to his top people and ensuring that in turn they were close to their top people, and so on cascading throughout that giant corporation. It had a profound impact on the culture of that company. 'Judging who will work best in which slot is one of the key tasks of leadership.'
THE ECONOMIST: SURVEY OF CORPORATE LEADERSHIP, OCTOBER 25TH 2004

As the title of this book states... *Do it Right: Do it Now!* is frankly not difficult. It takes an attitude of mind. And Doing it Right - Doing it Now is aimed at all levels through organisations where one person is in control of the working lives/working environment of a number of others!

This book was originally written in a pre-COVID 19 world, but post the global impact of 9/11, and post the global financial crisis of 2007/08. In my 49 years of professional life there has never been anything close to the impact of COVID 19! Impact not only on global business and world's financial markets, but frankly of much greater importance is the impact it has had on the lives of people, on the massive rise of unemployment, on the massive destruction of SMEs being simply unable to withstand the impact of lockdown, reduced consumer spending, reduced cashflow, on the massive impact on the need for government intervention for survival!

And finally Bob Iger, Chairman and CEO of the Walt Disney Company published a book, *The Ride of a lifetime*, with the sub-title 'Lessons in Creative Leadership', a wonderful book full of sane, pragmatic, practical, ideas which in many ways resonates with the contents of this book. A fabulous read, one that I would strongly recommend. In particular his Appendix 'Lessons to be Led By', pages 225-233 are an excellent summary of his key lessons on leadership and not a million miles from my summary of *Do it Right: Do it Now!* chapter by chapter at the end of this book.

1. THE HUMAN CAPITAL EQUATION

Human Capital has at last achieved recognition on a global basis to the extent, as shown by the above quote, that The World Bank has initiated a major global project aimed at a global effort to accelerate more and better investments in people for greater equity and economic growth.

The functional area of people management has gone through numerous changes during the course of the past four decades or so. And yet the core equation has still not been achieved:

$$P=AAA$$

where P=people and A= triple A rated asset! The reality in the majority of companies of varied size, form, structure and nationality is that:

$$P \neq AAA$$

Irrespective of what may be said, or what may be written, people are rarely treated as valuable, triple A-rated assets. There are of course exceptions, but in the vast majority of businesses people are hired to do specific tasks, get paid as little as the organisations can get away with, are provided with little or no leadership as such, receive little or no training, development, respect, or care. Don't ask, don't question, don't initiate, don't think, just do as you're told and be grateful that you've got a job!

I am absolutely not about to promote any notion of a Socialist State because frankly people are treated as badly and often times much worse in Socialist environments. I am merely advocating putting the triple A back into the people equation and behaving accordingly.

In 'Think', London Business School's Review journal 2019, Alex Edmans's article 'How Great Companies deliver both purpose and profit' contained the following:

'Human capital is more important than ever before and departures of key employees severely damage a company's competitiveness.'

A dramatic statement confirming in yet another way that P really should be AAA!

PERSONNEL TO HR TO HC

When I started work in 1972 there were personnel departments whose prime focus was the administration of the workforce. They dealt with all things related to the formal processes of employment: record keeping, administering policies and procedures, monthly pay and one's personnel file. They lived by the book, were not expected to be creative or develop original thinking. These personnel departments were run by personnel managers, usually well down the internal command and control chain, removed from the senior executives/decision makers and the board. They were functionaries.

As people issues began to grow in importance around the early 80s, personnel departments made way to HR departments. Although the cynic would say that this was just a subtle re-branding exercise, in reality there was a shift taking place of some considerable magnitude. HR moved up the hierarchy, HR directors were appointed carrying a significantly higher degree of authority than many of their 'personnel manager/director' predecessors.

The focus shifted to people resource planning, compensation planning and reward and incentive schemes. In brief, hiring, firing, retention and reward, as well as many of the core administrative and process centric functions of the old personnel department, were now pooled into HR. Tangible change was happening with the best and the brightest HR directors beginning to secure a seat at the board table, although this was still extremely rare. And more recently a further shift has taken place with the introduction of 'human capital'.

Human capital is not a new concept. It was first introduced by Theodore Schultz, an agricultural economist at the University of Chicago, who developed ideas on human capital in the 1960s as a way of explaining the advantage of investing in education to improve agricultural output. Gary Becker, 1962 Nobel Prize winner for economics, further built on the idea, but it only entered management speak in the 90s to further demonstrate the professionalisation of all things to do with the effective planning, deployment, and management of people within a business; a recognition and acceptance that people are assets of enormous value, that need as much care and attention, if not more than, the traditional physical assets such as plant and machinery, trademarks and brands.

This transformation was fuelled by the events of the 90s in which, more than ever before, ideas could be commercialised with little capital investment, where ideas could attract a massive following and venture capital investment, where intellectual property was recognized as a balance sheet item. The people transactions that took place in the 90s further underlined the notion of human capital. Capital assets are tradable, and so it became with teams of investment banking analysts and specialist equity research teams being bought from one bank by another. Given the millions involved in many of these transactions, there was no doubt that they could have been classified as 'capital transactions'!

And so it was with football teams too, where star players were 'traded' for enormous sums of money from one club to another. Equally CEOs of companies grew in recognition as 'valuable assets' who needed to be retained with specially devised incentive packages.

Of perhaps greater importance is the underlying recognition that people could be of immense value to the organisations they are employed by. To use a gardening metaphor, they are expensive to seed (recruit), need regular and on-going watering (training and development, appraisal and feedback) and regular weeding out (selective retention) to ensure that the best are grown and developed into full bloom (advancement & promotion).

Pilita Clark of the FT wrote an article on 22nd December 2019 comparing politics with business in which she highlighted the utter shambles within the White House under Donald Trump with some 80% of the top 65 jobs having turned over; and what Michael Bloomberg would focus on in his first 100 days if he got the keys to the White House… 'Build a team,' he said. He went on to state that one of the reasons for his mayoral success was a relatively stable team of experienced staffers with ideas, who could attract talented people to work for them and ultimately effect change.

PEOPLE AS ASSETS

Unlike other assets they have legs that enable them to walk, they go home at night, they have brains that enable independent thought, senses to make them aware and have intangibles such as feelings. The way they are managed impacts directly on the business's bottom line like no other asset category. All of this means that it is a mightily complex activity, requiring attention at the very top of the company.

No longer can or should people issues be delegated down the organisation to relatively junior functionaries. No longer is it appropriate at board meetings to allocate significant chunks of time to issues to do with numerical/financial performance, capital projects and strategic matters and then ignore the very thing that drives all of these, that makes all of these a reality: people. No longer is it just the appointment of a new Chairman, CEO, CFO, or board director that should get airtime at board meetings, but the strategically key issues that determine the effectiveness, the drive, the motivation of the company's people, all the people employed in the company!

I was struck by the approach taken by some of the leading investment banks where 'graduate recruitment' was de facto considered part of the bank's strategy department, not HR's – 'graduate' meaning both graduates straight from university at the age of 21 who become analysts, and postgraduates from business schools aged 28-30 who become associates. These recruits were perceived by the banks to be of strategic importance. Their intake and development were therefore managed with utmost focus and care. They were treated very much like assets to be invested in.

Unfortunately, the vast majority of the graduate intake of 2008 got dumped by both Barclays in the US and Nomura in Europe, the two banks that acquired most of Lehman Brothers from the receivers. And yet one year on, there was an interesting small piece in the *Financial Times* noting that many of the 2008 graduates that had been dumped had subsequently been re-hired! And that trend seems to have continued. So, despite the massive crisis in global financial markets in 2008/09, those financial institutions that have survived, that have recovered, are recruiting their talent again, well aware of the equation P=AAA!

Another example of an exceptional company that believes its people are of strategic importance, where P=AAA, is the Unipart Group of Companies (UGC). John Neill, UGC's CEO, cares passionately about all his people and does not just talk the talk, but absolutely walks the talk as is evident in virtually everything he does and the way things are done within UGC. It takes about a nanosecond to be aware that UGC is a people centric organization from the moment one walks through UGC's front door in their head office in Cowley. There are outstanding service awards, cuttings from media, photographs… all focused on the achievements of UGC's employees. There is significant focus on UGC's university, on training and development of employees at all levels within the organisation. It is simply impossible not to be struck by the care, attention and investment devoted to the employees of UGC.

John Neill doesn't just pay lip service to his business being people centric, he practices it every single day as is evidenced when he comes to meet a guest at reception and then walks them personally to his office; with little bits of conversation on the way with many of his employees whom he knows by name as well as the fact that they've just passed an exam, celebrated a milestone birthday, recovered from an illness or just returned from a funeral of a loved one!

Another successful entrepreneur, Julian Richer has shared his success in his book *The Richer Way* (Richer Publishing, 4th revised edition, 24 Sep 2001), in which he emphasises success in business being based on the effective development of all employees, and ensuring that they are treated well and with respect. Simple and 100% accurate! He absolutely put his beliefs into practice when in 2019 he implemented the effective sale of 60% of his business into an employee owned trust, EOT, passing a large share of his company to all his employees.

From the 80s onwards many schools of management, many writers of management ideas and concepts were driving in the direction as described by amongst others Prahalad, Hamel, Covey, Porter, or Labovitz and Rosansky. All had identified the need to ensure that an organisation's people and the way they were rewarded, incentivised, developed and communicated with had to be part and parcel of the organisation's strategic objectives and direction. The hugely successful, and at the time influential, book *In Search of Excellence* by Tom Peters and Robert Waterman (Harper & Row, US, 1982), demonstrated the characteristics of the most successful organizations and what differentiated them from the rest with eight key identified factors. Of these, the fourth factor 'productivity through people – treating rank and file employees as a source of quality' is in line with this chapter's core theme.

The Financial Times quoted the billionaire entrepreneur and successful NY mayor Michael Bloomberg saying, 'You can't do anything, I don't care how smart you are, if you don't have people' (FT 23rd December 2019). He stressed the importance of having the right team of people in place and focused his first 100 days on ensuring exactly this when he became mayor of NY, and would do the same again if he were elected President in 2020!

I have the following tucked away with my collection of quotations:

EFECTIVE INDIVIDUALS make a difference.

EFECTIVE TEAMS make a business.

Despite all of the above, is practice catching up with theory? I doubt whether those who paid lip service to ascribing real importance to their employees in the past will have changed their spots, even if they have imported the term 'human capital'. There has been, and there continues to be, abuse at all levels within organisations.

In professional service firms and investment banks, is it necessary to require employees to work 'overnighters' on a regular basis? Is it appropriate for employees' vacations to be cancelled at the last minute? What is this about? Rites of passage? No one can suggest that people can work effectively without sleep! No one can suggest that there is such a degree of urgency that it is an absolute imperative to complete tasks requiring working overnight on a regular and consistent basis. Bad planning and scheduling, certainly! Appalling management and leadership, absolutely! Is there censure on the perpetrators? No, the reverse - they are considered heroes and go on to make their mega-bonuses.

Just to add weight that this is still a reality, even at the end of 2019 there was newspaper comment about a certain EY partner who since 2009 was complained about for 'unsustainable pressure... setting unrealistic performance targets... that drives a bullying culture' and the said partner not being reprimanded or removed but promoted! Really quite extraordinary for an organisation that allegedly aims to 'provide an inclusive workplace culture free of discrimination, intimidation and harassment of any kind for our 14,500 people and partners in the UK'... interesting that the person quoted felt that EY's partners were separate from their people! Kind of speaks volumes!!

THE WHYS

Why do certain employers continue to treat their employees on the shop floor as hired labour, not to be communicated with, not to be trained and developed? Why do employers still so frequently pay lip service to people being their most important asset when in reality they are prepared to condone bad management, bad management practices, disrespect and abuse?

So let's examine what all this is about. Let's examine the finding and recruitment of people, their retention, motivation and incentivisation; let's look at how talent is managed on entry and on exit; at how people are communicated with at various levels in the hierarchy; at what levers are pulled to build loyalty; at how diversity is dealt with. And along the way let's ask a whole series of questions such as:

Why can't people be honest with each other?

Why can't people be on time?

Why can't people respond to calls, letters, e-mails?

Why can't there be a basic respect for each other irrespective of seniority?

Why can't people say 'thank you' and 'please'?

Why can't people offer help and support to others in need?

Why can't people be judged on performance?

Why does it matter that someone is under 30 or over 50 if they have the skills and experience required?

Why can't people talk the walk and walk the talk?

Why is it so difficult to deliver as promised?

Why can't expectations be managed better?

Why is there a tendency to build false expectations?

Why can't bad systems be ignored, bad processes be changed, bad procedures be dumped?

Why don't people learn to listen?

Why do people have to say 'If I do this for you, I'll have to do it for everyone'?

Why can't people say 'sorry'?

Why can't people say 'no'?

Why is it so hard to say 'You were right'?

Why do bosses forget what it was like to be at the bottom of the pile?

Why don't otherwise intelligent people understand how de-motivating some of their actions can be?

Why can't people remember that what is important to them may not be important to others, and vice versa?

Why can't Boards do away with rewarding for failure?

Why are there 'caps' on some bonus payments/commissions, and not others?

Why is it so difficult for some to recognize incompetence and act on it?

Why can't there be basic respect for each other?

Why is kindness seen as a weakness?

Why is WHY not asked much more frequently?

Why is selling considered to be a low level activity?

Why is there so little passion in business?

Why are more bad bosses not exposed more frequently?

Why did it take gross sexual 'bullying' for the #metoo movement to gain momentum?

In concluding this chapter let's focus on the few steps that could make a real difference immediately.

Do it Right: Do it Now!: Ask the questions

Do it Right: Do it Now!: Keep asking the questions

Do it Right: Do it Now!: The only assets that have legs and can walk are people. Treat them fairly with dignity and respect, and the payback is immediate

Do it Right: Do it Now!: Treat ALL employees with respect, not just the executive team

Do it Right: Do it Now!: Talk with as many of your employees as possible, get them to talk to you, invite them to talk with you randomly and frequently

Do it Right: Do it Now!: Treat people as AAA assets on day one, and always!

Do it Right: Do it Now!

2. PASSIONATE ABOUT PASSION

Why is there so little passion in business, one of the 'whys' raised in the previous chapter? People have said that I can get very passionate about things. One close friend only gets excited about something once I pronounce that 'it's fantastic', then she knows that I think highly of 'it,' whatever the 'it' may be. Life's too short, so let's enjoy it and put the maximum into it and get the maximum out of it at the same time. *Carpe Diem*: Seize the day! **FAN-TAS-TIC!**

Nevertheless, passion has become one of the most overused words in business! Passion is everywhere, almost in every issue leading business magazines/websites there will be articles on the importance of passion, business schools and management courses shriek passion, the FT and other business focused publications repeatedly sound-off on passion. Type 'passion in business' into Google and immediately almost a billion entries emerge…

> Passion is what drives you to succeed because you are completely dedicated to making your business work no matter how hard the process may be.

…passion may be an overused and abused term. But PASSION sells!

Despite all the noise I believe that passion is a vital ingredient for life, which by definition includes work. Without passion it is very difficult to maintain enthusiasm. Without passion, how can one maintain an enquiring mind? Without passion, how can people keep on going even when the going gets tough, and sometimes very tough? It's passion that differentiates the exceptional, that provides the adrenaline, that makes one go the extra mile.

PASSION IN CAREER CHOICE

When I was considering career options as I was approaching completion of my MBA programme, I was in the fortunate position of having to choose between two excellent alternatives, both of which had real attraction and were - to me - good means to re-enter employment. I was however more attracted to management consulting than international banking as I had undertaken a consulting assignment during one of my vacation periods and found it hugely challenging and intellectually rewarding. In addition, the offer came from McKinsey which already in 1975 had an established reputation for excellence. But one of my professors and a number of acquaintances who had knowledge about the organisations strongly advised me to reject their offer and take the offer from the international bank, also a well-regarded major corporation , Bank of America: 'McKinsey will ruin your life', 'You've only just got married, don't you want to stay married?', 'They may pay well, but they'll expect their pound of flesh', 'You'll be expected to travel non-stop', 'Your private life will cease to exist, it'll be work, work, work!' and so on and so forth!

So what to do? I turned to my wife (we had been married only a few months) who simply asked 'What would you do if you were single?'. In other words, where does your passion lie? 'Consulting,' was my reply. Her answer was equally clear, 'Do it!'. Hence very early on I put into practice the notion of pursuing a career option for which I had passion, rather than doing what may have seemed at the time to be the preferred option by some. My wife and I have recently celebrated our 46th wedding anniversary so having chosen the option that many advised me to reject was not such a bad decision after all!!

Similarly, some 25 years later, when my wife and I were discussing careers with our children as they were approaching that time of choice in their respective university careers, we concluded by saying, 'Do what you passionately believe in, try to find a career that fulfils the destiny in your dreams. For the first few years do what you really, really want to do, not what you think you should do. If the dreams come to naught after a couple of years you can always revert to pursuing other objectives, but at least you've given yourself the chance. At least you won't look back in five, ten or fifteen years' time with the feeling, if only! You will not feel that you had a great idea that you should have pursued. Grab life and everything it has to offer with both hands and go for it.'

In a similar vein the NY Times journalist, Thomas Freidman, in his keynote address to a graduation class of Yale University, said that those who pursue their dreams, who can build their professional lives based on doing what truly interests them, will be much more likely to achieve success, both in their careers and financially. Passion is important.

Passion is also the key to sustained performance, to maintaining the drive, the enthusiasm that successful people possess. Passion helps to inject fun, understanding, and often times tolerance… not that all successful people show these qualities. Passion does not die with age; not in the workplace, nor out of it. Gerald Ronson, the owner of one of Britain's largest private companies, Heron International, now in his 80s, still has all the drive and passion for his business that he had at the age of 14 when he started work!

And so does Sir Richard Branson. When interviewed in the FT and asked about how he differentiates between work and play, he responded by saying, 'There is no difference'. His passion for his business is still as great as ever.

Also true for Sir Martin Sorrell who created what became the world's largest advertising and PR group, WPP Plc, and after being ousted in April 2018, (at that time being the longest-serving chief executive of a FTSE 100 company) set to creating another venture, S4 Capital, which is already growing at a fast rate through a series of acquisitions. Having accumulated a net worth in excess of £370m, Sir Martin doesn't need to work to pay for either his grocery bills or his retirement; he's doing so out of drive and passion for what he loves!

I recall a conversation of many years ago when a crowd of us were having dinner in a restaurant in Battersea. The crowd consisted of five couples, one of whom was relatively recently married, and was about ten years younger than the other four couples. I really do not recall how the conversation wandered on to the topic of passion but it did, and the recently married Mrs stated that 'Of course once you've been married more than ten years, the passion in a marriage is gone', at which point probably the least extrovert, the least aggressive member of the party exploded with, 'What a load of total rubbish, you haven't got a clue what you're talking about. Passion need not fade away, it can continue to grow and grow…' And how right she was!

THE WHYS

Why are people so judgemental so early?

Why does the glass so frequently seem half empty rather than half full?

Why is it so difficult to look in the mirror and be honest with at least oneself?

Why is there such trepidation about allowing natural talent to blossom?

Why is there such a perceived sense of security from doing the expected rather than the desired?

Why is *Carpe Diem* not taught at school?

Indeed, to digress for a moment: Rabbi Colin Eimer, who officiated at my marriage ceremony, gave a brief address to us, the newly married couple. His words have lived with us ever since; I have even borrowed his words as part of a speech I made to another couple on their wedding day. Very simply he said that one of the problems of the marriage ceremony is that for many couples it represents the pinnacle of their relationship. He went on to say that he wished for us that the ceremony should merely present the first little plateau, and that we should continue to climb the mountain ahead of us, never ever reaching the peak. Because once the peak has been reached there is only one way to go! A very eloquent way of saying – keep the passion burning! (On a personal note I have to say that it is still burning even after 46 years of marriage!)

Passion will turbo-charge your career; will overcome periods of difficulty, stresses and strains; will provide the sustenance to keep on going when the outlook is bleak. But passion alone is not enough. There has to be competence, there has to be ability, and there has to be some talent too.

Take the case of Crena Watson, an only child, from a single parent family. She grew up with no family support structure, limited funds, and suffered from acute dyslexia which greatly inhibited her academic progress; but she was a natural artist, to the extent that at school teachers were happy to allow her extra time in the art room instead of her doing the maths or science class. She even made a bit of money as some of her teachers actually bought her work. She became part of an elite group of established photographers commissioned by leading magazines, fashion houses, and advertising agencies. She created her own studio, which became one of the most frequently used studios for shoots of all sorts. She re-built and re-designed a beach bungalow which was also used for designer shoots. She created her own success, by her own passion for what she did, by her own abilities, her own talent, focus and determination. Passion with ability and determination is a mighty powerful combination!

PASSION IN WORK

It's tough to talk about passion when work for many people is about earning the money that they need to survive or survive and just a little more. Work/employment is not about satisfaction, it's about being there and doing what is expected. Can one get passionate about working in a call centre, on the underground, or on a production line in a factory? As Professor Charles Handy explained when he was Director of the Masters programme at London Business School during my time there, for most people real work, passionate work, is their hobby – the work on the allotment, the DIY they do on their home – not what they get paid to do but what they do because they want to. Real work is what takes place not between 9-5, but before and after. This was reality in in the mid-70s, and for the vast majority it is probably the reality today. But, as I will show later, yes one can get passionate about working in a call centre, the underground or production line, it all depends on the quality of leadership and communication.

In capitalist society, be it in the UK or the USA, Germany or France, Brazil or Peru, Japan or China, Russia or Vietnam, there is an ever increasing population of people for whom employment by others is no longer the answer. Many people are taking a significantly greater degree of control over their destiny than in the past. The web has been a great leveller and has facilitated development of private enterprise. Some go for it, others don't and allow themselves to become ever more enslaved for the monthly salary. Sad but true.

Some years ago I was taken by a small piece of empirical research conducted by Gary Hamel, one of the world's leading management gurus, who asked business school audiences around the world whether they wished ultimately to pursue entrepreneurial activities, or to pursue an executive career as an employee? In the United States, the majority opted for entrepreneurial activities, whilst in Japan the majority opted for an executive career. Clearly there are massive cultural and social differences at work, nevertheless there is a momentum pulling towards taking greater control over one's own destiny.

An executive search (headhunting) business that I was advising went through very difficult times during the post 9/11 economic downturn largely because the demand for senior executives went through a decline. There were a number of people employed by the business on a good basic salary plus certain benefits, plus of course bonus payments based on the revenue delivered by each individual fee earner, often referred to as 'eat what you kill'. Given the very nature of the business one would have thought that fee earners would have a large degree of confidence in their own abilities, in their abilities to generate revenue even in what was a tough market environment.

As the downturn really kicked in, I advised the owners that their fixed costs were too high, very substantially due to the large fixed salaries they were paying their executive search consultants. It was agreed that I would meet with these employees and suggest that they should reduce their fixed salaries by 60% and at the same time doubling their bonus payment to over-compensate for the risk sharing they were entering into. This would have allowed the search firm to massively reduce its break-even point, and, at the same time, to give the individual fee earners an equally massive up-side with a substantially increased split of revenue between the individual fee earner and the business. I really thought that given this win/win scenario all fee earners would jump at the proposed change. How wrong I was. Only one of the team agreed that the proposition was attractive; the others declined. They wanted their security blanket of a regular monthly payment into their bank account and simply failed to see outside the blinkers of years of being 'salaried'. They simply did not have the confidence in their own abilities.

They lacked the intelligence to see that the business simply could not survive given the costs it was carrying and that by refusing to accept to change and have greater control over their own destinies they were about to lose it all! They lacked the passion that drives entrepreneurial initiative. It takes passion and self-confidence to be able to shake off the shackles of a salary.

Think back to the late 90s and early 00s, to the period of the white heat of the dotcom era. There was a sudden outburst of enthusiasm for small start-ups, for the entrepreneur with a bright idea to pursue, even though there were relatively few with well-articulated business plans. People with many years of experience from the most reputable backgrounds were throwing away what they perceived as the shackles of employment to be free, running their own businesses. (Many were also throwing away the core fundamentals upon which they had based business decisions up to then).

The very best investment banks, (Goldman Sachs, Lehman Brothers, Morgan Stanley, Warburg, Lazards), the very largest financial institutions (Deutsche Bank, CitiBank, UBS), the leading consulting firms, (BCG, Bain, AT Kearney, McKinsey, Booz Allen & Hamilton, LEK), were all haemorrhaging some of their best and brightest to tiny start-ups. The Global Head of Accenture gave up his job to become CEO of a dot com virtual grocery store that was funded to the tune of many millions of dollars, and even more hugely valued at billions of dollars… which has since died along with many other such enterprises.

What drove these people to jump ship? Search for wealth and fortune? Certainly. Boredom in their previous jobs? Almost certainly not. Remember that after the dotcom boom there were many that followed 'B2C' i.e. back to consulting, and 'B2B' i.e. back to banking. Greater control over their own destinies? Definitely yes. The desire for real passion in their daily lives? Absolutely spot on! I knew (and know) some of these people, and the sheer energy they ploughed into these embryonic organisations had to be seen to be believed!

ENTREPRENEURS AND PASSION

Without passion many would have given up a long time ago. But some are still pursuing their dreams. The business models have been adjusted, the growth curves diluted, the drive for cash brought into primacy, but many are still there doing what they believe in and finding life outside the comfort of being an employee more challenging than anticipated, but also a lot more rewarding, and not only, or necessarily, in financial terms. Although that too usually follows if the dream has been sustained, if the business has continued to grow, if growth has been achieved in profitability as well as revenues, and if real sustainable positive cash flow has been secured.

A good example is a small start-up in the Spring of 2001, called

Steel Business Briefing (SBB). This was born out of the collapse of a Sweden located, web-based steel marketplace Steelscreen AB that was going to revolutionise the way steel was traded and purchased across borders based on the possibilities created by the internet and e-commerce. An additional service that was being constructed for the benefit of Steelscreen's members was an online information service about the steel industry. When Steelscreen, the marketplace, collapsed into bankruptcy, so did the then embryonic online information service. Except that one of Steelscreen's executives, Patrick Flockhart, passionately believed that there was a market for a dedicated, specialised, sector focused online information service. Patrick also managed to attract one of the leading steel journalists, Roger Manser, to join the embryonic venture to provide the editorial gravitas required. In other words, Patrick's passion was contagious!

And so the tiny team was formed to buy the intellectual rights from the receiver, re-brand as Steel Business Briefing (www.steelbb.com), and re-launch as a dedicated online information service. The team, Patrick Flockhart and Roger Manser, not only had a belief in the viability of what they were doing, they had the passion for being independent, the passionate belief in their ability to build virtually from scratch a value-added daily information service that people in the steel industry would be prepared to subscribe to.

A decade or so later revenues climbed in excess of £10m, and a loyal team of over 150 people and 'stringers' in various parts of world were feeding through 'exclusives'. By this time they were not only able to show that they have been able to remain cash positive from day one, but were continuing to grow their subscriber base month by month, did so even through the tough years of 2008/09, and were growing their profitability little by little year by year. They were able to demonstrate an expanding list of advertisers, a growing number of interesting consulting assignments, and had also developed a highly successful and well regarded conference business on the back of their accepted sector expertise and global network.

Their passion for their enterprise enabled them to pursue their goal even when they faced barrier after barrier. Their passion enabled them to sacrifice taking a salary month after month during the early days to ensure there was sufficient cash in the business; and the contagiousness of their passion secured their respective wives' support for their actions! It's the passion of the founders that attracted others to join an embryonic business start-up, and it is the contagiousness of the passion that results in their staying with it. Many came from significantly larger organisations, arguably more secure, but it's the passion, the vision of the founders, the sense of being able have some degree of control over one's destiny, that together produced very a powerful magnet for the right people. Then along came a major global media corporation that clearly had done its homework on SteelBB and made an offer to acquire the entire business. After some lengthy and detailed negotiations Patrick and Roger agreed the sale… creating a number of very wealthy people! So passion helped to create the business, grow it and make it successful and fulfil the dreams of many people who joined the journey.

Another executive turned entrepreneur developed his idea whilst he was employed as marketing director of the large Anglo-French cross channel transport company, Eurotunnel. He was an excellent marketing director, but for years he had a dream of creating his own business. And that was exactly what he did when the whole board, and most of the senior executive team, were removed following a disastrous vote by shareholders at the company's annual general meeting. He collected his pay-out, and set about developing his business, a pancake shop, called Crêpeaffaire, started in Hammersmith in 2004. Some seventeen years on, Daniel Spinath, Crêpeaffaire's founder, has grown and expanded the business spreading the joy with stores from Brighton to Newcastle, and Netherlands to Kuwait!

From the original Crêpeaffaire's London base, they are opening stores across the UK – and abroad in increasing number of countries. Daniel really grinds it small, and ensures that he fully understands every part of his business, and only when he is fairly sure he's got it right, pushes further forward. When you speak with Daniel, his enthusiasm, his belief in what he is doing, his total passion, is striking.

It is difficult to imagine entrepreneurial activity without passion. As entrepreneurialism is the main global driver of economic activity, of economic growth, passion is clearly alive and well, at least in the SMEs.

But how to retain, inject and stimulate passion in larger organisations? This requires leadership. This requires conscious effort to ensure an appropriate environment is created throughout the organisation. A tough task, but not impossible! Google had it and has retained it. Virgin had it and has retained it. IBM had it, lost it, and has tried to get it back. Nokia, Vodafone, and GE are trying hard to retain it, with at times significant degrees of change along the way. ASDA lost it, got it back, lost it again under the ownership of the American giant, Walmart, and maybe will regain it with their new multi-billionaire entrepreneurial and private equity owners.

Apple had it, lost it totally, and massively recaptured it when Steve Jobs returned, and has managed to not only retain it but drive it further under the leadership of Tim Cook who's succeeded in creating the first trillion $ company! Chrysler lost it, got it back with Lee Iacocca, and subsequently lost it. UK's GEC had it and lost it forever. WPP had it, lost it and is fighting to retain some of it. Microsoft had it then started to decline after Gates handed over to Steve Ballmer in 2014 but very much has recovered it under Satya Narayana Nadella's leadership.

One cannot of course be passionate about everything and everyone all of the time. What I'm arguing for is for you to release your passion, both professionally and personally, don't keep it locked up and hidden, buried with the baggage of the past. Let it out! What I'm arguing for is the injection of passion into things that matter, into things that matter to you.

Without passion, this book would not have been written, irrespective of whether it's a success or not. Without passion, charitable institutions would not be able to gain the support not only of those that support them financially, but more importantly of those who give hugely of their time – often people who are massively busy but nevertheless give freely. For example, Norwood, a fantastic organisation that provides residential care for those with disabilities for the rest of their lives, has support from some of the UK's most outstanding business brains, free and gratis. These established business leaders provide their time (and of course money too) because they passionately believe in the cause. And this is repeated in so many not-for-profit organisations around the country, as it is repeated in so many different forms of human endeavour.

Just look at the annual London Marathon... the vast number of ordinary people running for their particular cause. That is passion at its best! 'The 2019 Virgin Money London Marathon raised a record-breaking £66.4 million for charity, setting a new world record for an annual single-day charity fundraising event for an incredible thirteenth successive year...' truly magnificent and impossible to have achieved without passion not only of the individual marathon runners, but all involved in making the event happen!

Take for example the Women's Institute (WI) in Ripley, Yorkshire. That now world famous calendar, (Nigel Cole directed film *Calendar Girls*) would never have seen the light of day and the leukaemia ward of the local hospital would have been £500,000 the poorer had it not been for the passion of just a couple of ordinary women to do something different! The passion to withstand the barriers of village conservatism, the passion to address a massive national WI annual meeting!

Passion, or something similar, has penetrated the thinking some of the leading business gurus of our time. In the book of the mid-1990s by the late Sumantra Ghosal and Christopher Bartlett *The Individualised Corporation*, they suggested that some of the world's leading corporations such as ABB and General Electric were no longer forcing employees to conform to a rigid conception of what an employee should be and do, but were reconfiguring the organisation itself to fit around the talents and abilities of their employees; and that by doing so these organisations were 'releasing entrepreneurial hostages' – allowing and facilitating the individual employee to rediscover passion for his or her work, creativity, thereby adding real value to the business.

By far the most dramatic example of creating a truly democratic environment in the workplace is that of Ricardo Semler in his business, Semco, in Sao Paulo, Brazil. He has detailed his journey from an authoritarian, command and control style of leadership to a relatively laissez faire style of democracy, in his wonderfully readable and enjoyable book *MAVERICK!* (Tabletun Inc., 1993). The highly respected management thinker Charles Handy is quoted on the back cover: 'The way Ricardo Semler runs his company is impossible, except that it works, and works splendidly for everyone. I relish this book. It revived my faith in human beings and my hope for business everywhere.' Semler totally re-wrote the rule book for Semco, provided a genuine sense of ownership, belonging, and passion to his key team, and to the whole company. And despite the odds it worked!

The Department of Trade and Industry in the early 00s identified six essential elements of inspirational leadership:

- Inspirational leaders genuinely care about their people; they talk about honesty, respect and trust so that their people feel highly valued

- Inspirational leaders involve everybody to create the climate and structure in which passion can grow

- Inspirational leaders listen

- Inspirational leaders show appreciation by saying 'thank you'. These two words are tremendous motivators

- Inspirational leaders ensure work is fun; they celebrate success and enjoy outstanding performance

- Inspirational leaders and their employees are deeply committed; they are passionate

AS A 'STRAP LINE'

The hugely successful sandwich shop, Prêt A Manger, which changed the concept of ready-made sandwiches, had the words 'passionate about food' incorporated into the company's value statement. I recently saw on the sides and back of a Ford van the name of a cleaning company with 'A Passion for Cleanliness' written underneath. An advertising campaign for one of the world's largest financial institutions, Deutsche Bank, has 'a passion to perform' as part of its strap line... which still continues even with all their difficulties. The merged property asset management business, F&C Reit Asset Management, which was led by the consummate property entrepreneur Leo Noé, introduced a new strap line: 'Passionate about adding value'. Major car manufacturers spend millions on advertising, and many have turned to include 'passion' in their adverts: FIAT - *Driven by passion*; MASERATI - *Excellence through passion*; RENAULT - *Passion for Life*. Even a medical practice had an advert stating - *Passionate About Medicine - Compassionate About People*. Passion is becoming part of the currency, a recognition that it needs to be part of the DNA of successful organisations. Or as Jeffrey Immelt, General Electric's Ex-Chief Executive, was quoted as saying: 'People have to know that the leader cares about certain things. It is as important that they see the passion as what the passion is.'

I believe there are a few truly important and easy actions that can be taken:

> *Do it Right: Do it Now!:* Help the next generation to do better in their pursuit of careers; give them options that were perhaps not available to us; facilitate them to think outside the box
>
> *Do it Right: Do it Now!:* Give the simple advice to 'follow your dream' early – if not straight after school/college/ university then it may be too late
>
> *Do it Right: Do it Now!:* Combining a real desire to do something with true ability has a better chance of

success than just following what seems to be the right thing to do

Do it Right: Do it Now!: Passion, plus ability, plus determination, plus tenacity makes a powerful combination

Do it Right: Do it Now!: Passion is not a 'here today, gone tomorrow' thing; it can be with you throughout your life, and grow in substance and intensity

Do it Right: Do it Now!: Passion is a key driver of entrepreneurial activity

Do it Right: Do it Now!: Economic growth and passion are closely linked

Do it Right: Do it Now!: Passion can to be released in the corporate world; passion should be released in the corporate world

Do it Right: Do it Now!: Be an inspirational leader by fuelling passion within your organisation

Do it Right: Do it Now!: Passion enhances creativity and adds value

Do it Right: Do it Now!

And get animated about things, get passionate, get angry if things go wrong, make your views heard, get thrilled when things go right, let others know how pleased you are with whatever they did to put a smile on your face, or make your life that little bit easier.

Passionate also means being passionate about others, about their achievements and their successes. Passionate in rewarding success, celebrating success, passionate about being a caring organisation. This is not a dream, it happens; such organisations exist, and they don't need to be large multi-national corporations, they can be small local businesses employing a handful of people.

Over a decade ago I heard a piece about a small Midlands based engineering company on Radio 4's *You and Yours* (Wednesday December 10th 2003). This company had decided that it would compete not on price, or product, but on its people, i.e. the quality of its service. They decided to implement a wholly new approach to all of their employees. Everyone was expected to work from 08.30 to 17.00 only. No overtime, no weekends, no pressure to stay longer. Everyone was expected to be fully trained in whatever was their specific area of focus. Everyone was expected to take their full allocation of vacation time. Everyone was communicated with openly about everything going on in the business, and everyone was expected to be able to help colleagues as required. Every employee had a fortnightly review meeting with the company's boss at which everything was open for discussion, at which the employees were encouraged to be constructively critical. The net result since this change was implemented? The company has achieved 25% annual growth in sales and profitability, a stable work force, and a much greater ability to recruit people than previously. People are actually queuing up to work for the company! This example doesn't age with time, it fully dramatizes the power of leaders with passion about their people and their business.

There are examples amongst some of the world's biggest corporations, too, where enlightened people policies have been successfully implemented over time, and where they are now very much part of the organisation's culture. Google, Apple, Netflix are three global corporations that come immediately to mind where the passion of the founders is still very much present.

Make the difference! Get seriously passionate about what you do, how you do it, and especially about the people you are doing it with and for. Only then will you ask the red-hot question, why it can't be done even better!

3. FINDING GREAT PEOPLE

As everyone knows it is mighty difficult to find, attract, and retain good people. Irrespective of the state of the economy, irrespective of the length of the unemployment queue, irrespective of the type and nature of the business, attracting, identifying and recruiting the right employees is not only of paramount importance, but also massively difficult and massively expensive. The great search for talent is an on-going relentless process for which there is no obvious scientific solution. Despite what some may suggest, there are no proven methodologies. This is an art, an art that needs real insights and sensitivities, some of which I hope to provide in this chapter.

> *'Finding the right person to lead a big company is as important, in terms of its effect on human lives, as choosing the right leader for a small country. Yet the decision often seems to be taken in a curiously random way, and to judge by the brevity of many new chief executives' term of office, boards find it extremely hard to get it right.'*
> THE ECONOMIST: A SURVEY OF CORPORATE LEADERS, OCTOBER 25TH, 2003

And it is not only important to get this right, or as right as possible, for 'big companies' but for ALL companies, no matter how small. In fact it is probably of significantly greater importance to get recruitment right in small companies as smaller companies' resources are by definition much reduced and hence the impact of wrong decisions can be disproportionately greater!

PERSONAL NETWORK
By far the easiest, the fastest, and the least expensive way to find the right people for your organisation is through your personal

network. People you have come across whom you know, or who are known by others whom you know. People who come recommended by contacts and acquaintances you trust. People who know you and who understand what you are trying to create. Friends from the past, school, university, earlier work environments. Keith Willey of London Business School said at an Entrepreneur of the Year Master Class: 'Lots of the best appointments do not come from head-hunters, but through networking. …During your regular business activity, you should always be keeping an eye out for someone who might be suited to your business.'

Indeed many of my own appointments to boards came from introductions by people I worked with or interacted with in the past in a professional capacity. The decision to actually appoint me was that of the board of the relevant organisation, but the initial introduction came from my personal network.

The world of venture capital and private equity (VC & PE) is not only well funded with money, and access to money, but also with people and access to people. Most VC firms actively build their own databases of people through their own networks, so that as they need to identify someone to join a buy-in team as a potential finance director or CEO, they have instant access to people they have cultivated over time, people whom they have referenced, and developed some sort of a relationship with already. The same goes for the leading PE firms. They too actively develop their own 'little black books' of people they may be able to turn to for differing situations. Networking is the rule.

The most prolific development capital provider in the UK today is British Growth Fund (BGF) which has provided funding to over 310 small to medium sized enterprises (SMEs) in the UK. As such it has invested in establishing its own 'Talent Network'…i.e. BGF's external network of Board Directors; and plugging this network into a wide range of opportunities to partner with BGF's current and future investee companies.

> *'BGF is continuously challenging and disrupting the traditional approaches to deal making; and taking a fresh approach to building our Talent Network, and the way we introduce highly experienced people from a wide range of backgrounds to our investee companies is no exception. It is hugely exciting to work with some of the UK's most successful business leaders, and give them the opportunity to help the next generation of success stories'.*

The personal network is also potentially important for solving many other business related issues: which advisers (accountants, lawyers) to choose, which bank to bank with, which property to rent, who to invite as non-executive directors, etc. The importance of a personal network cannot be overstated. As such it is worth focusing on the development of your personal network from a relatively early age – people with whom professional contact has been established, contact which is then retained over the years. People often progress their careers at similar rates, so that someone who was a junior banker when you were a newly qualified solicitor, when Fred was an account executive, and Mary had her first managerial appointment, move at roughly similar rates through their respective hierarchies; until, as you become a partner of your law firm, the banker becomes a managing director in Morgan Stanley, the account executive becomes account director at JWT, and Mary has become CEO of a FTSE 250 company... hence creating a wonderful instant network of potential value to all concerned. This will not happen automatically; it takes a certain degree of time and effort. It takes investment of energy.

Some people have a natural gift and can lock into networking almost automatically as they mature and develop, having started the process subconsciously at school and university. Others have first to be made aware, and then have to work at it. For some people this is more difficult than sending man to the moon.

Interestingly the importance of personal networks/personal contacts and relationships was highlighted in a Lombard piece by Kate Burgess (FT 22nd January 2020) when she wrote about Bernard Looney, the new CEO of BP who rapidly brought in senior colleagues with whom he had worked in the past '…Mr Looney is collecting his own band of older, greyer turtles around him'. And the article makes reference to António Horta-Osório who 'drafted in Santander workmates known as the conquistadors to aid his speedy shake-up of Lloyds when he became the high-street bank's chief in 2011'; and Jes Staley who brought in ex-colleagues from JPMorgan when he was appointed as CEO of Barclays. So personal networks matter and can make a difference.

In 1989 my brother started a new business called IDOM that morphed into an IT consultancy advising the banking sector of Central and Eastern Europe. By 1990 he had secured his first major mandate with the Foreign Trade Bank of Hungary ('MKB'), but he rapidly needed to resource up with people who had a first class understanding of both banking and specific banking IT 'packaged solutions' e.g. Kapiti, Leo, Bankmaster, etc. But where to find them without spending a fortune on head-hunters or specialist recruitment agencies?

Fortunately he had a personal network based on his 15 years with a major UK clearing bank and being an alumnus of INSEAD (a leading European business school), he had networks that he was totally prepared to use. Most people rarely mind being called for assistance by people with whom they have some connection, where there is some common base, some understanding that one day they may be helping you, and the next day you will be helping them. Calls were made, many of which led nowhere, but some of which led to further calls as people referred others that were part of their networks. That's how networking works. Eventually my brother was put in touch with a man, Mark, working in Barclays Bank's IT department who was 'dying in the institutionalised and bureaucratic environment' and couldn't say 'yes' fast enough to join a tiny one year old company with no track record. 'I believe in what you are trying to do, to hell with it I'm in for the ride!'

Not suprisingly Mark had his own network within the banking IT sector, and was able to use it to attract others to join the adventure of working in what was, at that time, perceived to be the 'Wild East' of Eastern and Central Europe. (Remember the Berlin Wall had only just collapsed, and the old communist regimes were only just beginning to pass control to more democratic governments). The result was that through networking an initial team was brought together who then used their own networks to reach others, and so the ball rolled on and on.

I joined the business in mid-1990. Between 1989 and 1995 IDOM grew from one man and a secretary, to a highly successful and recognized specialist IT firm with over 350 people employed working out of ten offices in as many locations, and not once was a penny paid to a professional recruiter, not once was there a need to mandate an agency or search firm! Each person employed came through a personal network, a personal recommendation.

During all these years IDOM didn't lose a single professional member of its staff, nor anyone else. We did occasionally ask people to leave where we made recruitment errors, but not one person left to join a competitor. We asked one person to take 'leave of absence' and go to business school because we felt that she had terrific potential to grow even faster, and we offered to be as supportive as possible for the application process and a guaranteed return ticket on graduation, if she wished to return. (She did and became our CFO).

In 1995 the magazine *Business Central Europe*, part of *The Economist* stable of publications, rated IDOM as the #1 IT consultancy of the Central European Region, ahead of EDS and Accenture! Not a bad achievement for a firm that was just 5 years old, and a fantastic accolade to the quality of people working in IDOM.

But we all know it can't carry on like that for ever; sooner or later resourcing needs to become more structured, and inevitably will involve third parties.

KNOW YOUR EXISTING RESOURCE

Having spent some years involved with the world of head-hunting I have frequently been amazed at how little effort is made by so many companies to really understand the quality of their existing resources ('Okay, we employ 1,000 people, and none of them are any good for the very important new position I now need to fill'). And guess what happens time after time? After having employed the services of a head-hunting firm, after having paid a search fee, after having invested a significant amount of senior management's time interviewing short-listed candidates? Just like magic, an internal candidate appears. An internal candidate with the right expertise and experience, plus the advantage of proximity and invested knowledge of the existing business. This however is a lose-lose scenario! The company loses the money that it has paid out to the head-hunter (although this is *de minimis* in order of importance); the head-hunter loses by not being able to close its search (bad for internal statistics but otherwise no big deal); and above all the company loses the opportunity to provide significant staff motivation by creating internal promotion, and hence effectively celebrating its success before having mandated the head-hunter.

This is a big deal, as the organisation has lost out on an important opportunity to be able to make a positive statement about itself, mainly internally, but also externally. In other words, this is an admission that the internal systems were not able to identify competencies available within the organization. And equally, that the systems were not able to identify competencies as the need for them arose. Resourcing from within requires that you know your talent pool, that you know your people! It requires that you know your star performers and how they are progressing through the organisation.

Unfortunately the above is not an unusual scenario. The above is not restricted to the very largest corporations. It happens in many businesses across the spectrum. Some organisations make a virtue out of formally benchmarking internal with external candidates. They want to ensure that they place the very best people into senior roles, irrespective of whether the best is internal or external. That's fine, as long as it is undertaken proactively, and internal candidates are included in the formal process from the start; but the real missed opportunity is when internal candidates are ignored: when perfectly able internal candidates exist, but are excluded from the process. Or, when internal candidates are only included either by default, or because they may have threatened to 'walk' if not given the chance to be part of the process.

And this is despite the result of formal research that has identified succession planning as an issue of significant importance in many smaller organisations, quoted and private, as well as the larger organisations. Numerous surveys both in the US and the UK have substantiated beyond any doubt that succession planning is a serious weakness in many major corporations. Why has this core issue been so neglected for so long? Surely planning for succession in all key roles is of the very greatest strategic importance, not just top management, but throughout an organization. Why have nominations committees not been held accountable for succession planning?

It is therefore not surprising that one of the world's most respected corporations, GE, led for decades by one of the world's most respected CEOs, Jack Welch, had succession planning as one of the core measures against which all executives were judged.

> *'Executive talent has been the most under-managed corporate asset for the past two decades... Companies that manage their physical and financial assets with rigor and sophistication have not made their people a priority in the same way... only 16% think that their companies even know who their high performers are.'*
>
> THE WAR FOR TALENT, ELIZABETH G. CHAMBERS, MARK FOULON, HELEN HANDFIELD-JONES, STEVEN M. HANKIN, AND EDWARD G. MICHAELS III.
> THE MCKINSEY QUARTERLY, 1998 NUMBER 3.

If they don't know who their 'high performers' are there is little chance that they have a clue about their sub-performers, or indeed have any sort of knowledge about their staff, performance-wise or otherwise!

A small personal example of how important it can be to know the talent within the organisation: I had been on the board of a relatively small business, (40 people) when the incumbent CEO was 'removed' and one of the executive directors was appointed as 'interim CEO' during the process of 'separation' from the incumbent. This was a fairly lengthy period during which the 'interim' went about providing a changed leadership to the organisation. The changed leadership was very well received by all and essentially re-set the internal culture. When the process with the incumbent was completed and it was time to 'appoint' a new CEO, a number of board members suggested mandating a search firm and 'going out to market'. I was horrified as we clearly had the right person in place! Why mandate head-hunters, why go fishing outside, when we had made the right decision and the decision had been proven right! It took some 'negotiating' but the board came to recognise the power of what we were telling the organisation and that there was absolutely no requirement to do anything else. The 'interim' was formally appointed to the role and has proven to be very effective.

SUCCESSION PLANNING

The above McKinsey Quarterly quote may now seem to date from a long time ago, and yet in July 2009 one of the leading stories in the corporate/financial world was the alleged lack of proper succession planning in Marks and Spencer Group plc (M&S), one of UK's premier corporations. Sir Stuart Rose, with the support of the board of M&S, defied prevailing thinking and guidance on corporate governance by combining the roles of Chairman and CEO, to the outcry of most institutional investors and other city bodies. This largely occurred because there was no proper succession planning in place. In fact it took until 2010 before a new CEO was finally appointed!

The lack of effective succession planning seriously undermined confidence in this historically very well respected, leading retail chain. Indeed, at Sir Stuart Rose's final AGM he was berated by shareholders over the lack of succession planning, and the consequential cost of head-hunting Mr. Bolland as the new CEO. Sunil Pal, another private investor, complained that M&S had been 'forced to pay Mr Bolland, the former Heineken and Wm Morrison executive, such a hefty sum because it did not – unlike

Tesco – have a successor in waiting in its own ranks' (*Financial Times,* July 15th 2010 p16). This issue was given full vent by the then National Association of Pension Funds ('NAPF', now known as the Pension and Lifetime Savings Association, 'PLSA')...

> *'Key investors have been told to press Britain's leading companies to explain how they would cope with the departure of their chief executive or other senior boardroom figures. The National Association of Pension Funds (NAPF) has recommended that its members, who oversee about £900bn of investments, check boards' leadership and succession plans, especially at complicated companies with long-serving chief executives'*
>
> **SEAN FARRELL, THE GUARDIAN, 24TH JUNE 2014**

'When clients talk to us about chief executive succession, it's usually too late', said Tony Couchman, a head-hunter with Egon Zender. That was the case at Boeing where the departure of Phil Condit with no natural successor led to the retrieving of a previous president to run the company. That was the case at Vodafone when Sir Chris Gent announced his decision to leave and Lord MacLaurin, Vodafone's then chairman, discovered that the company had no succession strategy.

In September 2009, Micro Focus (a UK quoted company) shares plummeted 14% on the announcement that its highly respected CEO, Stephen Kelly, had decided to step down. His announcement and explanation that it was time for him to 'step back' was, according to the *Financial Times*, '... a blow to the business and the board which is only just beginning to search for a replacement. The importance of succession planning, even when you have apparently a tireless boss, has rarely been emphasised more vividly' (Lombard, 1st September 2009). And rarely have I come across a better substantiation of the point I am making about the critical importance of effective succession planning in all organisations!

In the January 2010 issue of the magazine *Director*, Jane Simms has an article dedicated to the issue of succession planning entitled *Leading Questions*. The debacles of the late 2009 succession-induced problems at ITV, Channel 4, and Marks & Spencer are well documented, as well as contemporary data from surveys by Korn/Ferry Whitehead Mann, and PwC; yet again confirming that despite succession planning being 'recognised' as an issue of key importance to boards and CEOs alike, nevertheless in reality (in terms of well-structured actions, and well implemented successions) actual strategies were very few. Given how frequently the phrase 'people are our most important asset' is to be found in Chairmen's and CEOs' statements in annual reports and accounts, one seriously needs to question the validity of their words!

And so it continues decade after decade in large FTSE 100 and smaller companies… incumbents leave with no succession plan in place and the search only then commences!

> '*Marks and Spencer Group plc (LON: MKS) today announced that Humphrey Singer, Group Chief Financial Officer, has decided to leave the business and a succession process is now underway. Humphrey will work with Steve Rowe, Group Chief Executive Officer, and the Board to ensure an orderly transition. A departure date has not yet been decided and this will be confirmed by the Company in due course and, until then, Humphrey will continue with his responsibilities*'
>
> GILES ARBOR 23RD SEPTEMBER 2019.

> '*Insurer Lancashire Holdings Limited (LON:LRE) has kicked off succession planning after its chief financial officer, Elaine Whelan, announced plans to retire from the group next year*'
>
> CALUM MUIRHEAD - 08:14 FRI 24 MAY 2019.

The FT had a brief article 31st October 2019 by Richard Milne – 'Sweden's Atlas Copco has lessons in success to teach the world' – the article first established that Atlas Copco was at that time the largest company on the Swedish stock exchange as measured by market capitalisation, then within the body of the article there's a stunning paragraph:

Inside Sweden, the company is known as the leading finishing school for executives, akin to the role General Electric once played in the US. The future CEO of ABB, the chairman of Electrolux, CEO and chair of door-and-lock maker Assa Abloy and the CEO of Sandvik all hail from Atlas Copco. Mr Rahmstorm (Atlas Copco's CEO) noted that 85% of the group's leaders are recruited internally, with 'most in my team here for 10-20-30 years' He said that there is no succession planning at Atlas Copco; instead there is an internal job market with budding leaders receiving coaching on what the gaps are in their CV.

Now that's an impressive finishing school! Now that's a super impressive record of promoting from within!

Succession happens with or without planning. Clearly planning is much better and much more desired than no planning but data suggests that change at the top does not lead to better performance! Bankers reckon it takes about two years before investors can expect a boost to their returns from a new CEO; and PwC analysts say successors to a long-running chief executive often underperform and can have relatively short terms…at times even with succession planning being in place!

THE WHYS
(So in general what are HR departments doing?)

Why are they not fully on top of knowing everyone in their

organisation irrespective of whether there are 20 or 200,000 employees?

Why don't they know their stars, and superstars?

Why don't they do a thorough internal evaluation of resources suitable for development and promotion BEFORE reaching out for head-hunters?

Why have they not mapped succession candidates?

Why is there no internal talent map?

Why are there no structured executive development programmes in place?

Why are there no pre-planned succession planning development programmes?

Why is there no formal induction programme?

Why does the organisation not have a bottom up path for high-flyers, supervised top down?

Why does $P \neq AAA$?

Why is there inadequate knowledge of the organisation's human capital?

Interestingly I was informed recently by the head of recruitment for a FTSE 100 company that he was aghast at discovering when he took over, that the company had over 30 search firms working for it, that internal appointments were rare and that there was generally little knowledge of the nature of the internal talent that may have existed! How utterly appalling!!

But the very best corporations and professional firms do exactly as per the above list of 'whys' and some of them a lot more. The very best know exactly who they have, their relative strengths and weaknesses, their performance track records, their development needs and achievements. They track and project their people assets in a highly focused and professional manner. They promote internally and reach outside only in a structured and organized way. And when they do need to reach outside, they know their market and frequently can find the people they need themselves, through their established networks.

> 'The role of human resources should be redefined and its capabilities strengthened. More than process managers, HR executives need to be effective, proactive counsellors with personal credibility and strong relationships with business units, but only 27 percent of corporate officers strongly agree that HR plays this role.'
>
> MCKINSEY RESEARCH.

McKinsey has grown consistently through the years and decades and has grown very substantially from home grown talent. It recruits at its entry level and pursues a rigorous up-or-out process linked to thorough career planning and development, performance evaluation, and relentless on-going training. Only *in extremis* did it go outside to employ search firms to fill vacancies, although in recent years this has changed due to both size and the need to locate specific expertise. In the 70s and 80s new hires were almost all MBAs; now over 40% are lawyers, doctors, economists, scientists, military officers, or former government officials.

Shell, BP, Tetra Pak, Unipart, GE, Mars, Compass, P&G, Fishburn Hedges and WPP are some best of breed examples that really try their utmost to have well-structured internal process linked to strategic external resourcing policy to 'refresh the gene pool'. Shell and BP are interesting examples in that although they are both perceived as good examples of enlightened managers of

HR within the largest of the multi-national corporations: they have adopted HR staffing policies almost diametrically opposed to each other. While Shell took the decision some years ago to run all its HR activities with its own people, BP farmed out most of its HR support to outsourcing consultants.

Little wonder then that McKinsey is consistently rated as one of the most desirable companies to work for globally, as was Fishburn Hedges, a relatively small UK domestic PR/corporate communications consultancy, which was rated consistently for over seven years as one of the best places to work at in the UK (more about Fishburn Hedges later) (*Financial Times: 50 best places to work in the UK*, 2009).

Little changes over time, people want to work in environments that are rewarding and challenging, where there is good training and development, where people are valued, as dramatized by the *Evening Standard's* list of the top 20 places in the UK to work in and what employees have said about them (Laura Hampson, Wednesday 5 December 2018) of which the top 10 were:

1. **Anglian Water**
    'Coming from other companies, Anglian water is head and shoulders above the rest. There is plenty of support, training and fantastic opportunities to further your career, for the first time in my career I feel more than just a number. Good rate of pay along with several benefits including bonuses.'

2. **Bain & Company**
    'Fantastic culture, smart, motivated, inspirational people who genuinely care about each other and their clients.'

3. **XPO Logistics**

    'Everyone helps each other to achieve success. The work atmosphere is relaxed but everyone is required to accomplish the high standards we provide.'

4. **Bromford**

    'Great colleagues, flexible working, excellent training, innovative and your opinions matter.'

5. **Salesforce**

    'Great to work in an exciting and fast paced environment. Teams are full of talented individuals and the company supports your career aspirations and development.'

6. **Sky Betting & Gaming**

    'Vibrant, exciting, fast-paced. A place to think big and really achieve things you couldn't in other businesses.'

7. **Hiscox**

    'The workplace is friendly and communications is open, technology is available to allow a fantastic work/home balance.'

8. **SAP**

    'Culture, innovations, self-development, career opportunities, brand, benefits, salary, SAP really takes good care of its employees.'

9. **Taylor Wimpey**

    'Fantastic environment, great culture, support, training opportunities, business direction and strategic approach to the industry.'

10. **Royal London**

    'Very people focused and encourages development and opportunities. Flexible working is offered and the working environment is great.'

These are many of best companies to work for in the UK, the States and Europe… what all of them have in common is a focus on People, Training, Development, Opportunities to grow, and increasingly in the world of 2020 diversity.

REACHING OUTSIDE

But even the most sophisticated may need to reach outside from time to time. Rapid growth, the need for specialist expertise, unforeseen departures and death may all lead to resourcing requirements that even the most well-structured internal development plans are unable to deal with. The desire to ensure that there is some on-going parity with the best available also leads to periodic external recruiting. Despite the success of its internal development effort General Electric routinely fills a quarter of its senior openings from the outside 'to calibrate its talent and raise the bar'.

Apart from need arising from exceptional circumstances, there is also a need to bring people in regularly at entry level to fuel upward mobility. Hewlett-Packard for example tended to identify its future graduate intake through its summer internship programme. Graduate and postgraduate (including MBA) recruiting is therefore a major feature of many organizations' recruiting; and one that has until relatively recently been executed internally but is now also being outsourced to professional recruitment firms.

At the other end of the spectrum, companies tended to do their own recruiting for non-executive directors, where personal networks and informal recommendations often led to suitable introductions and appointments. But all that has substantially changed. Following the huge scandals and collapses of Enron, Worldcom, Marconi, et al, 'corporate governance' became a very hot issue, and with it the role, selection, appraisal, and performance of non-executive directors. This has continued with even greater focus since the financial crisis of 2007/8 with the collapse of the Royal Bank of Scotland and its saving by the government and the tax-payers. Questions about the role of non-executive directors and their responsibilities for the bank's demise were rampant, and frankly remained largely unanswered.

Recommendations contained in the Higgs Review (Derek Higgs: *The Role and Effectiveness of Non-Executive Directors*, 2003), supplemented further by the *Tyson Report on the Recruitment and Development of Non-Executive Directors* (both commissioned by the Secretary of State for the Department of Trade and Industry) highlighted the need for boards to be able to attract a new inflow of suitably qualified people from a more diverse pool of talent to the boards of UK companies.

> *'Diversity in the background, skills and experiences of NEDs enhances board effectiveness by bringing a wider range of perspectives and knowledge to bear on issues of company performance, strategy and risk. Board diversity can also send a positive and motivating signal to customers, shareholders and employees, and can contribute to a better understanding of diverse constituencies that affect its success'*
>
> *TYSON REPORT, JUNE 2003*

One of the recommendations was that boards should retain the services of professional search firms to achieve the goal of increased diversity and professionalism amongst non-executive directors. But the report raised an area of concern:

> *'At the beginning of the search, a search firm can encourage its client to broaden, rather than narrow, the candidate profiles it is willing to consider. Ultimately, however, a search firm is*

driven by its client's remit. If the search firm develops a list of candidates that stray too far from this remit, it will risk its credibility without affecting the client's final selection'

TYSON REPORT, JUNE 2003

If search firms bend to their clients' instructions and do as they are told, the end result is unlikely to change. It will need more than professionalism on the part of search firms to bring about the sort of change envisioned by both Higgs and Tyson: change in terms of the stereotype currently occupying the chairs around the board tables of the UK's largest companies. It will need search firms to be prepared to take on chairmen and nomination committees when setting the criteria for suitable NEDs. But this is totally unrealistic. Search firms are service businesses, and as such will of course bend to the requirements of their clients.

I have recently had discussions with three different search consultants who told me that their preferred candidates were rejected by their clients' selection committees as the committees opted for what they perceived to be 'safe' candidates. That is, candidates in the mould, rather than candidates who would perhaps rock the boat! And the search firms were unable to affect the final decision, even though they tried to bring in new talent, talent of greater diversity!

Currently there is ever increasing noise for greater diversity, ever increasing frustration by institutional shareholders at the lack of women in C-Suite roles and non-executive roles, and the lack of recognition by boards of the impact that better board composition and better diversity can have on the performance of companies. Perhaps there is recognition just inadequate action!

THE NED NONESENSE

The standard criteria used when considering a NED role on the board of a FTSE 100 company of either currently being a CEO or main board director of a FTSE 100 company, or of having recently held such a position, needs seriously to be questioned. There is a pool of talent that does not fit this criterion, yet who have very suitable and relevant experience. People from top level management consulting firms, from legal practices, from audit and accountancy firms, from investor relation and financial or corporate communication consultancies, from investment banking, who possess experience of working with and advising FTSE 100 companies at the most senior levels.

Such people have often developed a deep understanding of board issues, have been asked to comment and advise on them. They have not held board level office within FTSE 100 companies, but so what? They fit the rule of independence, they fit the expertise requirements, they fit the need for delivering wider networks and they may provide increased diversity. They know how to probe and question. They know how to analyse. And they should know how to influence.

The exceptions to being ignored are politicians and members of the House of Lords. They are somehow found to be acceptable, even though they too may not have had FTSE 100 experience, nor at times any significant business exposure!

Had there been greater diversity would non-executives have been more able to question, interrogate, and perhaps forestall the very worst excesses of the credit crisis amongst leading financial institutions of 2008/09? There is a real need to break through the cosy club that has evolved over decades.

The Walker review of corporate governance in the UK banking

industry of October 2009 aimed to do exactly this and included the following two related areas of concern in its formal terms of reference:

- the balance of skills, experience and independence required on the boards of UK banking institutions

- the effectiveness of board practices regarding the performance of audit, risk, remuneration and nomination committees

Another source is people who have run very large and complex multi-national organisations, but in the private sector. I know an individual who ran one of the world's largest private companies, with annual revenues in the many billions, and with truly global operations. He was successful, and was generally recognised to have been successful, and yet for some three years he was unable to secure a non-executive role on the board of a major corporation. Why? Because he was perceived not to have been on the board of a major quoted company, hence not to have quoted company experience! How utterly absurd, and totally nuts! It took the 'out of the box' thinking of a relatively small local search firm in the USA to see through the crap, put his name forward to their client (one of the world's best known, and largest, fast moving consumer goods businesses) and the rest is history.

To quote Jane Simms again from *Director* magazine, this time in the January 2004 issue: 'Too many companies (and head-hunters) appoint very senior people based on their reputation rather than their achievements – and these people are often recycled round other top jobs without appearing to touch the sides.' She then went on to question the appointment of Barbara Cassani, ex-CEO of GO, the airline acquired by EasyJet: 'Does this track record justify her appointment as head of Britain's Olympic bid team or qualify her to be a non-executive director of Marks and Spencer?'

It is fair to say that one could dissect the boards of FTSE 100, 250, 350 companies and find a significant number of people who simply have no clear right to hold a non-executive role around the board table. Increasingly analysis is being undertaken by independent research organisations often on behalf of ever more frustrated institutional investors who are seeking to drive the governance agenda. Findings of governance breaches, be they exceeding the nine-year rule of 'independence'; CEOs moving into Chair roles; combined CEO/Chair roles; lack of diversity… are ever present. The following extract from '**Breaking down barriers: diversity and inclusion in the C-suite'** August 2018 (*Financier Worldwide Magazine*)

> The path to the C-suite is not an established, linear journey. On the contrary, it is challenging and oblique. This is especially so for women, ethnic minorities, the disabled, and the lesbian, gay, bisexual and transgender (LGBT) community.
>
> Testifying to the extent of the struggle facing this large slice of the population is a wealth of studies and analyses, and reams of anecdotal evidence, much of which characterises senior management teams as utterly lacking in diversity and inclusion. For example, the 2017 'Parker Review' of the ethnic diversity of UK companies revealed that over half of all FTSE 100 firms do not have a single director from an ethnic minority background, with only 8 percent of these firms' 1,087 directors being of non-white origin.
>
> In another review, the UK government commissioned 'Hampton-Alexander Review 2017', the extent of the work needing to be done to recruit women into senior business roles is highlighted, with 33 percent of women in senior

positions by 2020 the voluntary target. A similarly themed 2018 review by the Allegis Group – 'Talent, Business, and Competition: A New World of Diversity & Inclusion' – found that in Fortune 500 companies, women and minorities hold 31 percent of board seats… overall, almost 80 percent of board members are male.

In terms of LGBT representation at C-suite level, many studies reveal that LGBT workers continue to experience discrimination in the workplace, there being numerous barriers to entry…

Research consistently demonstrates a link between diversity and inclusion and a company's operational and financial performance… a 2018 McKinsey report – 'Delivering through diversity' – highlights a strong link, finding that companies in the top rank for executive team gender diversity were 21 percent more likely to experience above-average profitability than less-inclusive companies. In terms of ethnic and cultural diversity, McKinsey found a 35 percent likelihood of increased financial performance.

To disrupt the status quo and embrace the positives that greater diversity and inclusion in the C-suite can bring – such as money savings, revenue boosts and sustainable long-term value – attitudes, cultures and systems clearly need to change.

We have witnessed the disastrous events of the 2008 banking crisis. One of the core issues raised was the role of non-executive chairmen and directors. What were these supposedly highly experienced veterans of FTSE 100 companies doing while their companies were being driven off the cliff by their executive teams?

We are experiencing another period of so-called drought of senior talent. Almost daily the columns of the *Financial Times* have articles about how many FTSE 100 companies are searching for suitable chairmen, about the pressures on a small group who are in constant demand, and the need for some to give up current roles to take on new challenges etc, that then only create new voids. I really do find all of this quite amazing, as I have absolutely no doubt that there are a good number of outstanding individuals fully equipped, fully able, to take on chairs of FTSE 100 companies; that there are extraordinarily qualified, mature individuals able to take on chairs in major financial institutions. They may not come from standard routes, but they have all the expertise and more that may be needed. They have the intellect, they have the gravitas, and many have outstanding skills at questioning, challenging and evaluating, and above all real independence.

New provisions defining 'independence' for non-executive directors in a revised corporate governance code could affect one-fifth of FTSE 100 chairs

GAVIN HINKS, DECEMBER 11, 2017, 'BOARD AGENDA'

UK corporate governance code changes to hit dozens of chairmen: Reforms to improve accountability to affect 67 of Britain's largest listed companies

MADISON MARRIAGE FT DECEMBER 11 2017

And so it was and so it is still in February 2020 with a wave of Chairman roles about to become vacant for the above reasons and others…including Lloyds Banking Group and Aviva,

I want to digress for a moment. In 1986 I was chief executive of Valin Pollen, a corporate and financial communications business. My chairman, Reg Valin, was one of the two founders. Reg was (and is) a tall slim man of about 6'2, with a strong physical presence. I had arranged for my then eight-year-old son to come into the office to see where Dad worked. As I was showing him around we bumped into Reg and the following conversation took place:

Reg: Hello, and who are you?

Son: My name is Robert. And who are you?

Reg: I'm Reg, I'm the chairman.

Son: Does that mean that you decide who sits where, and that you move the chairs around the table?

Reg (laughing): An excellent description of what the chairman does!

Out of the mouth of babes!

It will need chairmen (and nomination committees) who are prepared to change the chairs around the board table, who are prepared to challenge conventional wisdom, who are willing and able to think outside the box, to bring about the magnitude of change required.

MORE WHYS

So, to repeat, why not actively attract people with the experience that can enhance the quality of strategic thought around the board table? Why not recruit NEDs from a much wider gene pool than hitherto, including the arts, academia, the professions, the sciences and medicine, and from the not for profit sector? And very specifically why not throw the net much wider to ensure an effective mix of diverse candidates?

People who have managed vast charitable institutions, who have been officers in the forces, who have been partners in law firms or accountancy firms, or who have held senior management consultancy positions advising CEOs and boards of large multinational corporations, could make impressive contributions; could bring fresh thinking, and true independence. All of which are needed and are perceived to be in short supply. This notion that there is a scarcity of NED talent is something I have doubted for a long time! There is a vast army of talent available, talent that can be effectively harnessed if the will exists! And especially given the relentless need,

> 'City head-hunter MWM Consulting caused a stir yesterday saying that there were not enough suitably qualified people to serve as chairman of our leading companies... it has become commonplace in recent times for companies to search for months to fill such vacancies'
>
> ANTHONY HILTON, *EVENING STANDARD*, 13TH JULY 2010

As I have already mentioned I fundamentally disagree! There is an abundance of talent waiting to be recognised. Men, women, black, brown, disabled, young, old, who have extraordinary skills and competencies. It just takes real focus to find them.

Interestingly a digital recruitment business called NUROLE now frequently makes reference to their client's need for diversity, their clients preference for diverse candidates... even to the extent that I wonder whether we have crossed the line and the need for re-balancing has allowed slippage into positive discrimination?

HELP AVAILABLE

Let's turn to the means available to find talent. There are four alternative routes available: search, selection, interim, and of course internal. I shall briefly examine each.

SEARCH

Executive search, or head-hunting, is a well-established service provided by a large number of organisations, some global, some domestic, and some very local. Despite the provision of this service being in existence for decades, it is time for serious questions to be asked:

- Why has the fee structure stayed so rigidly at the 'one-third' of total compensation level?

- Why are 'professional service providers' reluctant to question their mandates, specifically what they are requested to search for?

- Why are search consultants not prepared to actually consult, not just process?

The answers are manifold. Search is essentially a distressed purchase. A vacancy needs to be filled, and usually fast. Hence the fee is largely irrelevant (except perhaps in the climate of austerity of post Financial crisis 2008 to 2018). Search executives typically want to get the job done, the fee collected, and move on to the next mandate. And most clients really do not want consultancy from their head-hunter, just delivery. There are of course exceptions, but they tend to be rare.

Search consultants and their clients really need to get two critical issues resolved:

- Speed of decisions making: Candidates are essentially placing their future in your hands. They deserve to be communicated with promptly. To my mind it is utterly wrong for organisations to drag out their decision making process without any consideration for the impact they may be having on the candidates. It is incumbent on the client organisation, and the search consultancy, to have their process in order, to have their decision making procedures sorted, and be able to move with some degree of speed. As a head-hunter I placed significant emphasis on ensuring that the whole process was pre-agreed with my clients, was as tight as possible, and that there was clear and fast communication with the candidates. And it worked.

- Waiting: Keeping people waiting I find wholly unacceptable. Candidates who are scheduled to be interviewed at a certain time, should not be kept waiting! I believe that basic courtesies do not alter, irrespective of the nature of the relationship between people, irrespective of whether one is buying or selling, irrespective of relative wealth. If I invite someone for a meeting at 15.30 on a certain date, I will be available 15.30, not 15.35, and absolutely not 16.00. And frankly I would expect the same from people I had arranged to meet with! Relatively few things make my blood boil more than being kept waiting by someone I have arranged an appointment with. It is the height of discourtesy, and merely an attempt to demonstrate either relative power, or that their time is more important than yours. Yuk!

Pilita Clark of the FT recently had an article very much to this point 'When a rude boss keeps you waiting, why not walk out', 26th January 2020 and provided examples of people doing just that after waiting for some 15minutes past the agreed time. Keeping anyone waiting, no matter however great the individual might be, in my book is just wrong and unacceptable!

Attention to detail is critical all the way through the process. It is people's lives that are at stake, their careers, their aspirations, their future. It is so easy to deal with people correctly, and so easy to screw things up, so why not do the right thing?

Why not return calls quickly?

Why not ensure that candidates are properly briefed?

Why not communicate with all candidates, including those that have to be turned down?

Why not advise candidates of the outcome quickly and politely?

Why not ensure that every single candidate is dealt with in an efficient and proper manner, irrespective of status or outcome?

Why not extend basic courtesies to all?

Why not ensure that communications are clear and timely?

It is so easy, so why isn't it done? Believe me it is easier to do it systematically, in a timely and honest manner than to leave it adrift.

I really can't understand why some people find it so difficult to do the simplest of things effectively. It is also not unusual that the worst offenders are the mid-level functionaries, rather than the bosses. The old saying comes to mind: 'If you want something done properly, find someone who is busy'.

When I was chief executive at Valin Pollen I learned from my chairman, Reg Valin, what it meant to have an efficient office. The man was pulled in numerous different directions, had a vast amount of paper passing through his office (pre-internet and e-mail), internal and external meetings to attend, clients to serve, institutional shareholders and analysts to respond to and communicate with, and a non-stop flow of calls to deal with. And yet everything got done, every letter got answered, 'turned round', the day it was received, every memo and every internal document got responded to without fail and without delay, and similarly with every call and message received.

He had a very efficient PA with whom he worked in a well-structured manner, and he had an amazing discipline to get things done, and not to allow paperwork to accumulate. I have emulated that style ever since, all letters, e-mails, calls, get responded to without fail, and within 24 hours. This is not only a question of courtesy, this also happens to be the easiest and most efficient way for me to deal with this aspect of work. I recommend it, it really is by far the easiest way to keep ahead.

Dirk Schavemaker, as SVP Operations of MVCI (Marriott Vacation Club International) also led a pressurised life, running a global organisation with almost 13,000 properties, and yet managed to be able to return calls and e-mails without delay, and always within 24hrs! It is possible, it can be done; it is done by those that care.

Many years ago I was totally staggered by the way a young woman was treated by one of the leading communication firms of the world, Ogilvy. She had worked with Ogilvy in Toronto the previous summer (during her university vacation), had received an outstanding performance evaluation, was given a significant cash reward for her contribution, flowers, card, etc at the end of her internship, even though it was made clear at the outset that the role carried no financial reward (evidence of how highly she was thought of by the Toronto team). The following year she applied for the formal Ogilvy graduate training programme in the UK. She completed and submitted a detailed application pack which of course included reference to her work with Ogilvy in Toronto, and referees from Ogilvy's Toronto office, including the boss of the office who had specifically offered to act as a referee. She was rejected out of hand.

Okay so life is not predictable and the UK graduate programme may have been looking for something different from what she had to offer; fair enough. Surely it would have made good commercial sense to at least invite her in for a meeting? Someone who clearly had done well in another Ogilvy office, seems to have been rated highly by her seniors, and had accumulated some relevant experience of the business and the company. Who knows where someone like that will end up? Even a very real possibility of becoming a potential client one day!

Many leading professional services firms do take the utmost care with all applicants for exactly that reason! But to have been sent a letter that was untitled, undated, unsigned, contained a single sentence 'Your application is not being taken further' was the utmost in rudeness, and sloppiness. Zero attention to detail here! Ogilvy, the advertising/PR company, whose business is communication, how crazy is that? And what sort of lasting impression has that little experience left? (Sir Martin Sorrell, who was then CEO of WPP the owner of Ogilvy would have been be horrified, as he is the epitome of courtesy, and efficiency. Despite his highly charged schedule he manages to respond to letters, e-mails, calls etc. without delay!)

Search can be a valuable and effective means by which suitable candidates can be sourced. There are issues that need to be managed both with clients and candidates, and there are numerous questions that need to be resolved by a client mandating a search firm especially in terms of the sort of firm that best fits requirements, culture and chemistry. Never shrink away from asking why.

SELECTION

This is where jobs are advertised in selected media, and candidates decide themselves whether the advertised job is one that they feel qualified to respond to. Rather than search, where the executive search consultancy uses its expertise to find suitable candidates, selection passes the task of finding the candidate to (a) the appropriate media, and (b) to the candidate him/herself by requiring to take the initiative to respond to the advertisement. The recruitment firm's expertise is in drafting the advertisement, identifying the right media, which today is more than likely to be social media/LinkedIn/Facebook and processing and evaluating the responses, Skype interviewing and creating the short list.

The task of the selection consultant is to be able to sift through the vast inflow of responses in a relatively quick and efficient manner, sorting out those that warrant closer and more detailed evaluation.

Every single application by letter, fax or e-mail should be answered in a polite and timely manner. It is utterly inexcusable for applicants not to get a response, even if the response, as is likely in the majority of cases, is a polite rejection. It is not unusual nowadays for selection firm to merely state that if the candidate has not heard from them within the next 'x' days then their application will not be taken further. Why take such an easy cop-out? Surely if people have taken the time and trouble to apply, the minimum is to communicate directly with them too? Especially today, volume is no reason not to handle all responses/applications with courtesy and care as technology can help substantially.

Having sifted through the inflow, the selection consultant is now ready to go to the next stage and commence interviewing those who meet the cut-off criteria. From here on the process is virtually identical to that of search as candidates are interviewed, tested, referenced, and short-listed candidates presented to the client for final selection.

In summary, selection may be an appropriate methodology. Always remember to respond to everyone who took the trouble to write to you. Respond in a timely manner. Respond with attention to detail. Treat all applicants with courtesy and respect: you just never know when someone rejected may pop up in the future, as a customer/client, supplier, or recruiter!

INTERIM

Interim management has grown substantially and is fully accepted as an additional means of resourcing in certain situations. Think of it in terms of 'talent on demand'.

Interim is substantially different from both search and selection. The client is usually seeking to fill an urgent, immediate requirement. There is no time to undertake a fully-fledged search or selection process; the need is here and now.

The scenario could be a sudden departure at a critical time, a death or illness, a board decision to dispose of a business, a go ahead for a new project, a recognition of a need for a specific expertise… a whole mix of different factors could result in there being a need for qualified, experienced, senior management talent, now. For example a board decides that it wants to dispose of a certain subsidiary. But the existing managing director of this subsidiary has been with the company a long time and may not be prepared to do what is truly required ('turkeys don't vote for Christmas!') Hence an interim is appointed with a very simple and clear brief, with no conflict of interest at all. This is exactly the domain of the 2,200 interim management firms… the top 10 in 2018 being:

- Interim Partners

- Eton Bridge Partners

- Practicus

- Penna

- Odgers Interim

- Boyden Interim

- WBMS

- Solace In Business

- Green Park

- B2EConsulting

These firms cultivate data bases of proven management resource, specific expertise and with functional and sector experience, pre-referenced, and qualifications verified. So if the client happens to require immediately a qualified finance director with experience of the clothing sector, the data base should be able to rapidly produce suitable names and CVs.

There is a growing group of professional interims, people who have taken a lifestyle decision not to go back to full time employment but to have direct control over their lives and to undertake interim management assignments. They are professionals in their own right.

For the client however an interim means clarity of terms, no vacation payment, no worry over bonus payments, certainty in the cost, and total control. The client can turn the switch off, just as easily as requesting an extension. A good example is given by the head of a major European corporation: 'The incumbent wasn't up to the task, I needed somebody who could step in and get up to speed right there and right then... the interim executive I brought in succeeded in turning round the division... not expensive at all if you strip out holiday pay and all the other overheads associated with a permanent position, plus the speed.'

Using the services of an interim provider has many well documented benefits. Just make sure that you are working with a well-established and professional firm. Check their credentials. Unfortunately almost anyone can stick a plaque on the wall; it is not a regulated service, there are many of the 'unwashed' variety. Check out your interim firm of choice: do they have a track record; do they vet, reference-verify their interim-managers; do they have references that they can provide of both clients and interims?

And as of 1st April 2020 there is another hurdle that the interim sector, and specifically the interim executives, will need to navigate, that is UK tax legislation called IR35. According to Wikipedia 'IR35 refers to the United Kingdom's anti-avoidance tax legislation designed to tax "disguised" employment at a rate similar to employment. In this context, "disguised employees" means workers who receive payments from a client via an intermediary, for example, their own limited company, and whose relationship with their client is such that had they been paid directly they would be employees of the client.' The topic of IR35 is too complex to fully expose here suffice to reference it and link it with self-employed status of interim executives. IR35 can be managed legally and bona-fida self-employed can navigate without too significant barriers.

As business needs change ever faster, as the need for specific expertise in specific circumstances grows, as the urgency increases for talent on demand, for having the right person in position now, not in three months' time, as need for specific expertise AI, robotics, blockchain, just to name a few, explodes, so the demand for interims expand. One could almost argue that as the average tenure of CEOs is reducing, now just under three years, that they have themselves become interim executives!

INTERNAL

One often overlooked source of recruitment is from within the organisation itself. Frequently this is deliberate as management decides to find talent from the outside who can bring in new ideas, new ways of doing things, or new competences that are believed not to exist within the existing team. That's okay if it reflects reality.

Reality, however, is frequently that management simply has no clue as to what competences, skill sets and untapped talent may be lurking within their organisation. Hence mandating a search or selection is a convenient cop-out, especially if they advise at the same time that the search/selection will be open to internal candidates too. This way what appears to be a very equitable solution is found. Equal opportunity is given to internal candidates while the best of what is available in the open market will set the bar high to secure the very best available, and at the same time management do not need to deal with the process itself as it is outsourced to the selected executive search/selection consultancy.

The very best corporations and professional service firms do have a well-structured internal promotion policy. They do resource internally wherever possible, they do know the skills, competences, strengths and weaknesses of their people, and do plot their career development accordingly. It is argued that 'superior talent will be tomorrow's prime source of competitive advantage', or as AlliedSignal's CEO Larry Bossidy put it, 'We bet on people not strategies'.

In today's world of ever increased focus on diversity, equality of opportunities, ensuring professional management of any organisation's talent pool has to be one of the most strategically important role. As such 'Chief People Officers' are increasingly gaining seats around the board table, and frankly absolutely right too.

Resourcing is an on-going activity because of the very nature of human beings, whether internal or external, search, selection or interim methods are used. There are basic truths that should be applied in all circumstances, so here are my immediate Do it Right, Do it Now suggestions:

Do it Right: Do it Now!: Consider the suitability of your personal network

Do it Right: Do it Now!: Know the available talent pool, the existing internal resources

Do it Right: Do it Now!: Respect the individual, in terms of courtesy, timeliness, honesty

Do it Right: Do it Now!: Always respond, irrespective how many there may be to respond to, or how poor the application may have been

Do it Right: Do it Now!: Respond in a timely manner

Do it Right: Do it Now!: Always be on time; never keep candidates (or anyone else) waiting

Do it Right: Do it Now!: Learn to listen: we were born with two ears and one mouth and should use them in that proportion

Do it Right: Do it Now!: Move HR from process to value added

Do it Right: Do it Now!: Select external professional service providers based on need and demonstrable expertise

Do it Right: Do it Now!: If you use professional firms use them as professional advisers, not as body-shops

Do it Right: Do it Now!: Value independence in advisers

Do it Right: Do it Now!: Never forget that all applicants are also your customers, potential future competitors, regulators, tax inspectors, advisers etc!

Do it Right: Do it Now!

Let me finish this chapter by sharing with you an example of excellence, or pretty close to it. GlaxoSmithKline, the FTSE 100 leading pharmaceuticals group, some while ago was in the firing line because the pay structure proposed for its then CEO, Jean-Pierre Garnier included a massive reward for failure component. The shareholders revolted against this, and he/the company grudgingly accepted to restructure. But on a much more positive note the company is an extraordinary recruiter of talent. Every year the company needed to recruit something like 6,000 people, and by a simple assumption of the numbers that they would need to interview to get to this number of new recruits, they will have seen over 40,000 people. That is 40,000 people who will have formed an opinion of the company by the way they were treated through the recruitment process. Lou Manzi, the then vice-president of global recruitment summed it up: 'We can't give 100% of the people jobs but we can treat them with the highest respect... Even if they are turned down for a job with us, they should walk away with the feeling that this is a phenomenal company'. YES, YES, YES... exactly right! And this is exactly what Ogilvy got so wrong with their response to the young woman referenced earlier in this chapter.

It would do all companies a great deal of good if they stopped seeing their candidates just as candidates, but saw them also as future customers, competitors, opinion formers, etc.

Resourcing is a mighty challenge for most companies. It gets a little easier in a slack economy, but quickly becomes hugely pressurised in a rapidly expanding economy, as was the case throughout the late 1990s when the term 'War for Talent' first emerged. But once you've got the right person, the right team of people, how do you keep them? How can the right people be retained and developed; rewarded and generally nurtured for leadership? These issues shall be the focus of the coming sections.

4. KEEPING TALENTED PEOPLE

Once you've got your man/woman, once you've got the various members of your management team, once you've got your movers and shakers, your leaders, your entrepreneurial driven business developers, your finance specialists etc, how do you retain them and continue to provide motivation? These are issues that have occupied the minds of business leaders, business academics, and social scientists for a long time. Vast numbers of words have been dedicated to the debate of this subject matter.

Organizations provide specialist consultancy services to clients keen to find ever better, ever more contemporary means to achieve effective talent retention. For example, firms such as Towers Watson and Mercer specialize in the development of executive incentive compensation structures aimed to reward and retain. And many law firms have specialist teams engaged in advising on not just employment law in general, but specifically on EISs (executive incentive schemes), option plans, and all matters related to reward and retention.

DAYS OF SLAVERY ARE OVER

But the simple truth of the matter can be summarised by an experience I had back in 1985. At that time I was an executive director of a merchant bank, Charterhouse, and I had received an offer to join Valin Pollen, as its chief executive. On receipt of the formal offer I went to my direct boss, Bruce Fireman, and explained the opportunity that had arisen. Although we had become friends, he was my boss. He considered the offer and confirmed that it seemed right for me, a move up and a real challenge. At the same time he openly admitted that he would prefer for me to stay, but, 'The days of slavery are over,' he said, and 'Irrespective of how much I would prefer for you to stay, I will not stand in your way of pursuing something that is clearly right for you and your career.' I have used those words many times since, 'The days of slavery are over'. How simple, and how wise!

The days of slavery being over, retention therefore should not be about tying people in, but about creating the environment in which they wish to remain. The environment itself is hugely complex and involves the job, the colleagues, the compensation, the future growth potential, the challenges, the leader's vision, the quality of interpersonal relationships, the training and development investment, as well as the alternatives on offer. It is difficult to imagine a scenario where all of these factors are aligned to such an extent that if a phenomenal alternative arose, even the most motivated and loyal person would not seriously consider it, and if appropriate, take it! Except, where there is personal ownership of the business, not just personal ownership of some small equity percentage in a business, but real ownership and control of the business. And even here the alternative that may arise in the form of an offer to purchase the business by a third party would be seriously considered if the price and related circumstances were right!

The above is hugely underscored by the massive growth of Private Equity which has successfully bought many thousands of privately owned businesses, creating equally many thousands of millionaires in the process, and helping to grow and develop businesses beyond their original entrepreneurial founders and teams. But retention of the right talent is a huge issue for them too.

Retention can also be totally mismanaged as was dramatized by a company I was invited to chair some years ago in the mid-2010s. The company was reasonably large, just sub €1bn with some 5,000 people and had recently been acquired by hedge funds. The hedge funds decided that the incumbent executive team was of quality and should be retained and incentivised to remain. They implemented a simple time-based retention plan... stay for a minimum of 24 months and you'll be rewarded with a retention bonus €1m! No performance criteria, nothing apart from time! I was totally besides myself with disbelief, incredulity, that such incredibly super bright people could implement a plan so clearly flawed with the inevitable happening of certain key executives treading water just to get their bonus before leaving.

Not a good example of what to do! An excellent example of what not to do!

WHAT EFFECTS RETENTION?

So let's look at the environment. Let's look at it at various stages of a career, and the sort of factors that would significantly enhance retention.

The job is clearly of profound importance. Everyone from the very first day in their very first job wants to be doing something that they feel is using their abilities, stretching their abilities, developing them and their competencies. They want a job that they can do and that they are allowed to do. They want a job that they can see clearly will lead to somewhere, exactly where may not be that important at this stage, but one that has real potential for growth. People starting out on their career after school, or university, between the ages of 16-22, have an abundance of energy and enthusiasm. They want to come home at night feeling that they have been stretched, intellectually or physically, or both. They want to come home at the end of a week feeling that they have made a contribution, feeling that they have a voice and a voice that is free to express itself and be listened to. They also want to feel that the employer is prepared to put something into their development, to help them learn new skills and competences.

Consider the likely impact that the following experience would have. A graduate from Durham University secured for himself the job of the kind that he had been salivating after for the previous six months. He had seen a tiny article in the *Financial Times* about a new e-commerce strategy consultancy that was being started by M&C Saatchi. He immediately sent an e-mail and actively pursued the company until they relented and took him on as their first graduate trainee. As he had turned down an alternative job offer paying a 50% higher starting salary to 'pursue his dream,' he was promised a salary review after three months.

For the first few months he couldn't wait to get out of bed, he was with a relatively small team, in a sexy sector, working in a smart office in Golden Square, Central London. It was all new and exciting, and he felt he was learning something new every day. But when his request to participate at client meetings was turned down, even those for which he had done the analytical grunt work; when his request to attend certain relevant training sessions was turned down; when he realized that he had stopped learning, and that he was being used as a 'go-for', his motivation and commitment rapidly declined. This decline was aided in no short measure by the fact that the promised review after his initial three months with the company never took place. When three months had come and gone, he reminded his boss that a review had been promised. 'No problem, we'll get it done shortly' was the reply, and so it went on for months, lots of promises, no delivery.

At last, after repeated requests, he was given a review, and it was a good review, with praise for the work he had accomplished, his fit with the team etc. 'What about the salary review?', 'Oh don't worry we'll take care of that,' came the reply. When he was offered an annual salary increase of £96.48, being the calculated amount after a companywide percentage increase was applied to his salary, pro-rated for the remaining months in the year, his next move became an absolute certainty. The derisory salary increase was not the cause; it was just the final tipping point.

The real cause was the lack of recognition that a new graduate needs to be stretched, challenged, and included. (At the same time, management trainees in McDonalds were being recruited at salary levels well above what M&C Saatchi was paying their graduate!)

There is a real tragedy in today's economy. A tragedy in that there are so many energetic and enthusiastic young people desperate to find suitable jobs. And equally a tragedy in the number of young professionals who are desperate to get out of their first job. The huge first job excitement has wilted and been replaced by the reality of boredom, barriers, blockages, no entry signs, cul-de-sacs, and more and more frustrations. There are hugely talented and able recent graduates with excellent first and upper second degrees from top universities, Oxford, Cambridge, Durham, Manchester, Leeds, UCL, etc. who are screaming with frustration, who come home in the evening exhausted with anger and frustration. Who are paid modestly and yet have much to contribute. What a waste of talent, what a waste of energy, what a waste of creativity!

Here are two examples of the many:

- A highly talented, well educated, intelligent and articulate man just turned 30 explained, 'There are three matrices: money, work-life balance, and intellectual engagement. On money, my job is okay, but I worry about the future; work-life balance is if anything too cushy, a real 9-5 scenario; intellectual engagement is way below 50%! I am dying!'

- An equally talented and educated woman quit her job in a major corporation, despite having nowhere else to go, as she simply could not take the 'mental deprivation' any longer. When she raised the issue with her boss, the response was, 'We all had to go through it, so just relax and enjoy!'

The above is equally true for all graduates no matter which university they may have graduated from… arguably even more so as graduates from many universities feel a sense of rejection right at the time when they should be on a high from graduating. Many leading professional service businesses, many leading financial institutions and investment banks, many major corporations have a 'policy' of only recruiting from what they perceive as 'top' universities, thereby essentially immediately ghettoing a significant number of graduates. Quality can be found everywhere and with the technological advances available in 2020 there should be no excuse for not spreading the net wide, for not being fully inclusive!

THE WHYS

Why should this be the reality for so many?

Why can't employers structure employment for the young that takes account of their energy and drive?

Why don't employers see the harm they are doing and the opportunities they are losing?

Why can't employers create work environments that challenge and stretch the able and the willing?

Why is it so difficult to strike the right balance between stretching, demanding and rewarding work and lifestyle?

Why is there such a belief in pressurising the new recruits either by utter boredom, or by 20 hour work days?

Why do we accept this crazy situation that so many now find themselves exposed to?

Why the implied arrogance, 'if this was OK for me, it should be OK for others?'

Why is technology not better applied so that ever wider inclusion should be possible?

And why do we accept this even more bizarre, and frankly immoral, situation that many young people now have to endure... the so called 'work experience' situation. There are many different environments in which this applies, although perhaps it is seen most frequently in the world of media. Magazines and newspapers, advertising and PR companies, TV broadcasters and production companies, cable stations and satellite networks, auction houses and galleries, all have developed 'work experience' into a fine art! Companies know that there are thousands of willing and capable young people who are desperate to get started in their business. So they make available a handful of 'work experience' positions to the lucky few who are invited to take them up.

But you don't only need to be lucky, you also need to be able to support yourself financially because these 'work experience' positions are unpaid! They are not only unpaid, but they don't even provide cash for the expense of getting to and from the workplace, which as anyone living in London knows can come to tens of pounds per week. So, by design, by definition, only those who either have parents able and willing to continue to support their child, or who have other means of earning cash, can undertake these 'work experience' positions. Interesting that the media sector as a whole is not known for its poverty, nor are its bosses known for their thrift or modest compensation! And when the extraordinary does happen that someone on 'work experience' is offered a permanent position this is usually at the very most junior level, and at a salary that is a disgrace in comparison to other professional services businesses.

Let me give you just one example. A relatively small but well established and reputable PR company has at any one time some 8 to 10 young people doing 'work experience' out of a total staff of about 40. They are all unpaid. They are all expected to undertake full time work for pre-agreed periods of three to six months. They are all expected to perform and deliver during this time. The PR company's clients have no clue about who is on work experience, who is paid or unpaid, but get billed for all hours recorded by everyone. So the company earns fees, but pays nothing, and when one work experience person leaves there are plenty waiting in the wings to take their place. And when the situation occurs that a work experience person is invited to join the paid staff, they are offered a starting salary most people would find it difficult to survive on in London.

A friend's son was working in exactly this situation. After six months of employment he was given a performance review which was excellent, but: 'Unfortunately we are not in a position to be able to give you a salary increase, although we are delighted with your contribution, and would like you to take on more responsibility in certain areas,' said the boss. 'I'm truly grateful for my review,' was the employee's reply. 'I love what I'm doing and am so glad that my performance reflects this fact. But in all honesty, I simply cannot continue on my starting salary and sadly will be forced to look elsewhere if you cannot make an appropriate adjustment to my salary.'

That took guts. Amazingly, within ten minutes a ten percent

salary increase was granted. If you don't ask, you don't get!

Although the above is still a reality for many, the Government has been trying to make such practices illegal and has introduced a structured 'apprenticeship' programme for those over 16 who also wish to continue in education. A significant step in the right direction.

LOGIC NOT WORKING

When I have challenged this situation in the past it has been explained to me that it is all about basic economics, supply and demand. In other words, there is a vast supply of people who want to work in media and limited demand. Therefore, given the large supply, media companies can reduce the price! I then looked around and saw that there was also a huge appetite among graduates for jobs in investment banking and management consulting, a situation in which there was also a vast mismatch between supply and demand, and yet in both these 'professions' the young people that were successful at securing jobs were rewarded exceptionally well, were used to their limits, stretched (arguably sometimes too much), trained and developed. If they were taken on for 'work experience' they were also properly rewarded. So what's the difference?

It clearly is not about basic economics!

But it gets worse. As people mature, as they make progress within their organizations, the likelihood of things getting better should increase. How many times has a promotion been offered to you that you felt was going to really challenge you to your limits? How many times has your boss, and the professional support team of HR experts and managers, sat down with you to review what you've done so far, where your next move should be, how best to plan to get there effectively? Frequently promotions are offered when someone is already virtually doing that job, hence it is just a formalisation of a reality.

Often promotions are offered in title but not in fact, for example you've been made an 'associate director' but the fact is that your day to day activity has not changed at all. Words without deeds will only lead to frustration and disaffection. Underutilisation and poor career development will lead to the competent and able increasingly to actively pursue alternative opportunities.

It is a reality that the best are the most mobile and the most willing to terminate situations that are wholly unacceptable because they know they can re-locate.

Companies that can stretch, companies that can deliver on their promises, that can develop, that can properly review performance and work with their employees to mould their careers will retain the talent that they have identified, and wish to retain.

BIRDS OF A FEATHER

I also mentioned colleagues as a factor that can influence the decision to stay or go. The best like to be associated with the best. Companies that have poor people management have poor knowledge about who are the top performers and who are the weakest performers, about who to compensate exceptionally well for exceptional performance, and to whom not to give a bonus.

In McKinsey's The War for Talent 2000 survey of 6,500 senior and mid-level managers at 35 large US companies, 59 percent reported that they had worked for an under-performer. Of this group 76 percent suggested that this prevented them from learning; 81 percent that it hurt their careers; and a massive 86 percent that it made them want to leave the company!

The best will find such environments unacceptable and move on, leaving behind an ever-growing shift towards the lowest common denominator. The best fly on and find environments that are ever more testing and challenging, where only the best survive, and the weakest are weeded out, constantly refreshing the pool and maintaining an ever present upward pressure. Birds of a feather and all that, but the likelihood is that similar people will click better together, will enjoy each other's company more, be able to create a more productive and rewarding environment.

McKinsey & Co Inc is well known for its 'up or out' policy. In other words all consultants are expected either to keep on growing, keep on making progress along a set of pre-defined expectations within bands of time periods, or, after a number of clearly defined signals, start to take steps to move on outside and leave. Some view this process as hugely pressurized, tough and unduly severe, but it is this process that has ensured that only the best and the willing are able to progress, that there is such a unique culture for which so many have such extraordinary respect even though they have left, that so many friendships that last lifetimes have been established. What better proof of this than the number of people who gather at annual or bi-annual alumni events, and the number of people who gathered in June 2003 in New York, London, and other locations around the world to pay respect, in memorial services held for Marvin Bower who died aged 100, to the spiritual leader and effectively the man who made McKinsey into the unique and world respected organisation that it is. And despite the issues McKinsey has had to confront during the last few years issues about being mandated by inappropriate organisations, issues about the integrity of certain ex-partners et al… McKinsey's reputation is still largely intact… with thousands of alumni still gathering annually around the world.

Another organisation renowned for its staff loyalty, and surprisingly so given that it is essentially a massive call centre, is First Direct, the phone and online bank owned by HSBC. Its reported 14 percent staff turnover is massively below the industry average and it has been recognised as the best call centre in the UK. The key reason, as explained by First Direct's founder/CEO Mike Harris, is that 'at the heart of the business was a pledge to treat employees as individuals' or as articulated by a subsequent CEO Matt Colebrook, 'We have always celebrated the original nature of the individual. In fact, we celebrate here a lot.' First Direct's then Head of People, Stewart Bromley added: 'The idea was, from day one, to use peer support and employee engagement to drive customer service… the brand is based on people's perception and experience of dealing with us as a business… employee engagement is absolutely critical.' In fact, employee engagement (defined by David MacLeod as 'unlocking people's potential, enabling them to be the best they can be') has been the subject of much debate and research, with some interesting findings that suggest:

- 59 percent of engaged employees say that work brings out their most creative ideas

- 67 percent of engaged employees advocate their organisation

- Significantly better retention rates

- Higher productivity

- Greater customer loyalty

- And better overall profitability

The importance of employee engagement is recognised by the Department for Business, Innovation and Skills (BIS) which has articulated a belief that competent and engaged employees were key to helping 'UK plc' out of recession. This was supported by the then CEO of Sainsbury's, Justin King, who agreed that even in an organisation employing some 150,000 people, engagement is important, even if one needs to work 'very hard' to achieve it. 'Our starting point is that everybody wants to come to work looking to do a good job'. But why is it that some people don't do a good job? He offered three explanations: 'Either they don't know what a good job looks like, they don't have the tools to do a good job, or they don't have the context.' Justin King said organisations spent a 'tremendous amount of time' on the first two, but rarely provided staff with the context, or on 'giving people a real reason for why they are doing what they're doing'. (*Rules of engagement*, David Woodward. *Director*, September 2009)

CASH

What about money?

Money does matter, and those who cast it to one side are seriously out of touch with reality. People are motivated by money as it is a tangible measure of personal worth. How much am I worth to you? There is no logical yardstick, there are no logical comparatives. It is very much the law of the jungle. Who is to say that an accountant is worth more than a nurse, or a company director is worth more than a university professor? Or that the manager of the England football team is worth approximately 20 times more than the UK Prime Minister?

What is evident is that the more you have the more you want, the more senior the job the more important the package and all its components become... for example the *Times* newspaper reported the details of the package of a newly appointed CEO of a FTSE 100 company. This included a substantial basic salary of many hundreds of thousands of pounds, an annual bonus of up to a hundred percent of basic salary, a golden hello of stock worth many more hundreds of thousands of pounds, plus further stock options on an annual basis with potential values in the millions, plus significant pension contributions, and then it went into the minutia of school fees, private dental care, private medicine, car and chauffeur, accommodation allowance etc. Clearly money matters. A graduate I knew in the company at the time, on a highly selective fast track graduate programme, pointed out that the new CEO's school fee allowance was greater than his annual salary! Not the most motivational discovery.

Money also speaks volumes when a new recruit is paid many times more for agreeing to join an organization to fill a vacancy than an existing internal employee at the equivalent level. This can cause serious ruptures among internal parities if that were to matter. In a world where the search for the best is an on-going activity, the notion of 'we'll pay whatever it takes' however has currency: 'To get the people they want 39 percent of the top-quartile companies pay whatever it takes, compared with 26 percent of their mid-quartile competitors' (*The war for talent, McKinsey Quarterly* 1998, Number 3).

Those companies seriously determined to recruit the best, to maintain a relentless momentum to attract the best, are prepared to pay 'whatever it takes' irrespective of some of the potential consequences they may have to address and manage. It goes with the territory. And this was as true in the recession inflicted, debt burdened UK of 2010 as it was in the go-go days of the rapidly growing global economies of the mid 00s and as it is in the new decade of 2020.

There is an uncanny persistence in the old saying, 'Pay peanuts and you get monkeys!'

I had a discussion recently where the business owner said… 'I keep telling my senior executives it is much better to get someone exceptional, even if it is necessary to pay well above the odds, than someone kind of OK at a lower salary because the output, the drive, the proactivity will be so much greater. Probably one exceptional may equal three ordinary!'

A number of years ago I was asked to advise how a well-established research organisation could get the same sort of fees for its output than leading management consultancies were able to secure for theirs? When I delivered my recommendations which included hiring three senior consultants with compensation packages of around £200k each, the business's owner fell of his perch and said 'there is no way I'm prepared to pay those sort of packages to anyone!' He didn't and he didn't create a business that was able to compete with strategy consultancies and secure comparable fee levels!

OTHER FACTORS

There are of course many other factors that impact upon compensation. The type of performance-reward structure, the complexity of the incentive compensation plans and the degree to which these are tied to factors within the role's direct control; the extent to which accountability and responsibility are truly linked. I have seen many incentive compensation plans, some so complex that a PhD in applied mathematics would be a distinct advantage! Keeping things relatively simple, especially in an area that can easily lend itself to over complication, has huge benefits.

I was recently shown a 12 page document outlining the bonus entitlement of a candidate I was interviewing for a specific role. When I asked the candidate to explain it, he himself found it difficult, and in fact actually couldn't do it!

Retention has a significant impact on the architecture of these plans because they are deliberately crafted in such a way as to incentivise executives to weigh up very carefully the financial implication of jumping ship. But if the executive for whom the plan is developed doesn't understand it, then it is unlikely to have much retention glue. The reality is however that if a recruiting organisation really wants someone 'whatever it takes', they will be prepared to buy the individual out of any prevailing incentive contract with overlapping plans, options that only vest after certain time periods etc. The reality is therefore that there is little long-term glue in these plans. This was most aptly demonstrated by the appointment of Marks & Spencer plc's chief executive, Marc Bolland, who had previously been CEO of a competitor, William Morrison Supermarkets plc:

> *'In year one Bolland will receive £975,000 basic. He's entitled to the company's maximum 250pc bonus, worth up to £2.44m, if he outperforms the consensus of analysts' expectations. He will then receive an 'exceptional' award of shares under the company's Performance Share Plan worth 400pc of salary, or £3.9m. He won't be able to get his hands on this last bit of his £7.3m year-one package until 2013.*
> *But M&S is also picking up the tab to compensate Bolland for leaving his previous pay pile at Morrisons. This adds up to £7.5m. The ingredients of this little dish are £1.6m in cash and £1m in shares for his 2010 awards, plus another £4.9m granted as he walks through the M&S door for Morrisons shares not vesting until 2011 and 2012.'*
>
> DAMIAN REECE, *DAILY TELEGRAPH* 2ND FEBRUARY 2010

The world of FTSE 100 companies is full of such examples time and time again, all very unfortunate because they rarely deliver to expectations!

Other factors at play in motivating employees to stay or go include the quality of mentoring, training and the honesty and regularity of feedback. All add into establishing a certain style, a certain culture. All of these factors and the forgoing together determine whether this is a good place to be. Take for example, the following exerts from an interview with Jeffrey Immelt, when he was Chairman and CEO of GE (In Search of Global Leaders, Harvard Business Review, August 2003):

'HR at GE is not an agenda item, it is the agenda

I spend roughly 40 percent of my time on people issues

In the course of a year I will review, in detail, five to six thousand internal resumes

Recognition and reinforcement are immediate

We spend $1billion on training which has the most important benefit of connecting people across the company

I always ask people about their teams

You've got to develop people so they are prepared for leadership jobs and then promote them'

Jeffrey Immelt stepped down as CEO of General Electric (GE) on August 1, 2017 and retired from his position as chairman of the board of GE on October 2, 2017… and had endured a number of controversies in his later years, but he maintained his focus on the above, right the way through to the end.

It's relevant to quote another successful entrepreneur/leader, Bill Hewlett, who was one of the founders of the mega successful Hewlett-Packard enterprise. Way back in 1973 he wrote – 'What is the HP way? I feel that in general terms it is the policies and actions that flow from the belief that men and women want to do a good job, a creative job, and that if they are provided the proper environment they will do so'...how simple, how true!

WHO CARES?

But why worry about retention in any case? People come and go, they bring certain ideas and they leave; there are always plenty of others around to fill the gap. There is no such thing as being 'irreplaceable'. As long as there is an available workforce, there will be people to do the jobs required. There are indeed many examples of companies that have revolving doors, and although this is well known, it does not seem to have done them any serious damage either in terms of their ability to do business or recruit replacements.

In my brief period, 1996-1998, with a major international search firm, I had some interesting experiences. During this time I saw people join at partner level and leave at partner level with a degree of frequency that beggared belief. Of the 4 people who commenced at the same time as I did, within 18 months all 4 had left. It was a firm where, when you called a colleague in another office, in another country, to share new business with them, the first question asked was 'what's in it for me?' rather than 'how can we help you?' It was where after winning a vast international piece of business (literally from Shannon to Vladivostok and all places in between for a major world class professional services firm) that I had to fight with every practice in Europe to provide support and resources to service the client's requirements. It was where people came and went with an amazing frequency, and yet its reputation in the outside world was relatively unscathed!

But the above is not a healthy situation, irrespective of whether it impacts on the business's reputation or not. It adds considerable cost, it adds considerable uncertainty, and puts considerable pressures on those who do stay with the organization to maintain an even keel.

Who would have thought that 'bosses from hell' could recruit and keep people, but they can; certain types of people in any case. The Mirror Group of Newspapers, or MGN for short, managed to recruit the services of an amazing array of well known, well established and reputable individuals, even though MGN was run by Robert Maxwell whose reputation was known to all, even well before the scandal that led to the group's demise. Why would these people put their name to the support of such a man as Robert Maxwell? Position, title, power, money – in whatever order you care to place them. Being the director of a major national newspaper group provides a degree of perceived power and position; and no doubt Robert Maxwell paid well to get the people he particularly wanted. As I said right at the start of this chapter, the age of slavery is over, and those who accepted Robert Maxwell's invitation to join his company knew full well what sort of man they were joining and what to expect. And if it all got too much, the option to walk away was always there. Unfortunately there are numerous examples of 'Maxwells' in many other organisations including Government and not just owner managers, but employees in senior positions ready to abuse their juniors, bullying, undermining and micro-management! The FT had a number of articles on exactly this topic…

- High-profile banking consultant sacked by Deloitte over alleged bullying (7th January 2020)

- EY whistle blowers complain of discrimination (23rd December 2019)

- King of cloud computing faces claims of sexual assault 24th October 2019

…all sighting bullying in the workplace of one sort or another as a key issue.

There are numerous lessons in this chapter, yet none of them requires a PhD in people management; just a little forethought, just a little attention to detail, just a little TLC (tender loving care)! So here are your marching orders for chapter 4:

Do It Right: Do It Now!: Treat all people right, right from the start

Do It Right: Do It Now!: Graduates/young people have a lot to give: harness their energy and enthusiasm

Do It Right: Do It Now!: Really care about everyone in your business, not superficially but in words and deeds

Do It Right: Do It Now!: Be honest

Do It Right: Do It Now!: Know the skills, the talents and the competencies of your people

Do It Right: Do It Now!: Invest in training and development

Do It Right: Do It Now!: Do not treat training and development as a discretionary expenditure

Do It Right: Do It Now!: Better to exceed expectations, so manage expectations with great care

Do It Right: Do It Now!: Keep the best, remove the worst

Do It Right: Do It Now!: Reward generously, but not too generously

Do It Right: Do It Now!: Surprise and delight, rather than short-change and disappoint

Do it Right: Do it Now!: Pre-empt, rather than wait to be pushed to action

Do it Right: Do it Now!: Pre-empt, rather than be reactive by when it's too late

Do it Right: Do it Now!: Make your team want to stay, you don't need to tie them down

Do it Right: Do it Now!: Complex contractual arrangements are good for the lawyers only, keep it relatively simple

Do it Right: Do it Now!: One size does not fit all

Do it Right: Do it Now!: Stretch, promote to stretch not to fill a hole

Do it Right: Do it Now!: Days of slavery are over

Do it Right: Do it Now!: No bullying of any sort; no micro-management

Do it Right: Do it Now!

I have for long been totally against any form of 'micro-management' as I believe it reduces the ability of an individual to learn, grow and develop… which is exactly what we should all be seeking to achieve with our employees/team members. Mike Norris, the longest serving CEOs in the UK has grown Computacenter into a highly successful and respected tech/services business. He is quoted acknowledging the success of his tenure, and the business, to his ability to allow his 'team members to take responsibility for their actions' and to his total lack of micro-management! Or as Mark Bartlett, CEO of Stix said 'make sure you have the best people' and let them get on with what they are good at.

As I said before, and shall repeat a few more times, the most important *Do it Right: Do it Now!*: actions are not difficult to get right, nor are they difficult to get wrong, but the payback from getting them right is almost immeasurable. So why do so many ignore the obvious, why are there so many large and small companies getting them so very wrong? Especially as getting it Right is for most part not that difficult and certainly does not require a major investment of cash!

A FINAL RANT-ABUSE OF THE YOUNG

I cannot finish this chapter without just one final rant at the abuse of the young, this time not by lack of sufficient work of sufficient interest, although that may be the case; not because of poor compensation, although that too may be true; but by setting expectations so absurdly high as to make the whole process of the initial years like some sort of an initiation passage. Business analysts (BAs) joining investment banks are often referred to as the '*crème de la crème*', the very best of their graduating class. These carefully selected recruits are the chosen few, many having demonstrated their abilities and stamina during previous summer internships.

Summer interns are paid generously, treated well, flown from one country to another (absurdly) in business class, collected at airports in limos, and generally made to feel wanted and valued. A year later when the selected few start full time work as BAs their lives change beyond recognition. They are expected to work 16 to 20 hour days, often weekends, and occasionally/frequently through the night. For a first job after graduation they are paid a relatively vast amount of money… for example in 2019 base salaries of £65K to £90k for 1st Year Analysts at mid-sized and large banks… some elite boutique banks may pay slightly more.

When compared against peers working in other graduate first job environments, peers who are in good first jobs with good reputable corporations, can be paid also good starting salaries of £35k to £50k but are also able to start building their personal lives and not requiring to be at their employer's call 24/7. One has to ask the question: is it really worth it?

I know a BA who asked to leave (early) at about 19.00hrs to be able to attend a family dinner for a major religious festival and was told 'no'. I know of a woman who asked to have Christmas day off to be able to be with her family, was told 'no', and when she ignored the 'no', was passed over for promotion. I know a young man who resigned two years into his BA period as he had had enough of 16 to 20 hour days and weekends, no life other than work, and being utterly exhausted when he did manage to get time off. But he was highly rated by his investment bank and had been earmarked as a future star, so the bank did not want to lose him. His ultimate boss invited him for lunch with his girlfriend one weekend.

They arrived at his boss's palatial home in St George's Hill, a highly desirable residential area outside London, with the latest Bentley and Ferrari in the drive, a uniformed butler to open the door and greet them, with tennis court and swimming pool and all the creatures comfort money could buy. And yet when they left, this young man was more determined than ever to leave and stick with his resignation. Despite all the material wealth, the house was devoid of anything other than what money could buy. There were no family pictures; no wife, lover or children; no warmth, no emotion.

I have to say I believe that investment banks and some other professional service organisations (magic circle law firms, top management consultancies) have got it utterly wrong despite the huge amounts of money that can be earned. People need fulfilling lives, young people need time to build their lives, establish friendships and create relationships, all of which takes time. Working 16 to 20 hour days consistently is wholly unnecessary, and if it were necessary it would suggest a massive degree of mismanagement. No one can be effective on a consistent basis doing these sorts of hours. The sooner this practice is stopped the better, after all trainee/junior doctors don't have to endure such extreme hours any more either (or do they????!)

There is a growing healthy recognition of the importance of a good work/life balance... and the employers that are getting this right, the employers that are placing emphasis on this, the employers that are not just 'taking' work/life balance but are practicing/implementing actions accordingly, will have real competitive advantage when it comes to recruiting the best!

Let me finish with one other example. A 29 year old professionally trained and qualified young woman recently quit her job in one of the world's leading law firms. Yes, she was paid well; yes, she had status; yes, she was intellectually stimulated and challenged. But after numerous overnight sessions, after a number of pre-planned and agreed holiday arrangements having to be cancelled at the last moment, after frequent Saturdays and Sundays having to be spent in the office... and after seeing the results of all the work... she came to the conclusion that it really wasn't worth it. Life is too short to waste it in such a sterile environment. Days of slavery are truly over! She resigned and is now working in a highly fulfilling environment within the charitable sector, applying her legal expertise for good. Now that really is a positive outcome!

5. THE FEEL GOOD INTERVIEW

Interviewing: a core management skill, or a specialist expertise? Both. The process by which information and insights are extracted in conversation between typically two people, should be a core skill of all management. Interviewing is required in so many diverse situations that it is difficult to imagine anyone in a management role not being able to interview effectively. And yet that is exactly the reality.

Interviewing is not taught at school, nor at most business schools. It is assumed that because people know how to converse, they will be able to conduct sensible interviews. But this is not the case. Interviewing is a skill. There are ways to interview, there are methodologies to learn, there are pitfalls to avoid. Interviewing can be learned, but not everyone is suitable to be an interviewer.

LISTENING

One of the most basic skills that any interviewer needs to learn is the skill of listening. Listening both silently to what is being said, listening actively through body language, by repeating certain key words/statements, occasionally using an acknowledgement such as 'yes' or 'really'; and by carefully observing the interviewee's body language, by listening to the unsaid. Silence can be hugely powerful. Interviewers need to understand that there is no need for constant uninterrupted dialogue. It is an error for an interviewer to try to fill a silence, rather than allowing the interviewee time to think. Equally one of the most common errors committed by an interviewer is not just failing to listen, but effectively not allowing the interviewee enough airtime, wishing to 'hog the microphone', wishing to demonstrate to the interviewee how successful the interviewer is, how senior in the organization, how articulate etc. Egos can play havoc with an interview!

Equally it is important to allow the interviewee not just time to think, but time to speak! Interviewers should restrain themselves from interrupting the interview, allowing them the 'space' to collect their thoughts, to organise their ideas, to consider the question, to have as much 'airtime' as they need. Often interviewers are inclined to jump in the moment there is a pause in speech by the interviewee or to challenge issues too rapidly. As has been said many times… we have two ears and one mouth and should apply them proportionately!

THE JOB INTERVIEW

Interviewing job candidates takes on added importance. You are, in all seriousness, dealing with the destiny of the interviewee's life. The interviewee is there because he/she has already come through some process or another that has enabled her/him to secure the opportunity of being on a short list of suitable candidates, suitable enough for time to be invested in a face to face meeting. The potential job is important enough to the interviewee to take time off, time out, to come to the interview and be challenged in a detailed dialogue. This alone warrants careful consideration by the interviewer.

The purpose of the interview is to assess the candidate's suitability for whatever the vacant role might be. As much as it is expected for the candidate to have done a good deal of homework about the company, it is also expected for the interviewer to have done homework about the candidate. To have read the candidate's CV thoroughly, to have spoken with others who may already have interviewed the candidate, to have had feedback from the external search firm who found the candidate. To have thoroughly taken on board what the vacancy is about, what skills sets/competences are being looked for; who the selected individual will need to work alongside, report to, supervise; the sort of personality fit that will be required in addition to the skill set and experience. The actual interview can therefore be focused on getting to know the interviewee, getting to understand career decisions taken, using the interview to develop a sense about the candidate's strengths and weaknesses.

And above all trying to assess the extent to which the candidate would fit in with the rest of the organisation, the people within the organisation. In other words, would the chemistry work?

Unfortunately the vast majority of interviewers are lazy! Unfortunately the vast majority of interviewers will not have taken any time to study the CV, to chat to others, to try and get some sense of the interviewee before the actual interview itself. Unfortunately it is more than likely that the interviewer will commence by saying, 'Now just run me through your CV will you?' In other words: I haven't read your CV and am about to do so with your assistance. What incompetence! On the occasions when this has happened to me I really felt like saying, 'What exactly would you like me to expand on?' knowing full well that they wouldn't have a clue as they had only just picked up my CV for the very first time. This is wrong, this is discourteous, this is insulting and yet this is often the way it is.

The job interview should be about gaining as good an understanding of the fit between the interviewee and the company as possible, in terms of both technical capacity and chemistry. As I have said before I believe that getting a good 'technical' fit is relatively easy i.e. the extent to which the candidate has the required expertise; getting a good 'chemical' fit, i.e. the extent to which the candidate's personality fits with the rest of the organisation, the specific team, is the real added value, and this is what is tough, this is where the interviewer needs to get under the interviewee's skin. This is the subjective part where maturity, experience and a good degree of sensitivity pay off. This is where gaining the input from others who have interviewed the candidate is important… which by definition means that for most significant roles there should be multiple interviews.

I know numerous organisations where no-one gets hired unless at least six interviews have taken place, with each one being able to 'terminate' the process if it were felt that the 'candidate' was not right.

The above skills can be important in other forms of interviewing too, such as for internal performance appraisals, competitive analysis, customer/client satisfaction surveys etc. In most of these the key input comes from interviewing. Although each may require a slightly different technique and approach, all share the interviewer's core objective of getting information and insight from the interviewee. The purpose of the interview determines the extent to which probing may be required, probing questions such as: 'Can you elaborate on this/that?'; 'How exactly was this/that achieved?'; 'Can you give me an example of…?'; 'Can we be more precise here…' – i.e. the what, how much, how long, how and why type of questions.

APPRAISALS

Let's shift our focus to appraisal interviews. These are increasingly undertaken in all sorts of organisations and at all levels within organisations. They are therefore increasingly undertaken by all sorts of people. As with so many other actions it is not very difficult to get this right, and frankly it is even easier to screw it up completely. This form of one to one discussion/interview is however of the utmost importance, or should be, to those involved. It's a golden opportunity for the appraiser to really reach out, connect positively with the appraisee and help to constructively develop the appraisee and his/her competencies. To better understand problems and barriers to performance improvement. For the appraisee to gain quality time with the appraiser, to better develop their career, gain a commitment for training and development. To effectively forward manage expectations to a considerable degree. These really are very important discussions.

In reality few appraisers are trained in undertaking appraisals; few fully appreciate the importance to the appraisee; too few appraisers' own performances are linked to the quality and rigor with which they conduct appraisals of their subordinates; few allocate sufficient time both to prepare for the appraisal meeting, and to conduct the appraisal meeting itself; and few systematically follow up. A huge wasted opportunity to increase productivity AND commitment! A huge waste of time and resources. And worse as poorly conducted appraisals and poorly followed up appraisals can lead to disengagement by the appraisee and potential loss of key people in the organisation.

Lucy Kellaway, the then *Financial Times* journalist dedicated an article *On Work* to 'My appraisal of job appraisals: get rid of them' (*Financial Times*, July 12th 2010, p 16) on the basis that typically they are poorly executed, rarely if ever followed through, more de-motional than motivating! She also referred to a book authored by Samuel Culbert, a business school professor in California, entitled *Get Rid of the Performance Review* which also advocates the dumping of structured appraisals in favour of the simple, but massively effective, spur of the moment, real time, feedback ('Great job… well done… thanks') to ('think you could have dealt with the situation differently… have you thought of… suggest that…') Of course, the immediacy of this is fabulous, but a well-managed, properly structured and implemented appraisal process has real value and the two are not mutually exclusive.

We really should avoid throwing out the baby with the bath water! I have seen, and experienced, fabulously constructive, motivational, performance reviews. They can be done. They can be done well.

INTERVIEW ENIRONMENT

Another factor to take into account is the environment of the interview itself. The actual way the chairs are arranged, the physical layout of the room, the location where the interview takes place. I recall an experiment I undertook many years ago whilst at business school, the results of which have been with me ever since.

A classmate and I were doing a project on interviewing. There happened to be present a large contingent of middle to senior executives from BP undertaking an executive education course organised by the London Business School. We gained permission to contact this group to request volunteers to be interviewed. And there were a goodly number, so we got them together in a group and explained what we were doing and why. They were a nice bunch of guys (yes 100 percent male), all in their mid-30s to early 40s, happy to partake in our little experiment.

In they came, one after the other. One of us interviewed, the other observed and made notes. We changed our interviewing styles, we changed the room layout, we changed our appearance, we changed everything that we felt could have an impact. Now remember that all the interviewees were volunteers, understood the process, and for them the whole thing was 100 percent risk free! And yet many of them exhibited nerves just as if it had been for real. I recall one case in particular. I was to do the interviewing, and we decided to see the result of a relatively harsh, aggressive interviewing style. We arranged the room accordingly, table in the centre of this fairly large room, clean desk, no clutter, harsh lighting, and we decided to leave the chair for the interviewee by the rear wall so that he would have to physically move the chair to the table.

The interviewee came in, and sat down by the wall, without taking the initiative to bring the chair closer to the table. As the interview unfolded the interviewee got more and more nervous and was pushing his chair back against the rear wall to the extent that if it could have moved, he would have physically pushed the wall further back! Right towards the end of the interview I relaxed the tone, smiled for the first time, took my glasses off, and asked about his leisure activities. Exactly at that moment his whole body relaxed, he reached for the chair and actually moved it forward a few inches. We were utterly amazed at the power an interviewer, and the environment, could exert over an interviewee!

You will have noticed that I have not talked about 'online' interviewing anywhere in this chapter… be it by Skype or WhatsApp or any of dozens of different video-conferencing facilities available. The basic rules and requirements are the same in terms of preparation, being on time, providing airtime, etc. But the need to focus, to stay focused, to be super alert to the whole environment is even greater. Body language may be a little harder to read, mannerisms a little harder to capture, the setting harder to control. From the interviewer's side attention to detail remains hugely important.

Some interviewees think it's OK to be interviewed in a Starbucks with ambient noise; or in one's running kit… it simply isn't. Treat an online interview exactly as you would a physical face to face meeting.

STAYING FRESH

Interviewing needs time, focus, and lots of preparation. If one is undertaking lots of interviews one after the other, one must allow sometime between the interviews to make notes, scribble down certain key words as *aides memoire*, to ensure that differentiation between interviews and specifically the interviewees can be maintained effectively. Always make sure that you know who you are about to interview, what the purpose of the interview is; refresh your mind by quickly scanning the background papers. I jest not but it has been known to happen that only some way into the interview, an interviewer suddenly realized that the interview was being conducted with the wrong person.

Always stay awake! It is hard at times. Especially when one is involved in a crazy schedule of undertaking say six interviews in one day, one after another with little time between interviews. Or when one is interviewing straight after a long-distance flight with all the effects of jet lag, dehydration etc. But if you are interviewing, it is your responsibility, and only your responsibility, to ensure that you are awake and alert; anything else would be the height of discourtesy to the interviewee.

It does happen. It has happened to me when I was being interviewed. It is the only time that I can recall when someone interviewing me almost fell asleep, and as many will attest, I am fairly animated when I speak. The interviewer happened to be the CEO of Korn Ferry International at the time, who had just arrived that morning from the States. He had a sudden attack of jet lag and was visibly on the verge of dropping off, in fact did drop off for what amounted to a few seconds. It has nearly happened to me, but as I am so very aware, I take evasive action the moment I think I am entering the danger zone. (Evasive action includes drinking water, changing sitting position, becoming even more of an active listener, writing notes, even suggesting a natural break). Whatever it takes but stay awake and alert!

Interviewers should also ensure that the scene is properly set, right from the outset. Although the airtime should be substantially that of the interviewee's, the interviewer should take control at the beginning by relaxing the situation as much as possible, by building a sense of trust as fast as possible, and by putting things into context in terms of the purpose of the interview, what will happen as a consequence, timing, and confidentiality. Confidentiality is really important in many interview situations. It is beneficial to stress by repeating a number of times that 'everything that is discussed will be kept strictly confidential; you will not be quoted verbatim' (and ensuring that this is kept to), at the same time explaining that when quotes are used they will be used in such a way as to ensure that no one can possibly know who was being quoted (non-attributable).

Very often, only by ensuring strict rules of confidentiality, can one get the best results from an interview. Only by creating a real sense of 'feel good' can one ensure that the interviewee relaxes and is a willing and active participant.

This really was a lesson learnt at the relatively young age of 25, in my first job after graduating from London Business School. Interviewing is a core skill all consultants have to learn, and as such it was an integral part of our early training. It was an integral part of virtually every study (mandate/assignment) undertaken, and hence an activity every member of a study is exposed to irrespective of how new he or she is to the job. As a management consultant it is vital to get to the heart of the matter as fast as possible, as accurately as possible, hence getting the co-operation of people interviewed is critical. Making them feel 100 percent comfortable, making them feel 100 percent certain that everything said is 100 percent confidential is vital. If there is ever the slightest doubt about this it will immediately make the task of getting insights and pooling the collective wisdom of people within the client organisation exponentially harder, if not impossible.

There are of course many lessons learned over the years:

Do It Right: Do It Now!: Always do your homework well in advance

Do It Right: Do It Now!: Don't ask candidates to 'run me through your CV'

Do It Right: Do It Now!: Know the purpose of the interview

Do It Right: Do It Now!: Know how to probe, ask probing questions, ask open questions

Do It Right: Do It Now!: Stay awake and alert

Do It Right: Do It Now!: Listen, listen actively

Do It Right: Do It Now!: Understand that the environment has an impact

Do It Right: Do It Now!: Understand how you come across as an interviewer

Do It Right: Do It Now!: Take time between multiple interviews

Do It Right: Do It Now!: Keep notes

Do It Right: Do It Now!: Set the scene; set the tone

Do It Right: Do It Now!: Maintain high level of energy

Do it Right: Do it Now!: Be on time, never keep an interviewee waiting

Do it Right: Do it Now!: Take control, but don't dominate… be generous with 'wait time'

Do it Right: Do it Now!: Don't hog the conversation

Do it Right: Do it Now!: Always give airtime to the interviewee, especially at the end

Do it Right: Do it Now!: Silence is golden

Do it Right: Do it Now!

6: DAY ONE

Starting a new job is always both hugely exciting and somewhat scary. Starting the very first job ever is both of these multiplied exponentially. So much has already happened to get there. So many hurdles have had to be overcome, exams, qualifications, applications, interviews, tests, more interviews, waiting for the post, the e-mail, and finally the formal offer arrives confirming that you are selected, you are wanted, you are the chosen one. What fantastic elation, feeling of achievement; suddenly all that has gone before has been worthwhile. And immediately expectations start to be formulated about what's ahead, with all that has gone before providing little pieces of the jigsaw.

The great day arrives. What should I wear? What time am I expected to arrive? Will they remember that I am due to start working with them? What's it going to be like? Will I be able to cope? What are the other people going to be like? And a million more questions, doubts, concerns run through one's mind.

What is little understood by many organisations is exactly how hugely important the first day is to a future employee. And yet everyone had a first day. I genuinely do not think that the first day's importance can be over stressed. It can have a profound impact, one that can last literally a lifetime! Let me give you two examples from my life, one positive and one negative:

POSITIVE
A pack of information arrived at my home the week before I was due to commence, containing all sorts of simple but relevant information about the company I was due to start working with.

It contained a couple of forms for me to complete and bring with me on day one, a suggested arrival time on day one, and other bits and pieces about the immediate environment etc.

On day one, I arrived at the suggested time and was delighted when I was warmly welcomed by the receptionist who had clearly been briefed about my joining the company. The receptionist telephoned Harry (The Brigadier) who had been key in the interviewing process and whom I had met a few times already. He appeared within seconds to welcome me and whisked me away into the office.

Harry first took me to 'my office'. Well not exactly my office, but the office I was sharing with another person, to whom he introduced me. But it was 'my office' insofar as I noticed that my name was already inserted in the appropriate slot on the door, and there was a desk with all sorts of things already prepared for me, including a set of business cards already printed with my name on them, business cards with MY NAME on them, memo pads again with my name on, credit cards, etc. Wow, did all this feel fantastic.

The desk contained various files with almost every conceivable bit of information I could possibly require, from internal telephone directory, office layout, copy of a recent internal memo announcing my arrival (this was the pre-e-mail world) including background information on me, and company rules and regulations, to lists of local restaurants and bars, the nearest clubs and other services that could be useful. There were also the usual bits of stationery and office/desk equipment from pencils and paper clips to Sellotape and writing pads. On top of everything there was a file entitled 'Induction Programme'. Harry took this file and went through it with me, providing additional bits of information and explanation as he went through the programme.

The induction programme spelt out how every single minute of my time was going to be spent during my first two weeks with the company. It was extraordinary to me at that time how much thought had been put into the management of my arrival. I was passed from one person to another, each one allocating a pre-agreed time slot, who explained their activities, area of responsibility, focus and other information about themselves, how long they'd been with the company, etc. Each day I was taken to lunch by a different person, or group of people, so that by the end of my first week I had already met with a large number of people. Because I was not just whisked around the office on my very first day and introduced to everyone, I could actually remember most people's names.

Within the induction programme there was time allocated for certain formal activities, such as on day one in the afternoon I spent time with what at that time was still called 'Personnel', handing over the forms that I had completed in advance, being briefed about certain policies, having my terms and benefits summarised, being briefed about the way performance was regularly reviewed etc. During the first two weeks I had pre-allocated sessions with the most senior people within the company including two with the Managing Partner who was scheduled formally for a 45 minute slot on the Friday of each week. And yet he still took the time on my very first day to find me and informally welcome me. HE took the time to find ME; he didn't get his secretary to find me, he didn't get me to go to his office: he came to find me, greet me, and welcome me to the business!

At the formal scheduled session with the Managing Partner, at the end of my second week, he really wanted to have my first impressions, he seemed really interested to have feedback from me. 'Best time to get real initial impressions! Amazing how this feedback has helped us address certain issues over the years. A fresh pair of eyes can see things that, over even a short period of time, become invisible to us who have been around for some time.'

This was in 1975. This was an extraordinary experience. Nothing above has been exaggerated in any way whatsoever. The company still exists and has continued from strength to strength despite the fluctuating economic environment of the past forty-five years. And it continues to practice its structured welcome/induction programme today, clearly with changes to reflect the digital world we now live in, to reflect that it now employs over 30,000 people, to reflect the fact that in any one office and on any one day there may be numerous people starting at the same time. But fundamentally there continues to be focus and care for every starter!

And I have never experienced anything like it since.

I re-counted some of these experiences to the *Financial Times* feature writer on management, Stefan Stern, who in turn started his major analytical piece *Reinventing the spiel* (Friday 25th June, 2010) with 'On my first day at the firm…' followed by a verbatim account of the above. Clearly, a message that has traction!

I have imitated and implemented similar induction programmes in companies where I have held senior executive positions and could influence accordingly. But I have never seen or heard of other companies having anything close in substance, quality, or structure.

NEGATIVE

Twenty-one years after the above, in 1996, I experienced the very worst of the very worst.

After weeks and weeks of pursuit, and meeting after meeting in which the importance of the accumulated experience I could deliver was highlighted, the contribution to the firm's strategic development I could make and the importance that was being attached to attracting people who could really help the organisation change and move forward in a certain direction etc. I was finally persuaded to accept an invitation to join a certain professional firm with direct entry to partnership.

Although I was now in my mid-40s I was still excited at the thought of starting something new. I was flattered that they had pursued me with such vigour. I was excited by the challenges ahead, by the unknown. I was looking forward with anticipation to my first day. My ego was also well massaged with the expectation of being a partner, being part of this global partnership.

From the date that I agreed to join and returned signed copies of the employment contract to the day that we agreed I would commence, the radio went silent! No further communication took place at all. Not that at the time this seemed strange to me as I was too busy doing other things, but in retrospect it seems strange, especially in comparison to the almost frantic action during the chase. And remember that they were chasing me, they made it very clear that they wanted me to join their firm.

The day of commencement arrived and I arrived at my new address at around 8am. Surprise number one was that the building's security officer did not have my name nor the fact that I was starting as a new partner of the firm. He accepted my word for this (remember that this was years before 9/11 when there was still a good degree of trust in people's honesty) and allowed me to enter the building, but nevertheless my first impression on day one was not instantly positive.

And so it continued.

The firm's receptionist had no idea that a new partner was joining that day. In fact it only registered with her after searching through a pile of documents, 'Oh yes, here you are'. She had no idea that I was starting as a new partner, she had no idea which office was allocated to me, she had no idea what to do with me except to say, 'I'll get someone to come and show you to your office. Please take a seat and wait'. In due course a member of the administrative team arrived and I was shown to my office. The office was spacious, but totally void of anything of use: no welcome pack, no information folders, no stationery (only bits left by its previous occupant, including a rotting banana in the drawer); not even an internal telephone list. There was clearly NO preparation or forethought.

I therefore went and got hold of an internal telephone list (always good to know names and numbers of your colleagues) and a floor plan so that I could note down who was where; and I literally just walked around the office and introduced myself to everyone who happened to be around. Most were very pleasant, even though they were totally clueless about the fact that I had joined as a new partner. There had been no internal communication.

At lunch time I entertained myself by getting a sandwich and a coke from one of the many local sandwich bars, and ate alone in my office, reading a trade magazine I had collected during my earlier walk around the office. In the afternoon I continued my travels around the office, with occasional breaks in my own office just to make the odd call and read bits collected as I walked around the place. At about 4pm the phone rang. 'Hi John, welcome, it's great that you're here,' said the office's managing partner, 'we must get together for a proper chat soon'. And that was the extent of my official welcome.

In fact there were three of us who joined this firm on the same day, all as partners, and we all received exactly the same zero welcome, zero induction. At the end of the day we decided to have a drink together, and spontaneously we all concluded that we had just screwed-up our careers by agreeing to join this firm! When I got home I said exactly that to my wife.

By the third day I was beginning to wonder if I had joined a truly paperless office as I had received no mail, no internal memos, no circulating documents, you know the type with a long list of recipients each of whom needed to sign-off that they had seen the document/journal, etc. Nothing of any kind at all. I was surprised as I was expecting some mail. Only after I had made a number of enquiries did I discover that there was in fact a 'mail room' tucked well away in the back office, where everyone had a 'pigeon hole', and where everyone was expected to collect their own mail. When I finally located this room, my 'pigeon hole' was overflowing with both internal and external mail. What was even more frustrating was that there were actually numerous notes of welcome, unfortunately their impact seriously diluted by the time I received them!

After my first week I sat down and wrote a short paper of my first impressions. (Early impressions are often the most valuable, as was stressed to me 20 years earlier). I wrote about my initial observations as to areas requiring closer attention. I wrote about what differentiates a great professional services firm from an average professional services firm. In other words I wrote a paper on issues I thought the senior management wanted to have my input on. I sent the paper off… and never had a response, not even an acknowledgement of receipt, not even a 'don't bother with anything like this again'. The paper disappeared into a black hole! This was the response to a note when during the chase for me to join it was exactly my past experience and my accumulated expertise in professional service businesses that was highlighted as of major importance.

The only conclusion I drew was that they lied! They lied in expressing a desire to have me involved in the strategic direction of the firm, they lied in wishing my involvement with the senior management, the only thing that they really wanted was my contacts, network and developed relationships!

During the course of the coming weeks and months my fears were proven to be 100 percent accurate. All the promises made during the chase were rapidly forgotten. All the expressions of desire to 'get people with your experience on board to help bring about change' were blatant lies. Yes, I did become a partner in that I bought into the partnership and had a slightly bigger and better office than the non-partners, but that was as far as it went. There was no 'partnership' in the true sense of the word, of any sort. There was no involvement in the management of the firm, its stewardship, its strategic direction. And what was worse was the utter rejection of any ideas offered for consideration.

The leadership group had no interest in change, had no desire to take on board ideas from others.

That first impression on that first day was a highly accurate indicator of things to come. First impressions count. The way day one is managed matters. Irrespective of whether it is your first job or a career move, irrespective of whether it is a junior role or a senior appointment, the way you are welcomed on your first day, the way your entry is managed, has lasting impact.

THE WHYS

(It is so easy to get it right and yet so few seem to do so. Why?)

Why is so little attention paid to the arrival of new recruits, irrespective of seniority?

Why often is no attention paid at all to how new employees are treated on their day 1/week 1?

Why, especially given the complex task of securing new recruits, is no thought given to their effective induction?

Why is there no greater recognition of the massive damage that can be done by a poorly executed welcome?

Why is induction more about process and procedures, than about people?

Why are the most senior executives not directly involved?

Why are new employees not instantly made to feel valued?

Why do so many screw up so badly, and so consistently?

Why can't this simple activity be undertaken by all, and undertaken well?

All that is required is the investment of a tiny bit of time to think through the logical sequence of events that help to integrate a new person into your organisation; to think through the small bits of detail that would make someone new feel welcomed, feel special. What could be simpler, and yet what could have more impact on day one?

> *Do It Right: Do It Now!*: Has there been communication with the new employee about what time to arrive on day one, whom to ask for etc?

Do it Right: Do it Now!: Has there been internal communication to advise everyone about the new recruit (including the building's security), where he/she will be located, what he/she will be doing, who she/he will be reporting to, and providing a mini bio to all within the organisation?

Do it Right: Do it Now!: Has anyone been asked to mentor/buddy the new recruit for the first few days/weeks?

Do it Right: Do it Now!: Has an induction programme been created suitable to the recruit's requirements?

Do it Right: Do it Now!: Has a desk/office been set up, has an e-mail address been allocated, is there a computer ready and set up, has a mobile phone been allocated and set up, have business cards been printed (why wait until someone arrives before getting this sorted, there is usually ample time to get this done well in time to ensure that the new employee has her/his business cards ready for day one), is there a starter pack of required stationery/stuff, is there an internal telephone list, and internal floor plan?

Do it Right: Do it Now!: Who will be taking the new recruit to lunch days one, two, three, four and five?

Do it Right: Do it Now!: Who will be the most senior person to welcome the new employee? (Typically, but not always, the most senior person to have interviewed, or signed off on the appointment)

Do it Right: Do it Now!: When will the chairman/senior partner/MD/CEO/divisional director, or whoever is the most senior executive, welcome the new recruit?

Do it Right: Do it Now!: Is there time scheduled for a debrief with the new employee at the end of week 1 or week 2?

Do it Right: Do it Now!: Has the new employee been guided about how to portray his appointment on LinkedIn?

Do it Right: Do it Now!

None of the above actions require a first class degree in applied HR management. What is required is an attitude of mind that people are truly important to you. You've spent a hell of a lot on finding the right staff to be part of your company, your team, and you want to make absolutely certain that you do everything that you possibly can to ease the process of integrating the new member into the organisation. Getting it right is easy and inexpensive. Getting it wrong is just as easy but a great deal more expensive.

It really is extraordinary to me how easily some people forget that we all have the gift of mobility and many of us are prepared to exercise this gift if we feel little reason to stay, if there is little or no sense of belonging. Replacing people is expensive; replacing them frequently is very expensive, and makes a lousy advertisement for your company!

As we live in a world of social media everyone has a 'vote' and many use their 'vote' to share experiences without let or hinderance. They will be blatantly honest about their experience. There are some web-sites dedicated to exactly this, one of the better known is 'Glassdoor' - https://www.glassdoor.co.uk

Company Reviews and Ratings. Get the Whole Story.

Search ratings and reviews of over 600,000 companies worldwide.

Get the inside scoop and find out what it's really like from people who've actually worked there.

Companies no longer have total control over how their image, how they are perceived is the some of the external noise.

HELLO-GOODBYE!

Just to add substance to the above, Penna Sanders & Sidney, the career outplacement and career management consultancy, conducted research by interviewing over 1,000 people in London, Birmingham, Manchester and Edinburgh. Their finding is that over 30 percent of people start to actively search for a new job after their first day in a new job! After six months the figure rises to 48 percent (Simon Brooke, *Livewire Magazine*, December 2003). Powerful facts to substantiate the points I have been making in this chapter! And just totally crazy especially when one takes into account the cost, the time, the emotions involved in recruitment, in finding people, finding the right people to join your business!

Getting day one/week one sorted, making the new hire feel valued, may materially reduce these horrendous statistics, and it need not be restricted to an office environment. Getting day one right is just as important in all walks of life, from call centres to the Royal Mail, from hospital staff to doctors and nurses, from teachers to shop assistants.

Do it Right: Do it Now!: it really is not difficult!

Do it Right: Do it Now!

7: INSPIRING FROM THE START

As with the previous section we are still very much at the genesis of corporate professional life. We are at the start of a new job, at the start of a career. As before it is so easy to get it right and yet so few do.

'YOUNGISM'

The greatest area of frustration is the huge wastage of talent, of enthusiasm, of energy that occurs with such vast degrees of regularity that it is verging on whatever a collective corporate sickness may be called.

It is quite extraordinary to think that when a person is young is the time when he or she has the greatest energy, has the greatest ability to absorb, learn, be challenged. There are no Olympic champions in their middle years, there are no football stars in their 40s, there are no downhill skiing champions in their 50s. The reality is that young people are fitter, stronger, and tend to have more energy than older people. I know that there are plenty of people in their 50s, 60s and 70s with vast amounts of energy, who need very little sleep, and have all those years of experience behind them too. But on average, this is not the case. When a person is young, she or he has the most fertile and uncluttered mind, 'a sheet of white paper on which experience is yet to write'.

As Professor Gary Hamel remarked in a London Business School lecture, when the CEO of a company has an issue why doesn't he invite comment from his new recruits as well as his senior executive team? Crazy? No! Not if you think that your ten year old child is probably a lot more computer savvy than you, can navigate the web better and faster, is probably a lot more able to use the functionality of his/her mobile phone than you are, is able to text 'blind', and is probably much more able to use the full functionality of all his various digital equipment than you are. And this is not restricted to technology alone but has been substantially accelerated by technology.

Equally, it is the under 25-year olds that are fully 'socially networked'. They are the 'Facebook generation'; they are the ones who will not hesitate to participate in social networks, use them effectively both socially and for business. They are the early adopters of Tik Tok/Snapchat/QZone… and whatever else may have been introduced and marketed successfully. No fear, no inhibition, but knowledge of how best to use the networks and communicate, and also how best to retain privacy as appropriate.

Why is it possible for a man or woman in his/her early twenties to be responsible for dozens of subordinates and to have responsibility for life or death decisions in the armed forces, and yet be perceived in the business world as not sufficiently experienced to hold a managerial position? Crazy? Totally.

Is it the fear that we older people have that if we allow younger people too much responsibility too early, if we take them too seriously, then we are the ones who would be seriously challenged and threatened, as we would be the ones who would not be able to keep up. So better to keep them down, keep them shut out. There may always be a renegade, a Richard Branson, who will just get on and do his own thing, or a Michael Dell, but these are the visionary entrepreneurs, not your average graduate recruit. True, but only to some extent.

Over the years I have known many a young person just about to graduate from university with great aspirations, huge enthusiasm.

The world is going to be their oyster, they have been educated, they are now ready to be launched and make their mark on the world. Over the years I have also known many who are hugely bitter and frustrated a year on that they are being deliberately held back, they are being given menial tasks, being kept on the outside. I have known amazingly articulate and intelligent young people in their early 20s clearly ready to absorb at rapid rates, bursting with ideas, who have been treated as glorified office runners: 'Their time will come' but first they have to do their time, 'we did, and look at us now!' What a total waste!

Why do so many of our brightest go into professional services, accountancy, law, into management consulting, or into investment banking? Because these are the few areas where young people are stretched, some would say abused, others that they are given the opportunity to shine with few constraints. At the age of 25, on graduation from business school, I was immediately exposed to complex issues confronted by senior management of the very largest of quoted, FTSE 100, corporations, with clients typically at board level. Within a few months I was expected to be able to make cogent presentations, to be able to undertake sensitive interviews of senior executives, participate in undertaking detailed analysis and evaluation of identified issues and the development of recommendations suitable for implementation.

Children of friends of ours working in investment banking are equally stretched today and are expected to be able to make a real contribution through the quality of analysis they undertake. Others in law are expected to be able to rapidly and accurately get through vast volumes of documentation, in accountancy, undertake ever more complex audits.

The senior management of these organizations are prepared to listen to ideas, views and opinions of their junior colleagues and encourage their new recruits to think how to do things better and differently. They genuinely want input from all levels in their organization, as was the case back some 45 years ago in my first post business school job.

STUCK IN BOREDOM

In many other corporate environments this is very far from the case. Hugely talented young people are stuck in mindless endeavour, with no chance to express themselves or demonstrate their ability to originate ideas, let alone improvements to the way 'things are done around here'. The creative environments, be they publishing, PR, advertising, media, or journalism, are classic examples of where this is a fact of life. They are environments that are in great demand, where for every job opportunity available there may be dozens of suitable applicants from the hundreds or even thousands that are seeking to get in. And what happens when you are lucky enough to have secured a place? Utter boredom and often times extreme frustration at the way they are so underutilised. They go home at night ready to scream and shout at the way they've been treated, at the crass mind-numbing activities they've been allocated under the cloak of 'training'.

John Simpson's first book *Strange Places, Questionable People* (Pan Books, 1999) in which he refers to his early years at the BBC after graduating from Cambridge, is an excellent description of how a young man with an abundance of energy and ability had to learn to kick his heels, restrain his brains, make tea and wait! And although that may have been the BBC of decades ago, there are contemporary examples that would suggest not a great deal has changed.

These early years are precious. They are a wonderful opportunity to tap into a resource that has been carefully nurtured for the past couple of decades and is ready to explode with untold ideas, contributions, insights, questions, creativity of original thought. Young people should be encouraged to challenge, to ask 'why', to set their minds free from inhibitions. The fertility of these minds needs to be carefully cultivated and reaped, just like any good harvest. And the yield, just as from any good harvest, would be excellent. The yield would come in many forms, from the possible value-added contribution to the business itself. From perhaps the one simple 'why' could stream an improvement that yielded thousands, maybe millions, of pounds of savings, or a new way of satisfying demand, from having a highly motivated and enthusiastic member of staff whose enthusiasm could be contagious to others, both existing employees, and potential recruits of tomorrow.

Some while ago in the then Lloyds TSB's accelerated graduate programme, participants were asked where in the organisation they would like to spend some time, outside of London? One of the participants immediately answered 'New York'. 'But the furthest anyone has ever been sent is Bristol. International placings aren't included', came the reply. 'Why? If we are expected to be the future senior executives of the bank, surely international experience is not only important, but essential?' And yes, he did end up in New York! But only because he was willing to ask 'why?' and rationally defend his position.

Those in positions of responsibility today would do well to think back over their early experiences. If they were exposed to some of the above, they should aim to ensure that things are changed, that the same is not repeated with today's and the future's younger generation. I certainly try to.

It is not by chance that Glasses Direct, that became the world's largest online retailer of prescription glasses, was started by Jamie

Murray Wells while still at university. At the age of 21, he took on the whole establishment of opticians and won. Equally Brent Hoberman and Martha Lane Fox were very much at the start of their career when they created Lastminute.com, one of the real successes of the early dotcom era. It's the guts, the imagination, the passion, the lack of inhibition to rock the boat, and the clarity of vision for new opportunities that is demonstrated by these youthful entrepreneurs.

The billionaires of today were the 'child prodigies' of their era… be it Mark Zuckerberg, Bill Gates, Larry Page, Sergey Brin, Larry Ellison, Jeff Bezos, Michael Dell, Jack Ma, Elon Musk… they had the vision, the drive, they were prepared to challenge and confront. They were also prepared to bring in other likeminded people to work with them… at times with just a burning ambition and promise, at times with real capabilities yet untested.

It is not difficult to get it right, or more right than it is today, in far too many situations. Again, all it takes is just a little bit of planning, and thought. A little bit of planning to ensure that new employees actually have a worthwhile job to undertake, suitable to the level at which they were recruited. A little bit of planning to think through:

Why are we hiring this person?

How are we going to use the skills this person has?

How are we going to develop this person quickly to increase their value to the organisation as fast as possible?'

How are we going to stretch this person, create challenges to motivate?

THE WHYS

(So why is it such a major issue in so many corporate environments?)

Why is it not the most natural thing to do to ensure that all talent is used effectively?

Why is an inspirational environment not the norm?

Why is it not recognised widely that the young, the young and educated, have so much that they are able to contribute?

Why do board rooms not reach out much more frequently for the input, the advice, the insights of the newly recruited, the newly minted graduate intake?

A little bit of planning will ensure that the new employee has some sort of a defined role in the organisation, understands what is being asked of him/her and why, has been given some clarity of outlook as to where she or he is expected to be in the coming 6, 12 or 24 months, and that new ideas are positively welcome. The management of expectations is as real here as in any situation where one is dealing with people and their aspirations. The objective for all must surely be to harness the extraordinary abundance of energy, and to capture the spirit of youth.

Just a little focus on getting things right can have a major impact:

> *Do It Right: Do It Now!:* Hire the best for your organization, but then recognize that you've hired talent, and handle it accordingly
>
> *Do It Right: Do It Now!:* Foster an open environment in which to ask is good, to question is better, to challenge is best

Do it Right: Do it Now!: Making mistakes is okay, it's part of the learning process

Do it Right: Do it Now!: Pressure is better than leisure, you'd be amazed how much the young can cope with

Do it Right: Do it Now!: Provide excellence and you'll get excellence back

Do it Right: Do it Now!: Manage expectations; not everything can be challenging all the time

Do it Right: Do it Now!: Foster contagious enthusiasm, a high yielding harvest

Do it Right: Do it Now!: Harness their energy, capture their spirit

Do it Right: Do it Now!: And positively discourage mediocrity

Do it Right: Do it Now!

The very best do, and have done so. The very best seek to maintain an ever improving cohort because they know that their best and brightest represent their future. And the beginning of their future is the day the best and the brightest first walk through 'the front door'.

RE-REVVING

Enough of the young. Inspiring from day one is as relevant to the experienced as the inexperienced, it is as relevant to the mature hire, as to the first-time hire. There is, however, a difference. The difference is that unfortunately most of today's experienced work force have already had their expectations massively limited by their repeated familiarity with mismanagement/abuse/no management, so trying to get them re-revved may be tough. Getting people with a whole series of negative experiences, experiences in which they were expected to do as they were told, rather than take the initiative, is a much bigger job than getting it right to start with. But even this can be achieved, it is never too late for some. Mature people can learn new skills and can certainly learn and be encouraged to take a much more involved approach to their work. The turnaround of ASDA, the large UK retail chain subsequently acquired by the even larger US retail chain Walmart, was based on the empowerment of its whole workforce. The executive hired to save the business, Archie Norman, recognised the vast untapped talent present amongst the workforce, amongst the people that had day to day, real time exposure and interface with their customers. The workforce could develop a much closer understanding of the customers, as they were the same as their customers. All they needed was freedom, freedom to feedback, freedom to act, freedom to initiate, freedom to believe they could make a difference. A genuine belief that they would be heard, and their views would be acted on. And what a difference they all made.

As mentioned in an earlier chapter, employee engagement can have profound effects on the business, and the business's competitive position. Embedding employee engagement, especially in a large workforce is tough, very tough, takes real leadership in a consistent manner, but absolutely is achievable!

Creating an inspiring environment leads to inspired behaviour irrespective of age or stage in career. Creating an inspiring environment can be achieved, and achieving it really is neither too difficult, nor too costly!

Julian Richer, founder of 'Richer Sounds' which today is the UK's leading Hi-Fi, Home Cinema and TV Specialist retailer… was founded in 1978 when Julian Richer was just 19. Today there are some 53 branches. On 21st October 2019, the FT ran a 'How to Lead' profile on Julian with the headline 'Treating staff and customers well pays dividends'. The article is a gold mine of what to do right:…

- Most people you meet are decent and if you treat them well they'll treat you well back

- What this means in terms of leadership at Richer Sounds is a focus on engaging with staff and customers

- Every night if a shop has good figures, I e-mail them saying 'guys, great figures today, well done'

- All bosses including me don't say' thank you' and 'well done' enough,

And the results speak volumes…not just in financial terms but Richer Sounds' annual staff turnover is less than half of the average among UK retailers; staff theft running at 1-2% in British retail is under 0.1% at Richer Sounds. Julian Richer is a genuine beacon of 'walking the talk' and as he rightly says, 'This is not complicated'!

8: THE POSITIVE EXIT

Not everyone can rise to the challenge. There will be times when some people will either wish to leave or will need to be asked to leave. So how to achieve the best exit of employees? Getting this right can be almost as important as ensuring that the right people are recruited. Over the life of an organisation the number of people who have worked for it may well become significantly larger than the number of those who are employed by it at any one time. These past employees can be important in that they may have many roles that can impact on the company's wellbeing, and reputation.

EXs ARE INFLUENCERS

They may have become customers, suppliers, advisers, opinion formers, investors, even possibly regulators or inspectors. Their views about the company will have been formed during their time as an employee and to a considerable extent by how their departure from the company was handled, irrespective whether the departure was at their instigation or the company's. It certainly has a lasting impact. It certainly had a lasting impact on me!

When, after 15 months, I decided to leave the professional services firm that recruited me as a direct entry partner I had already decided that this was not a company I wished to be part of (remember, I reached the conclusion on day one that I had made a mistake joining this firm and decided that my tenure should be relatively short). I had already decided that its culture, its values and management style were not aligned with my own. So I went to see the senior partner, explained my decision to resign my partnership and when asked why I had come to this conclusion, as tactfully as possible gave my reasons. So far, so good. But when it came to discussing the details including payment of bonus due on revenues originated by myself, the whole thing came unstuck. It took real determination on my part not to give in, to continue to argue my corner for what was, by right, due to me.

In the end I got paid. But it was a struggle and a completely unnecessary struggle that only went to further sour a relationship that was already clearly not a particularly positive one.

Suffice to say that one way or another I have been supportive, after I had departed, of every single organisation I have ever been associated with, with one exception. I have never bad mouthed any organization I have been associated with, and have even been able to put business in the way of many of the companies I have worked with in the past, and have done so with pleasure, except…!

So it does matter… let's now consider the exit scenario.

TO DEMONISE OR NOT TO DEMONISE?

In some companies anyone who leaves is immediately thought of as a traitor. By definition all their actions and track record will have become coloured by the fact that they have decided to move on. They will not have anything positive credited to them, even if up to the point of announcing their intention to move they may have been seen as one of the company's star performers. This does happen. There are numerous examples of companies, often relatively small, often still owner run, where the above is a reality. The actual process of exiting from the company becomes a painful event for employees as they feel that all the work that had been invested by them is wiped from the record and that they will need to negotiate hard for whatever may be theirs by right. They are effectively demonized.

The chances of getting a fair, and objective, reference also becomes highly dubious. The result is clear in that the departed employee will do nothing supportive for his past employer or the business. In fact, the chances are that the opposite will occur. This may damage the company, the company's reputation, and in the most extreme case may even undermine its very existence. Remember the existence of social media and sites such as Glassdoor where employees rate the company… including ex-employees. I guess it is increasingly like being part of the 'Gig Economy' where user (employee) and provider (employer) both are rated…think in terms of Uber drivers and passengers, Airbnb, landlords and renters.

Clearly there are situations where a degree of demonisation of a departed employee may be appropriate. Situations where people have been fired because of gross misconduct, where people have been found with their 'hand in the till', where employees have lied, cheated or committed fraud; these are all situations where an amicable separation is out of the question, and correctly so. Equally and regrettably people are removed due to inappropriate behaviour to other employees, fraud, theft or failing to live up to the values of the business. But they are relatively rare, and much more often exit happens because:

Employer initiated:

- Does not fit the team
- Performance inadequate
- Role being integrated with another, redundancy
- Strategic change, redundancy

- Reached as high as can go, no potential to grow further, up or out
- Others are better suited, up or out
- New management, poor chemistry
- Doesn't want to take up new challenge, lack of drive
- Will not agree to move, lack of motivation
- Should never have been hired, mistake

Employee initiated:

- Head-hunted to bigger and better position
- Fallen out with management
- Blocked upward opportunities
- Passed over for promotion
- Disagrees with strategy
- Disagrees with actions being implemented
- Can't see the future for the business
- Can't see future personally
- Seeks greater challenge
- Feels uncomfortable with culture, style of organization
- Just doesn't fit in
- Wants a change
- Going for more money
- Finds the pressure too much

- Finds the pressure too little

- Work life balance

- Other openings arise elsewhere

- Goes back to full time education

- Undertakes re-training, switches to new sector

- Joins family business

- Should never have agreed to join, mistake (as was my reality with the firm I joined as a partner!)

There are no doubt many other examples for either employer or employee initiated reasons for exit. But the net result is always the same: the employee departs.

BY THE BOOK

In most cases the actual process of separation is handled in a relatively sterile manner ensuring that everything is done legally, to the 'letter of the law'. Companies do not want to spend time and money in court for wrongful dismissal and other related potentially legal actions, just because they made a small error in their internal procedures. So if they initiated the process they will try to make absolutely certain that everything is done by the book, leaving nothing to chance. For most companies the process is relatively well trodden, there is no emotion, it is just another part in the jigsaw of business life. One person goes, another one comes, and that's all. Generosity is limited to what is required based on contractual terms; end of story.

If the departure is initiated by the employee, typically most companies again play by the book, and refer to the terms as per the contractual requirements. Sometimes they may make noises suggesting that they would prefer to retain the employee, that they may be amenable to making certain adjustments to current package etc; in other words that they are open to negotiations. Sometimes much more overt and significant pressure is exerted to retain the employee, but usually to no avail. A story of too little too late!

Sometimes the opposite is implemented by the company, almost as a 'punishment' to the departing executive. They will not agree to release the individual from his/her contractual terms, they will not permit early exit. But at the same time, they do not want the departing employee around any longer for fear of negatively influencing others, or damaging business in a more general way. They will therefore insist on 'gardening leave' i.e. that the employee stays at home, on full pay, for the duration of the notice period. This could be up to a year, and hugely frustrating to the individual concerned. And the reality is that it simply doesn't work. There are plenty of examples where senior executives on so called 'gardening leave' used their enforced 'out of work but on full pay' time to plan and plot their next activity; plan their next major role; engage, very discretely, in planning sessions, meetings etc… all on your payroll! How utterly crazy for all concerned!

The more senior the role, the more complex the separation. Divorce of any kind is always difficult and often emotional. Business literature if full of examples of very senior departures with massive payments for unexpired contractual periods; and/ or where claims have been made for discrimination, wrongful dismissal, or other threatened or actual legal procedures.

The above is nearly always fuelled by complex legal structures and inherent distrust. Many employment contracts/service agreements can run to dozens of pages, easily 30 to 50 pages, of legal document that tries to spell out what can and can't happen. No poaching of staff, no poaching of clients/customers, no poaching of intellectual property! And there is a strong belief that the stronger/the tighter the contractual terms the greater protection there is for the company and potentially for the employee.

But frankly all that this achieves is massive extra cost for the company; souring of any relationship that may have been established, boost to distrust and any potential collaboration. The departing employee will not leave as an asset and will often end up denigrating his past employer. And in the fullness of time may well reach out to grab past colleagues and clients/customers once the exclusion period is over.

But it needn't be like this! There is a better way, and it really is not expensive either in terms of time or money.

RESPECT AND COURTESY

The better way is to treat an exit with exactly the same degree of courtesy, care and attention as someone new joining the company. An employee decides, or you the employer decides, that it is better that a separation takes place. Fine. But the employee has put in many loyal hours, has worked hard for the benefit of the company, and has had certain achievements. Okay, the employee was rewarded for these services, but now it's time to move on. So why not generally be more inclined to the positive:

THE WHYS

Why not create an atmosphere of support and understanding?

Why not extend whatever assistance may be suitable to ease the process of change?

Why not ensure that, rather than only meeting the absolute legally stipulated requirements, you go beyond and exceed expectations?

Why not treat each other as adults?

Why not be marginally more generous?

Why not surprise and delight?

Why not give more time?

Why not be as supportive as possible making exit as easy as possible

Why not be more understanding?

Why not help with the search for a new role, if that were possible

Why not come to an agreement rather than stick to terms?

Why not understand that gardening leave is good for no one?

Why not turn a negative into a positive?

Recently I had a battle with the CEO of a company I am chairman of, to agree to be generous with a departing employee. The employee of many years' standing had decided to leave. The instinct of the CEO was to observe the letter of the law precisely, not a penny more, not a penny less. The employee wanted to shorten the notice period to be able to depart sooner rather than later. It was only after extensive discussion and on pointing out that agreeing to be relatively generous was a win-win situation that the CEO relented. Phew!

And amazingly enough we got payback very quickly in the positive PR that was 'broadcast' as a consequence.

In 1984 I was invited for dinner one evening by the senior partner of one of London's leading executive search firms. Towards the end of an excellent meal he said 'John, tell me, how come that in all the years I have spent in search, I have never come across an ex-McKinsey employee who denigrates the firm irrespective of whether they resigned or were asked to leave? Totally unique in my experience, and totally baffling!' The answer was relatively simple. 'McKinsey has a very clear policy for people who leave, unless of course they are made to leave for reasons of impropriety, and that is that they are all potential clients, advocates, or introducers in the future!'

The reality is that some will become clients, some will be able to influence decisions as to whether to retain the services of consultants or not, and others will influence the general perceptions that people in business hold about the firm. Ensuring that departures are managed with tact, courtesy and sensitivity, therefore, is not just morally sound, but excellent commercial practice!

That was then in the early to mid-80s. Since then McKinsey has got very much larger and inevitably over the decades many thousands will have left the firm, and not all will have had either an exceptional experience or will have left with warmth in their hearts. But nevertheless despite a volume of bad press, McKinsey still stands out as an exceptional place to work and an exceptional firm to have worked at.

It is taken a stage further by retaining a special bond with all who have moved on from the firm. There is a McKinsey alumni organisation to which all ex-employees belong, associates, partners, and directors; and maintenance of this alumni body is taken very seriously. There are regular occasions organised for alumni to gather together socially; special access to online publications, online webcasts/webinars, journals, and other knowledge sharing programmes are made available to all alumni; there is a data base accessible only by alumni; a jobs board exclusively for alumni and lots more. McKinsey invests a significant sum each year into maintaining and further developing its alumni organisation. But the flip side is that McKinsey generates a significant percentage of its global fee income from direct/indirect alumni actions.

I have a special personal vignette I want to share to dramatize what it means to be part of this organisation. In the autumn of 2003 my wife and I together with another couple visited St. Petersburg for the first time. In preparation we wanted to (a) find a private tour guide with whom we could plan to maximize our limited time in the city, and (b) book seats for ballet/opera at the famous Mariinsky Theatre. I first researched Google to no avail: thousands of sites, spent hours surfing, but found nothing that was even vaguely of value. I called the hotel. 'Send a fax' was the response. I did. I am still waiting for an answer!

I then went to the Russian Tourist Office in Piccadilly in London. The office was located above the Aeroflot shop frontage, accessed by a side entrance. There were eight people seated behind desks, many smoking, chatting on phones, engrossed in discussion with each other. No one bothered to ask if they could be of help to me (glasnost/perestroika clearly had not yet arrived in Piccadilly!). Anyway I made my presence felt and asked for assistance in relation to both (a) and (b) as above. 'Impossible,' was the reply, 'you cannot get tickets unless you are there in person. You have to go to the ticket office. And sorry but we have no lists of authorised guides, only authorised tour companies.' Utterly useless!

So what to do? Suddenly a light went on in my brain. Why not ask for help from McKinsey's office in Moscow? So at two o'clock in the morning I sent a short e-mail explaining that I'm an alumnus, had been part of the firm from 1975 to 1980 and needed help with the following... By seven o'clock that morning UK time, there was a reply providing exactly the information required, with the following words, '…hope you find the information of use, but if you have any problems at all please get back to me and we will take care of your needs directly from the office.' Wow did I feel great! And it all worked out fine. We managed to book our tickets without any problems and made contact with a private guide.

On another occasion the alumni network proved of extraordinary value. Unfortunately we had a burglary and a section of our conservatory was shattered. We made immediate contact with the conservatory's supplier who advised the whole side had to be replaced for many thousands of pounds. Why, I asked, why not just replace the unit that's shattered? Can't be done was the reply! I felt that this was total nonsense… so decided to contact the supplier's CEO directly. I then had a second thought, I wonder whether the CEO is a McKinsey alumnus, and bullseye, yes, found the CEO in the McKinsey alumni directory, with all contact details. A brief e-mail, and within an hour the whole issues was resolved. The required part was replaced and installed at a total cost of a few hundred pounds instead of nearly £10,000! Alumni networks do work!

The above is just a great example of how well companies can retain contact and goodwill amongst past employees. And, by the way, past employees can also represent a highly valuable source of new business. Numerous professional service firms derive a significant percentage of their annual revenues from past employees, up to as much as 30 percent in certain cases!

The whole exit process can be undertaken in a civilized and constructive manner: the positive exit!

In total contrast a young woman I know was head-hunted to become CEO of a UN women related organisation. What she had to endure when she went on maternity leave; what she had to endure when she decided it was time to move on beggars belief… and it was an organisation aimed at improving the lives of women! She literally had to argue, negotiate, threaten legal action to receive the basic minimum… the negative exit!

VALUE-ADDED ON EXIT

One part of the process that unfortunately frequently falls by the wayside is that of undertaking exit interviews. No one would ever dream of making an offer to someone without interviewing the candidate. Why are so many so willing to see the back of people without sitting down and interviewing/talking with them? The exit interview should be as much a part of standard procedures as getting candidates to fill out application forms, or submitting CVs. The exit interview is a terrific opportunity to find out from the departing employee what she/he really thinks about the company, the management, the strategy, the strengths and weaknesses etc. Okay, so there will need to be a certain degree of interpretation and understanding of circumstances leading to departure etc, but nevertheless it could be a hugely valuable information/insight gathering exercise.

There are numerous lessons, lessons that are real, lessons that can be implemented with much ease, without great investment of resources, just some forethought and management time:

Do it Right: Do it Now!: Don't get mad, people come and they go

Do it Right: Do it Now!: The days of slavery are over

Do it Right: Do it Now!: Treat those exiting with the same degree of professionalism and courtesy as those joining

Do it Right: Do it Now!: Treatment of outgoing employees is visible to all and can impact on overall morale

Do it Right: Do it Now!: Exit interviews are valuable, can and do provide insights

Do it Right: Do it Now!: Your past employees can be valuable assets

Do it Right: Do it Now!: They can have a direct impact on revenues

Do it Right: Do it Now!: Don't turn them into liabilities, into enemies

Do it Right: Do it Now!: Turn ex-employees into assets, ambassadors

Do it Right: Do it Now!: Remember there are likely be more ex-employees than employees!

Do it Right: Do it Now!: Avoid litigation if at all possible; it sours the relationship, costs a lot of money!

Do it Right: Do it Now!

The positive exit is totally achievable.

Let me finish by one final example. In 2007 the managing director of one of the companies that I chaired asked to meet with me prior to a board meeting, so we met for an early cup of coffee. He then advised me that he had been offered an exciting new opportunity with a larger company, with potential for equity participation. I quoted my old ex-boss, Bruce Fireman: 'The days of slavery are over' and after due consideration wished him well and supported the move. I then asked whether he was prepared to tell me where he was going? He did. At which point I became not only angry but saddened.

I had introduced him to another company as our managing director, given that there could be potential synergies between the two businesses worth exploring. Synergies that could be strong enough to consider a potential merger? The merger never happened, but he got nicked to join the other company. Unprofessional on both parts, but I was still not prepared to stand in his way. So, despite the adverse circumstances, a positive exit nevertheless in that no damage was incurred, and that we essentially said goodbye to someone, without cost, who clearly did not want to belong any longer!

So do everything in your power to secure a positive exit. It is achievable and doesn't necessarily cost a lot either! A truly win-win situation!

9: PURSUIT OF Y

So far in this book I have asked 'why' in every chapter and will continue to do so in all remaining chapters. But this chapter is entirely dedicated to 'Y', why, dedicated to underlining why it is so imperative to question, to question requests, to question orders, to question the status quo.

> *'In particular students are not taught to pose the question 'why' and to keep asking why until they cannot ask it anymore...'*
>
> **WHAT BUSINESS NEEDS FROM BUSINESS SCHOOLS,**
> **JOYCE DORIA HORACIO ROZANSKI AND ED COHEN, *STRATEGY BUSINESS*, FALL 2003**

Leadership is very much about creating a clear vision for the future, with the road map, and the right team of people. Without asking why, getting clarity of vision can be difficult; without asking why choosing the right route may be complicated; without asking why getting the right crew on board for the journey may be impossible; without asking why developing the right strategy could be a big ask!

There is a reason why toddlers when they begin to be able to talk very quickly get to asking 'why?'. Because only by asking can they begin to make order out of their world, can they begin to learn and understand. As per Sir James Dewar's quote...'Minds are like parachutes. They only function when they are open.'

CHALLENGING THE STATUS QUO
Most advertisements/role descriptions for both executive and non-executive board roles nearly always specify an ability and willingness to probe, question, and challenge. Seems blatantly

obvious, and yet it needs to be spelt out. It needs to be spelt out because we are conditioned from a relatively early age not to challenge, not to probe and not to ask why but to accept the way things are.

For me, asking why is at the core of everything. Only by asking why one can fully and totally recognise that 'People are the essential ingredient for success' and frankly it is only the people that makes the difference between success and failure. It's the people and their management and leadership that differentiates exceptional organisations from the rest.

SHEEP MENTALITY

One morning I decided not to use my car but to take public transport instead. I had an 8.30am meeting in Canary Wharf so I had to take the train from my local station, Wimbledon, to Waterloo, and then the underground Jubilee line, to Canary Wharf. As at that time I wasn't a regular user of public transport, I did not have a season ticket, so had to buy a ticket for the journey. I decided to buy a day's 'Travelcard Ticket' (this was in the pre-Oyster card times) that for £6.20 gave me unlimited usage of all public transport in London, zones 1-4. There were automatic machines available through which these tickets could be purchased.

When I arrived at the station there were queues of five or more people at each of the three machines on the station's forecourt, and slightly shorter queues by the machines visible at the far end of the station lobby. But as I walked into the station lobby, I noticed that there were no queues at all by the machines just hidden from view from the outside on the inside of the outer walls. Why? Why are people so into queuing? Why are people so ready to accept that there are queues everywhere and that it is not worth looking around for a shorter queue, or better still no queue at all?

Still staying with queuing, at Stansted Airport a colleague and I were in line for a Ryanair flight to Trieste, Italy. The queue was 80 yards long and moving very slowly. There was a much shorter queue of about 10 yards to our right, leading down to another check-in desk, above which was also the sign for Trieste. I hesitated for a nanosecond, then walked forward to join the much shorter queue. Within a minute many others had followed, so by the end both queues had equalized to about 45 yards each. But why didn't someone go across before me?

How many times have you come out of a theatre with the person in front holding the door open for you and you in turn for the person behind you etc, and failing to see that there is another door available for all to go through, too? I simply cannot tell you how many times that has happened to me, until I open the extra door and create a new flow. I am constantly amazed how sheep like we all are!

OUTSIDERS REQUIRED

EasyJet and Ryanair are fantastic example of mould breakers. They stormed on to the air travel market and did the impossible. They drastically re-structured the business model, and as a consequence dramatically reduced the cost of travel and remained profitable at the same time. Why did it take so long for other airlines to react and adjust to this new competition? Why could they not see from day one the threat presented by these upstarts and do something meaningful about it?

Theodore Levitt wrote in his seminal *Marketing Myopia* back in the 1960s about the demise of the US railway companies who simply couldn't see the competitive threat posed by the then new airlines, Pan American, TWA, etc.

And yet exactly the same happened right in front of our eyes! When Ryanair's market capitalisation is greater than that of British Airways', doesn't that suggest that something dramatic is happening? Why can't highly intelligent and experienced businessmen see what is really happening, especially given the vast resources at their disposal and the army of professional advisers? And why does it always take an industry outsider to shake an industry up? Why can't it be done internally?

Why can't those with vision and imagination, those who have the ability to see beyond the limitations of their existing business, be given airtime to develop new ideas and concepts? BA did allow and sponsor the development of its own low-cost airline, GO, that it failed totally to make a success of and relatively fast decided to exit by permitting a management buy-out. The then management team of a bought-out GO also failed to make a real success of it and fairly rapidly decided to sell to… yes you guessed it… EasyJet!! And BA was essentially forced by competitive pressure to recreate a strategy of low prices and online booking a year later.

BA struggled for many years trying to combine a legacy airline 'flag carrier' with the realities of low-cost, no frills competition. It took the arrival of Alex Cruz as CEO of British Airways to restructure the airline to be able to compete which resulted in providing competitive pricing at a much-reduced level of in-flight service. Interesting that Alex Cruz came from a low-cost airline purchased by BA's owner, IAG, Vueling, i.e. he came with experience of building and running a low cost airline!

Glasses Direct, as already mentioned, is another mould breaker, taking on the long-established market for prescription glasses as delivered by opticians. Prêt A Manger in the sandwich market also fought hard and won; as did IBM with computers in the late 50s when it was forecast that the total world demand would be less than 100! Did Mr. Dyson not have the same sort of problem with his centrifugal vacuum, and then had to defend his innovation from blatant copying by well-established massive corporations in the domestic appliances business? Innovation is tough but getting market penetration and defending that market is even tougher.

THE WHYS

Why are we not more welcoming of innovation, more supportive of innovators, of market leaders, of entrepreneurs?

Why does there continue to be such a gulf between the UK and the USA in how entrepreneurship is perceived and valued?

Why do governments not create a more favourable environment for entrepreneurs, especially given the understanding that it is small business that drives economic growth and development?

Why are big corporations so unable/unwilling to embrace out of the box thinking?

And yet in the world of May 2020 with a global pandemic and the global economy in lockdown it is quite remarkable to observe how the business world has been able to respond with agility and extraordinary speed to the extraordinary set of circumstances it was forced into. The reality of the COVID 19 pandemic has led to millions of people around the whole world 'working from home'; to millions of businesses around the world rapidly pivoting to digital technology; to millions of people and businesses establishing a new way of work to be able to maintain some degree of 'survival'!

So agility and speed of change are possible but why does it take a Global Crisis of the magnitude of COVID 19 to make it a reality?

THEORY vs. PRACTICAL

At business schools around the world, and especially at the leading business schools Harvard, Stanford, Wharton, London Business School, Insead, IMD et al., huge amounts of time and academic focus are placed on the development of learned research papers, often of an esoteric nature. Academics need to publish to further their careers. To publish they need to undertake research to be able to create new insights into un-researched or under-researched areas. Subject matter that does not lend itself to research is often considered of little significance. It does not capture the imagination or the fire of the academics as the more mundane everyday subject matter fails to provide the opportunity for them to develop reputation-making, promotion-promoting, article-publishing material.

An analysis of the course schedules also demonstrates the focus on strategy, financial analysis, marketing, organizational behaviour, and related subject matter, all of which have been around for decades, are considered to be the heavyweights, and are perceived to be the 'in-demand' areas requiring concentration of teaching. But I wonder how frequently in their future careers do the students of business schools need to be able to apply 'beta factors', capital asset pricing models, statistically valid market segmentation?

I do not question the validity of any of the core subject matter. I do question the validity of failing to include as a core plank in business school programmes a range of 'life skill' related courses, non-researchable perhaps, not helpful to academics for advancing their careers, but fundamental skills for the rest of the students' lives. Courses on writing, presentation, selling, basic problem-solving techniques, interviewing, listening, giving feedback, and mentoring, to mention just a few. Why? Why not!

Interestingly enough, when I was Chairman of TACK International Limited, a sales and sales management training company, I managed to get London Business School to agree for us to run a couple of pro-bono courses on 'Selling' for the graduating MBA class. The classes were a complete 'sell-out' to the extent of 'standing room only'! The two one-day seminars received rave reviews with comments such as 'this was the most valuable one day I have spent in the past two years!', 'wow, what an eye opener!', 'this has given me a real sense of confidence', 'why did we have to wait for two years to receive something so practical and pragmatic?' and lots more along similar lines. So why not include selling skills as part of the core curriculum, along with a selection of the other 'life skill' related topics? Why not indeed?

Despite the strong and positive reviews and frankly overwhelming enthusiasm by the MBA students, the school totally ignored the noise and failed to include selling skills in any programmes.

I heard the head of one of the world's leading consulting companies say recently, '…we do recruit heavily from business schools because we know we'll get a quality product, but they only start learning the tools of real value when they join us, and it takes us another 18 months to develop them into professionals…'. And don't I know it, as that is exactly what happened to me. My post business school training in interviewing, writing, presentation, and analytical skills were those that have actually stayed with me throughout my professional life, all of which I learned at McKinsey, not at London Business School!

So why don't the business schools get a lot closer to their customers, both the students and their future employers, and find out what they really want/need, and start to align their courses accordingly?

If issues of ethics, environment, and climate change, and 'ESG' are top of the agenda for politics and business, why are they also not high on the agenda of academic institutions, not just business schools but all academic institutions? Why are schools and colleges as well as universities not able to deliver thoughtful matter for discussion and debate on topics that are forming the agenda for our world of tomorrow? Is education not supposed to be forward thinking? Is education not aimed at our leaders of tomorrow?

Amazingly some progress has been achieved at arguably the world's best known business school, Harvard:

> *'Harvard University picked Nitin Nohria, a specialist in leadership and ethics, to be dean of its business school, charging him with transforming management education after financial catastrophes and scandals shook public faith in business. Nohria, 48, a professor of management at the school, was named dean by President Drew Faust, president of Harvard in Cambridge, Massachusetts. He will begin after Jay Light, dean since 2006, steps down in June. Nohria, who will be tenth Harvard Business School dean, said in an interview that he will emphasize responsibility and the positive role companies can play in society.'*
>
> BY JOHN LAUERMAN, MAY 4, 2010 *BLOOMBERG*

One of the largest, if not the largest, asset class in the world is that of property. More fortunes have been made via property than any other asset class. More fortunes have been lost, and more businesses destroyed because of disastrous property decisions. (You only need to think back to September 15th 2008, and the collapse into bankruptcy of Lehman Brothers, very substantially as a consequence of disastrous property investment decisions.) So why are there so few, if any, courses on property investment/ management at business schools? It seems totally crazy to me that an asset class of this magnitude is virtually ignored.

I make no apologies for the above as perhaps being too simplistic. My objective here is to raise the issue, in the hope that perhaps it may just result in some change.

In business the early 00s were full of ethical issues. From 'Fat Cats', to 'Corporate Rape', from governance, to compensation for failure, and lots more. How many professors of business, how many MBA courses, how many research projects have there been in these areas? Where are the 'Chairs' in ethics? Yes, there are references, there are seminars, there are electives, but the subject matter has not been included as part of the core curriculum. This is a little like having the token woman, or the politically correct racial mix, on the board of a major quoted company. There is a nod in the right direction rather than a root and branch change. Ethics should be a part of every course, ethics has relevance to finance, marketing, HR, strategy; indeed, ethics should have relevance throughout business behaviour.

Equally climate change is perhaps the single greatest issue confronting the world, even as it is struggling with COVID 19. The huge difference between the pandemic and climate change is that for the pandemic there will be both a cure and a vaccine; for climate change there will never be a vaccine and the cure is for the world's major businesses and governments to agree Net Zero as a core target!

CSR IN PRACTICE

Thank goodness, then, that there are some leaders who are totally committed to change and are putting their money where their mouths are. In October 2003 I had the privilege and pleasure of listening to the then Chairman and CEO of Unilever, Niall FitzGerald, deliver a fabulously powerful speech at London Business School (Distinguished Speaker Series, Sponsored by Lehman Brothers – 2nd October 2003). His focus was very much on Corporate Social Responsibility, 'CSR':

'embracing and valuing differences'

'diversity is essential to our company's strategic future'

'corruption-zero tolerance' ... 'there is no appeal'

'we trust our managers, if not we act decisively'

CSR is core to the company's future, it is core to the company's strategy and as CEO & Chairman he made everyone in the audience believe 100% that he was personally totally committed to seeing the effective implementation of a whole range of policies that pragmatically embrace the full spectrum of what CSR is actually about. It's about being ethical with employees, suppliers, customers, about treating everyone equally, irrespective of whether they are employed in Sri Lanka or Switzerland, about being fair and honest, not accepting the morals of the lowest common denominator, but seeking to be the very best in everything, and that includes ethics and morality.

Niall FitzGerald concluded that, despite some of the increased burden CSR may place on the company, it ends up winning the high ground, and along the way produces products that people want to buy, at prices they are prepared to pay, in volumes that beat competitors, producing results that please shareholders. Not a bad virtuous circle! So it can be done. But why by so few? And why are so many still prepared to 'go with the flow', to accept unethical behaviour, to leave unchallenged corruption, backhanders and cleverly constructed ways of 'oiling the wheels'?

Why is it not standard practice at more companies to ensure that corruption of any sort is deemed to be wholly unacceptable, with zero-tolerance? As a senior executive from Ghana's Central Bank once commented, corruption is the global AIDS of business. Why is the eradication of corruption not a core issue of discussion and debate in business schools? Why is corruption not a key issue around the board tables of the world's largest corporations?

Similarly, in the 21st century more and more senior executives and entrepreneurs are questioning the single minded drive for profit as the ultimate goal. We have responsibilities for our environment, we have responsibilities for the carbon emissions by our actions, we have responsibilities for people diversity, we have responsibilities for our planet.

Many companies and their executive teams are facing up to these challenges and formulating strategies that can accommodate profit, people and planet, the three Ps of the triple bottom-line! There was an interesting article in November 2019 in the FT written by Jude Webber about the transformation achieved by Daniel Martinez-Valles, CEO of Orbia, a Mexican company that was totally revamped to do just that. It just proves it can be achieved.

Equally there is a growing recognition that ESG…(environmental, social and governance) issues have grown to the top of the pile, are now very much within the board rooms of most major corporations…and certainly major asset managers.

The simple conclusions are:

Do it Right: Do it Now!: question

Do it Right: Do it Now!: question everything

Do it Right: Do it Now!: question the status quo

Do it Right: Do it Now!: question the established wisdom

Do it Right: Do it Now!: nothing is ever set in tablets of stone forever

Do it Right: Do it Now!: zero tolerance for corruption

Do it Right: Do it Now!: think profit, people, planet; think zero carbon; think ESG

Do it Right: Do it Now!

Only by asking why can one find the route to a better mousetrap, and there is always a better mousetrap! As the famous Japanese business thinker and world renowned strategist, Kenichi Ohmae once said… '…always ask the why whys!…'

10: *DO IT RIGHT: DO IT NOW!*

'*Carpe Diem*' - Seize the Day! Time is totally perishable; it can never ever be renewed. Some do seize the day, they do seize every opportunity presented, they are action-orientated and refuse to wait until they are sure there are no alternatives or being told to get on with it. They take the initiative, they live their personal and professional lives to the absolute maximum absolutely on the basis that there may not be a tomorrow, or a tomorrow nearly as good as today! I very much try to live my life accordingly, and it's amazing how much you can get done, how much you can see and learn, and how much fun you can have along the way!

INACTIVITY IS NO-ACTIVITY

It is so easy to delay. It is so easy to put things off until another day. If you put it off for another day that day may never come and hence the day when action is required can be avoided. This is easy. It's like the manager who never replies to phone calls, voice-mails, e-mails, letters, on the grounds that if it is really important the caller/writer will call/write back. Somebody else will chase.

Well, that's fine if it is not important to you. That's fine if your business does not benefit from interaction with others. But it isn't fine in all other circumstances and I'm not aware of many businesses that are not dependent on active and constructive interaction with others.

In virtually any walk of life the only person that will have real control over your own destiny is you. Hence there is no merit in delaying action for another day. By the time you get around to it the opportunity may have passed, circumstances may have changed. Of course, there are times when holding back makes sense, there are times when deliberately leaving a certain action for a specific date in the future is not only appropriate but the sensible and a strategically sound action to take. But in most situations inactivity is equal to no activity.

As I said earlier, Reg Valin, the founder and Chairman of the VPI Group PLC (100% owner of Valin Pollen Ltd.) polished the notion of *Do it Right: Do it Now!* to a fine art. In the late 80s we were still in a pre-personal computer world, in which vast volumes of paper flowed in, around, and out of companies. Letters, faxes, memos, proposals, pitches, shareholder documentation, legal documentation, weekly/monthly management accounts, performance evaluations, CVs, work schedules, and lots more. This was the pre-paper-free world (sic). Given the volume of paper that flowed across any senior executive's desk it would have been so easy to let vast proportions go unanswered. Reg was extraordinary in that everything was dealt with, and was dealt with on the day it arrived, even if only to acknowledge receipt with a date by which a more considered response would be forthcoming. I learned the art of getting through vast volumes of paper from Reg, and it was really neither difficult, nor hugely demanding of time. Either at the start of the day, or right at the end of the day, all the volume of paper from the previous 24hrs was dealt with by the following:

- Each document was read/speed read.

- Each document was actioned by a dictated reply;

    - a pencil note of action to be taken by my PA;
    - a note to my PA requesting the document to be brought forward on specific date for more detailed consideration;
    - a copy of the item to be sent to another executive for

action; 'vertical filing', i.e. bin (if it required no action
and was of no value)

The net result was that (1) everyone got a speedy reply and (2)
there was never the danger of a build-up of paper that by definition would have meant that lots got lost or was never replied
to. This did have an impact on everyone within the company
because they knew that the CEO kept abreast of what was
going on throughout the business and was well briefed when
he attended meetings. It also meant that the actual volume
of irrelevant and poorly thought through internal documents
rapidly decreased, with the originators learning quickly that it
is not in their interest to send anything half baked!

And the above lessons are as appropriate for the world of smartphones, Blackberries, iPhones and specifically e-mails with the
constant flow of messages, data and information...of value and
often times of no value!

It is perhaps worth mentioning that having a good PA, and
having a well-established working relationship with your PA,
was certainly a key component of making the above possible, and
effective. Both Reg and I had outstanding PAs. Rita Buckley was
my PA for many years, and indeed despite not having worked
together since the mid-90s we are still in touch. And to this day
she still remembers my children's birthdays although they are
now in their 40s! In today's world PAs, or as they are now called
EAs (executive assistants), are increasingly rare except with senior
executive roles. It is exactly at this level that they can function
effectively and that a positive and well-structured relationship can
increase an executive's productivity by many order of magnitude.

THINK IT, DO IT

At one of the companies that I chaired, Coffee Point PLC, a newly appointed main board director, Charles Trace, was totally committed to the concept of *Do it Right: Do it Now!* The impact he made in a few short months after joining the business was palpable. He didn't just ask 'why', he got on with the action.

Why are there no visitor parking spaces? By the end of that week two parking spaces had been designated for visitors with Coffee Point branded signs attached 'COFFEE POINT – VISTORS' PARKING'. Done. Why don't we have better brochures, more suited to the needs of our customers? Done. Why don't we have a more contemporary, ecommerce-based website, where our customers can both place orders online and can trace their orders online? Done. Why isn't our external image better positioned? Done, PR companies short-listed and a winner selected with a schedule of work agreed, and implemented. Why don't we have a showroom serving our customers in the South of England? Done, southern showroom opened. Why don't we have a much closer working relationship with caterers? Done. And so on and so forth.

All of the above being just the tip of the iceberg, all of the above being done alongside his main focus of being the company's sales and marketing director, securing opportunities to compete for major national accounts that required massive and complicated proposals, formal presentations and detailed commercial negotiations. Done. A significant number of major new accounts were successfully secured. *Do it Right: Do it Now!* Done!

Charlie rapidly took on extra responsibilities and became Coffee Point's COO. And when Coffee Point was acquired by Bunzl in 2007, Charlie's energy, focus and drive was rapidly recognised by his new colleagues, as he was appointed COO of the much enlarged merged vending businesses.

As with most issues dealt with in this book it isn't difficult to get it right. All it takes is focus, and a positive attitude of mind. My take on leadership has repeatedly been shown not to be difficult nor complex; it just requires a readiness to act now and act positively.

During the extraordinary times of the global COVID 19 pandemic some organisations made rapid decision that spoke volumes about their culture and the 'Think it, do it' nature of their leaders.

- Admiral, an independent UK insurance business announced that they would be making a refund to all their motor insurance customers of £25/vehicle covered 'because people are driving less during lockdown'. An excellent initiative driven by Admiral's CEO David Stevens.

- Similarly many businesses in the luxury sector made relatively fast decisions to provide support be it Pernod Ricard's 70,000 litres of sanitizer gels; Claridge's Hotel offering free accommodation to NHS workers; LVMH providing 28 million medical masks; Jaguar Land Rover providing 160+ cars to the emergency services…each and every one being decisions taken and implemented fast.

Irrespective of the size of an organisation, 'Think it, do it' can happen as long as the c-suite is engaged and on-board!

Delaying is very often perceived to be an easy option. It isn't. All this does, unless of course it's for well thought-through reasons, is defer decisions and actions that could have been made earlier. Deferring is not a solution. Frequently deferring decisions just compounds their complexity and often increases their acuteness, leading to poor decisions being made out of necessity and time crunch. No time left to consider alternatives, no time left for thoughtful reflection, no time to undertake analysis of issues contained in the original proposal. Deferring does not provide space or time; it does exactly what the word means, putting things off. Out of sight, out of mind.

John Gapper of the FT wrote (October 16th 2019), 'There are rewards for being decisive, beyond the risk of the company drifting and you losing your job... Investors and the media are drawn to confident stories and dislike uncertainty. There is no point in holding a strategy day if you cannot settle on a strategy, or say how it will be executed... decision will at least prove right some of the time; indecision is always mistaken!'

The *Do it Right: Do it Now!* mentality is so appropriate for virtually all aspects of management. It is especially so for the really tough decisions that need to be taken. There are none tougher, none more difficult, than having to tell someone that they no longer have a career with the company. But many times this decision is delayed and delayed to the massive detriment of the organisation as a whole and in all fairness the individual who is to be sacked, made redundant, asked to leave, too. Delay, hesitation, procrastination, helps no-one.

I have been very forceful with many CEOs that I have worked with in the past on the above issue. I cannot tell you the number of times CEOs have discussed with me, in total confidentiality, the need in due course to remove a sub-performer or the person who doesn't fit any longer, or whose job is no longer required. Why in 'due course' I ask? With the usual responses of timing, just needing to get certain things completed, other more pressing priorities that need to be addressed first and etc. NO!!! There can be nothing more pressing than to deal with the lives, well-being, of employees.

If the CEO has identified the need for an individual to be exited from the business the very high likelihood is (a) that there are many other people in the organisation who have already come to the very same view and (b) that the individual themselves will know that things aren't right! So the correct action is ACTION. Deal with it, do not put it off, do not delay, do not procrastinate especially about people related issues!

Interestingly enough Lucy Kellaway's article in the FT (January 12th 2004) had the title 'Let this be your productivity slogan: just don't do it'. In this she argues not against a *Do it Right: Do it Now!* approach, but against doing things by rote, just allowing oneself to go with the flow. So by saying 'don't do it' she is arguing for people to seriously question whether they need to attend all the meetings they have got accustomed to attending in the past year, whether they need to attend conference calls with more than three people, whether making all those trips are really necessary, whether all the lunches are important, etc. In this she is effectively underpinning a core part of this book, which is to question everything, but in no way diluting the *Do it Right: Do it Now!* concept of this chapter.

Lucy Kellaway was absolutely right in her observations… and little did she know how a global pandemic can suddenly bring so many things into focus. Why get on planes when using video-conferencing works so well? Why have people to commute for hours to and from an office when working from home works so well? The COVID 19 pandemic has focused minds and will certainly challenge the way we work and the things we do in the future.

Buying into Lucy Kellaway's thought process creates a neat reciprocal relationship between the whys and the do its! There are so many activities that managers/executives are expected to undertake that absolutely require the question 'why?' But once an activity has been accepted, then there should be rapid action, even if the rapid action results in the cancellation of previously unquestioned events, activities, processes and procedures. So the simple set of 'why' and *Do it Right: Do it Now!* for this chapter are:

THE WHYS & DO IT RIGHT: DO IT NOW!

Do it Right: Do it Now!: Always question

Why are things the way they are?

Do it Right: Do it Now!: Challenge the status quo

Why should we spend more time analysing the past than preparing for the future?

Do it Right: Do it Now!: Because the alternative is unacceptable

Why is the unacceptable wrong?

Do it Right: Do it Now!

On my first day back after one Christmas break with one of the companies that I chaired, one of my board colleagues came up and said, ' I thought of you during the term-end show at my son's school just before Christmas. One of the kids read out a poem by Edgar Guest, a poem I thought you would love especially as it sums up your attitude to life.' 'How wonderfully kind and thoughtful of you, thank you so much,' was my reply. And then I read it and asked him to ensure that it is fully circulated at the next board meeting to all board directors. And here it is for you:

It Couldn't Be Done
by Edgar Guest

Somebody said that it couldn't be done,
But, he with a chuckle replied
That 'maybe it couldn't,' but he would be one
Who wouldn't say so till he'd tried.

So he buckled right in with the trace of a grin
On his face. If he worried he hid it.
He started to sing as he tackled the thing
That couldn't be done, and he did it.

Somebody scoffed: 'Oh, you'll never do that;
At least no one has done it';
But he took off his coat and he took off his hat,
And the first thing we knew he'd begun it.

With a lift of his chin and a bit of a grin,
Without any doubting or quiddit,
He started to sing as he tackled the thing
That couldn't be done, and he did it.

There are thousands to tell you it cannot be done,
There are thousands to prophesy failure;
There are thousands to point out to you one by one,
The dangers that wait to assail you.

But just buckle it in with a bit of a grin,
Just take off your coat and go to it;
Just start to sing as you tackle the thing
That 'couldn't be done,' and you'll do it.

Peter Thompson, thank you so much for finding this and thinking of sharing it with me. The poem says it all. A positive mindset, a 'can do' attitude, and nothing should be too difficult to undertake – *Do it Right: Do it Now!*

In another way the poem also resonates with another set of words that I have come across, that I had framed and hung in my office, written by *Sydney J. Harris*, (permission to reproduce by TREND enterprises, Inc. 300 9th Ave SW New Brighton, MN 55112).

The winner is always part of the answer.
The loser is always part of the problem.

The winner always has a programme.
The loser always has an excuse.

The winner says 'let me do it'.
The loser says 'It's not my job'.

The winner sees an answer for every problem.
The loser sees a problem in every answer.

The winner says 'it may be difficult but it's possible.
The loser says 'it may be possible, but it's too difficult'.

The winner sees a green near every sand trap
The loser sees sand traps near every green

The winner uses mistakes to learn from.
The loser uses mistakes as an excuse to give up.

There are very few actions that need to be deferred. There are very few things in life that have to be put off. '*Carpe Diem*, seize the day, *Do it Right: Do it Now!*, be the winner!

It is therefore critical to re-boot one's mind to believe that things can be done. We should all aim to embrace the essence of '*Carpe Diem*'.

11. THE 3 'Cs' - COMMUNICATE, COMMUNICATE, COMMUNICATE!

'It's all about communications.' The reality is that it is virtually impossible to over-communicate. In every company that I have consulted, worked with, or advised, communications have always been one of the recurring themes of perceived weakness. And even when communications are given priority, even then there will be some for whom there is not sufficient sharing of information.

THE WHYS

Why is it so difficult for so many to 'PUtFP' (pick up the fucking phone) and make a call?

Why is it so difficult for so many to speak one to one?

Why don't people recognize that e-mail is not communication?

Why does it seem to be so challenging for so many senior executives to walk from one office to another, to walk out of their office and go down a corridor, and even more challenging to walk down some stairs to the back offices, or the shop floor?

Why isn't 'MBWA' as coined by Lord Rayner, Chairman of Marks and Spencer (1984 until his retirement in 1991), Management By Walking Around, practised by more senior management. Is it fear or what?

Why do senior executives fail to understand that the people they employ (largely) would like to have an understanding of the business they are working for and can (in the large) be trusted with shared information?

Why do people forget that in effect they are communicating all the time, even subconsciously, and frequently non-verbally, by their actions and behaviour?

Why is there a growing dependency on 'electronic messaging' rather than face to face?

Why are so many people in leadership roles not willing to be leaders and meet and greet their staff?

PHONE INERTIA

I know a successful entrepreneur who is inhibited by the phone. He completely relied on faxes, and then progressed to e-mails for all forms of communication, supplemented with the odd face to face meeting. He would send faxes and e-mails relentlessly, when all he needed to do was to call someone. Often these written bits of communication would get the tone wrong, creating avoidable and unintentional problems because the recipient misread the meaning, or thought there was an implied meaning, when there wasn't. It was all so totally unnecessary and so totally avoidable. And yet this individual has an amazing gift of the gab, can be very witty, and is a confident and able talker, so why does he have this fear of the phone? Is it something to do with control?

E-mail is a fantastic technological invention. E-mail has vast power to reach and facilitate contact between people and institutions. But it is NOT communication in the truest sense. E-mail is the transmission of information, it is possible to share vast amounts of data, of knowledge, of research findings, words and pictures. But it is NOT the same as walking down a corridor, walking into a colleague's office, and saying face to face 'thank you'. It is not the same as having a video call where the person can be seen, where even electronically one is able to look into the other person's eyes.

There is vast e-mail overload, and not just from junk mail, but from everyone always copying everyone on everything they write, and then hitting the 'reply to all' key so that everyone knows what was said in response, and so on the numbers grow exponentially. 'I've been out of the office for two days and I've come back to 1,400 e-mails in my inbox!' …and people start to compete, 'Oh that's nothing I had over 2,200 in my inbox after just three days!' Has the world gone mad?

I have recently heard of a research project being undertaken in a major 'bulge-bracket' bank exactly into the issue of e-mail over-load. Early data is indicating that for a relatively small team, the volume of incoming e-mail traffic in one working week was in access of 13,500,000; and it gets a lot worse because this 13,500,00 of received e-mails then generated a multiple of outgo-ing e-mails precisely because the 'reply to all' was pressed! A huge waste of time! And potentially dangerous in that occasionally the importance gets buried by the volume.

This e-mail overload causes a loss in effectiveness in its potency, but even if this overload were not to exist, it would not be a satisfactory replacement for real one to one, one to small group, contact and real communication, where you are communicating with words and emotions and your whole body.

WALKING AROUND

In all the companies where I have worked, where I have held executive or non-executive positions, I have tried to 'walk the corridors', be they corridors or subsidiary businesses, shop-floors or gravel pits. I rarely asked people to come to my office when it was just as easy for me to walk to theirs. This should not be about positioning, making points about seniority, but frequently that is exactly what it is all about. In fact the more senior the person, the greater the need to walk the corridors, the greater the need to get out and about among the troops.

In a world of 'lockdown' where people are working from home and offices are standing empty, one can still 'walk around' except the walking around is done electronically by engaging with people in groups and one to one via WhatsApp, Facetime, Zoom, Microsoft Teams, WebEx… or any of the other means by which one can communicate visually and by voice.

In 1980 I was appointed to the board of Amey Roadstone Corporation Ltd., at that time a major construction materials business, by its parent Consolidated Gold Fields, a FTSE 100 company, as the 'shareholder's board appointee' and as executive director responsible for the business's strategy. I wanted to really get to know the company, not just from reading the management accounts, the monthly board papers, attending management and board meetings, not just by wandering about head office, (although that too was a novelty for many) but by actually visiting the operations. I decided that in my first year I would visit every single operation wherever they might be in the world. And I did exactly that, visiting every single ready-mixed concrete plant, quarry, gravel pit, concrete-block site, black-top operation, and so on and so forth, in the UK, in Europe, and in the USA. I learned a phenomenal amount about the company, its people, its strengths and weaknesses.

Actually taking the time to talk with the people at the sharp end, to listen to them, to genuinely give them the opportunity to chat about the business is hugely instructive. It is critically important to ensure that they are given 'airtime', that they feel they have someone who is prepared to listen, who is really interested in their views. Unfortunately it is often forgotten or ignored, that the people at the sharp-end have quite amazing insights about the business. How things can be improved, where certain core issues are, where there is waste and inefficiency, after all they are the ones doing the work on a daily basis!

One of the interesting observations I came across in this journey was that many of the workforce could not name the boss of the business, felt that they had never heard from him, and that the whole senior executive group had no interest in their employees apart from ensuring that the job gets done and financially the business achieves its objectives.

A few years back I was undertaking a consulting assignment for a large travel-related business. I was working for the division that provided the rest of the organization with services, from purchasing to IT, from accounting to property services, etc. My mandate was to improve the quality of the internal service delivery. I shall not go into details of this assignment except that one of the key recommendations to my client, (my client being one of the company's main board executive directors, who was later appointed CEO), was to 'just get out of your office, go and meet with your staff, walk to meetings in other buildings, meet and greet people whether you know them or not'.

I was suggesting that as head of this division my client should set an example of getting close to 'the customer', and in that sense the division head's 'customers' include the division's staff. The recommendation was accepted, and - along with a number of other things - it worked. But there was a degree of a resistance, a degree of fear, fear from meeting someone whose name has been forgotten, fear of meeting someone who could have asked a difficult question, fear of the unknown, and perhaps fear of the loss of total control that staying in an office seems to provide.

Getting about a business is business. Lord Rayner visited at least one Marks & Spencer store a week, always unannounced. He wanted to see for himself what was happening on the shop floor. How else can the boss really get a feel for the business? Irrespective of whether the business is retail like Marks & Spencer, or construction materials like Amey Roadstone, or professional services like Valin Pollen, the boss needs to get out and about both with the staff and their customers. No amount of market research, sophisticated consulting assignments or staff reports, will provide the feel, the sense, the insights!

Some while ago I read about a CEO who actually went 'under-cover' to really understand what it was like being an employee in his business, and what the employees really thought about the business.

> *'At just 42, Stephen Martin is the recently appointed chief executive of the Clugston Group, a major force in construction, building roads, schools and supermarkets. But the industry is in crisis as a result of the recession - hundreds of companies have folded and nearly 30,000 construction workers have lost their jobs. So Stephen has decided to trade in his suit and expense account for a hard hat and a canteen lunch and, armed with a cover story, he visits his construction sites to work alongside his frontline employees. He pours concrete, works in blast-furnaces, tries his hand at carpentry and does freezing night-shifts repairing roads, while searching for the best way to run the business. He confronts the consequences of his executive decisions and hears exactly what the workforce thinks of the management.'*
>
> **FIRST BROADCAST: THURSDAY 25 JUNE 2009, 9PM ON CHANNEL 4**

The above is somewhat extreme in my view, although I can see the value especially in a large service-based business. I am advocating something much simpler, something much less covert, something that takes just the smallest degree of planning, scheduling, something that can actually be undertaken on the spur of the moment. Walk out of your office, walk to meet with your colleagues in their offices, walk randomly to various parts of the building, drop into your remote offices, workshops, factories, distribution units etc. Go unannounced. Speak with your employees. Reach out to the employees, not just management, talk and listen.

Do it Right: Do it Now!: Get out of the office, meet those at the sharp end, meet the customers

Do it Right: Do it Now!: Walk to other people's office rather than getting them to come to you

Do it Right: Do it Now!: Get a random group to meet with you over a sandwich lunch from time to time

Do it Right: Do it Now!: MBWA

Do it Right: Do it Now!: There is no substitution for direct contact, for direct feedback, for direct dialogue

Do it Right: Do it Now!: PUtFP!

Do it Right: Do it Now!: Call to congratulate on a job well done

Do it Right: Do it Now!: Talk to your employees as you are walking around

Do it Right: Do it Now!: Meet with your employees let the talk to you, listen to what they have to say some of it could be 'gold-dust'!

Do it Right: Do it Now!

An article by Scott Blanchard featured in March 2020's edition of BA's 'business life' on board magazine was entitled 'It's good to talk' and was focused on the importance of engaging with employees, actually 'talking' with them… the manager's role is to simply… ask questions such as 'How's it going?' or 'What's on your mind?' with the net result being significantly reduced employee turnover! So it really is good to talk!

NO COST

I could have suggested in this chapter that you should be allocating a significant budget to internal and external communications, PR and advertising campaigns. This may or may not be required in your particular business or organisation. But what I have suggested requires zero incremental investment of cash, requires no board decision, no meetings to review, only a simple decision to act. An attitude of mind that says… 'yes people are important' and as boss I need to ensure that I am accessible and that I am connected with what's going on, that there is as good a degree of transparency for all as possible.

When I was in senior executive roles I did exactly as I'm 'preaching'. I arranged with my PA to schedule time when she would kick me out of my office and told me to go for a walk around; when she would schedule informal sandwich lunches with a total cross-section of employees, no agenda, just open chat; when she would schedule my attendance at client meeting, just to be there; and she would schedule client lunches with a number of non-competitive clients to have an informal discussion that included their view of our business and our people.

12: THE POSITIVE 'NO'!

Everyone says it.

All children learn to say it very early in their development.

Everyone needs to learn early on in their career how to say it.

'NO'.

TINY WORD BIG IMPACT

We are conditioned from an early age that saying 'no' is unaccept-able. As tiny tots we are expected to do as we are told, to eat what is put in front of us, to wear the clothes given to us, to be nice to people we are introduced to, to go to events that we are told to attend and so on and so forth. In some cultures and in some societies these expectations go on for a long time, right the way through to adulthood, and frequently include core life-shaping elements such as religion, marriage, and work.

So is it really surprising that this tiny word should take on such giant proportions in our minds, in our professional environ-ments? Saying 'no' can be very tough. In many respects the ability of an individual to say 'no' effectively is a determining factor in their personal development, their personal maturity. The ability to say and mean 'no' is a critical part of growing up both personally and professionally.

CHILDREN NO

Let's just revert to childhood for a second. When a small child rejects something, it is not always because of being stubborn or difficult, or just being contrary. Children often reject certain things naturally because of some innate, biological or physiological reason. They reject certain foods because their digestive system can't cope with it, or they haven't developed the suitable taste buds; they reject certain clothes perhaps because they have a natural reaction to its smell or feel; they reject certain people because they have an automatic internal warning system making them alert to unsaid, unknown, vibes.

As adults of course we know better and frequently try to force our better knowledge and expertise on to our children. I know that as a child I automatically rejected fatty food, meat with bits of fat I would spit out, despite the fact that in the early 50s lean meat was almost unheard of in Budapest. The reason became known later that I simply did not possess the sufficient mix of digestive chemicals to deal with fatty food effectively, hence my body's automatic reaction.

My daughter from a tiny age virtually threw up when in contact with certain fabrics, to the extent that whenever she was taken shopping as a little girl, she would first smell clothes before trying anything on, even down to school tights. Unknown by us at that time, but became clear a few years later, she has an aversion, almost an allergy, to rubber, hence any clothing that contained elements of rubber, even of minute proportions, she would reject.

As a child, a friend refused to show normally accepted behaviour towards one of his parent's close friends. Occasionally he got into trouble because he refused to kiss them, refused to sit on their laps, and tried to stay well out of this couple's way and reach. Amazingly enough years and years later it became obvious that this couple did have a problem, not a huge problem but a problem nevertheless. Being childless they enjoyed the company of children, not in any extreme sense, they weren't paedophiles, but they enjoyed just a bit too much cuddling and stroking to overcompensate their childless status. Perhaps because of an early experience, perhaps because of innate self-preservation, my friend sensed this and went into avoid mode by saying 'no', whatever the consequences.

'No', therefore, is not always a negative. In the above cases, 'no' is a strong positive warning mechanism, one that adults fail too often to take sufficient notice of. Hence the notion of 'THE POSITIVE NO' …but more on this a little later.

ADULT NO

In adult life saying 'no' has huge implications. Again there is the positive and the negative version. I shall not be focusing on the negative version, the 'no' that is deliberately destructive of established society, the anarchistic 'no', the 'no' that is associated with unacceptable behaviour that leads to criminal activities. Although even this type of 'no' has an important role in society, and there are plenty of historical examples where it would have been better for the world as a whole had society been less compliant and more prepared to stand up and be counted, to challenge the establishment and the government/law makers of the day: Nazi Germany, Nazi Austria, the Balkans, Iraq, Afghanistan, to name a few and more recently even the USA under Trump's presidency! But perhaps this is a bit too political.

It took a lot of extraordinarily brave individuals to say 'NO' to apartheid before that particularly abhorrent system collapsed, it took the phenomenal bravery of Nelson Mandela and F.W. de Klerk, to bring about a bloodless revolution; it took huge commitment by a few to stand up against the ingrained interest of the many in the southern United States and a bloody war to bring slavery to an end and then years later it took a Martin

Luther King and his 'I have a dream' to push for equality in what was a hugely prejudiced society. And it took the electorate to put a black man into the White House, to finally put America's racially divisive history to bed by electing Barack Obama as their 44th President. Or did it?

In all societies, in all ages, there is a need for the brave, for the alert, for the unconventional, whether it is a Gandhi, or Rabin, the Suffragettes, or the righteous gentiles. In Burma, Aung San Suu Kyi represented hope for the people, even though she had been imprisoned for over 20 years and a 1991 Nobel Peace Prize laureate – BUT despite all the apparent good once in power she could not stand in the way of her Government's genocide of the Rohingya and the prosecution of journalists and activists who are opposed to her party! Critics say Ms Suu Kyi did not do nearly enough to condemn the military, she simply was not prepared to use her extraordinary position to call the military out, and say NO!

In our democracy saying no can be a powerful weapon, but it takes real conviction. Sajid Javid the Chancellor of the Exchequer in Boris Johnson's new Government of December 2019 resigned on the 13th February 2020 as he refused to be bullied by the Prime Minister into accepting to dismiss his advisers and be guided by his special adviser, Dominic Cummings. Sajid Javid showed real strength of character in doing so, clearly a man of principle!

THE WHYS

Why are the vast majority so sheep-like and merely follow, never taking control of their own lives?

Why are so few prepared to think and act, including saying 'no' when appropriate?

Why does our educational system not develop a greater degree of independence in us all?

Why does our education system not encourage critical thinking and the support to saying no as a discretionary response?

Why do even the independently wealthy not say 'no' more often, and allow their voices to be heard more loudly?

Why is 'complaining' which is a form of 'no' frowned on by so many?

Why do we allow relationships to drift endlessly for so long before saying 'no'?

Why do we accept being pushed around by those in authority or perceived to be in authority?

Why do we accept the negative 'no', when we know we are in the right?

In a constructive and positive sense being able to say 'no' is a critical management skill. Knowing when one has to pull the plug on projects that have gone bad, knowing when haemorrhaging cash flow cannot be sustained any longer, knowing when a business plan is unacceptable, knowing when the future has to be different from the present and hence being able to say 'no', and mean it, is critical. Being able to say 'no', 'you do not have a future with this company', is hugely tough and at the same time hugely important.

LEARN EARLY TO SAY NO

When one is relatively young and new in a corporate environment being able to say 'no' to one's boss is very tough. But this is sometimes required and is sometimes important and will in most situations merely establish that here is one person who will not allow themselves to be totally pushed around and dominated! This is so important especially in the over-demanding society. Let me replay here a scenario I have already referenced… a graduate whom I knew was working for a leading American investment bank and had been there for about three months. The first month was dedicated to training. Excellent. Since the formal training ended, this new employee was expected to work 7 days per week, week in, week out, getting home at 02.00 on a regular basis, and sometimes 04.00, only to be back at work by 07.30 the latest! This was utter madness.

The worst type of management imaginable is one that actually condones and promulgates this type of behaviour. And unfortunately there is a lot of it around. I really do not understand why. Is it to prove some sort of endurance? It then got even worse! The new employee advised the relevant superior that a certain evening and the following day she wanted to take off to observe Yom Kippur, the day of atonement, the most important day in the Jewish calendar.

Unbelievably the superior called saying ' I need to have a piece of work done by tomorrow morning. You must do it. I haven't got time to discuss further as I'm on my way to Church', and cut the line. This conversation with the new employee was on a Sunday morning. The new employee was totally compromised, and stayed till the small hours to get the work done rather than joining other members of her family.

The key problem was (a) bullying by the boss, and (b) the new employee's inability to say 'no'! Saying 'no' by a new employee, especially in a highly charged environment, especially in what is perceived to be a privileged and highly paid position is extremely tough and especially in the first few months when the new employee is trying to get established. And yet that is exactly when it is important to stand one's ground and to establish certain basic ground rules. That is exactly when the positive 'no' is required.

The fault, and there is a fault, is wholly that of the organization and the senior executives in the organization who permit this type of an environment to exist. They are the ones who should be saying, and meaning, 'NO'! No longer are we prepared to tolerate this abuse, no longer are we prepared to accept this inefficiency, because that is exactly what it is!

Ultimately the fault lies with the CEO and the board for not taking action to eradicate this type of unacceptable behaviour. And while life in the 20s may be different, and expectations may have altered, these practices still exist and are perpetuated by certain individuals and organisations. (Perhaps in the world of lockdown caused by COVID 19 there is a temporary respite as the vast majority are working from home, but I doubt that it will have been eradicated!) I will never forget back in the late 70s Harry Langstaff walking the corridors of McKinsey's office in St. James's Street in the early evenings, say between 8.00pm and 9.00pm, and asking those around, 'don't you have a home to go to?'. What a terrific example to all!

Let us now look at other positive 'no' situations:

'No' to people: There are many circumstances in which it is positive to say 'no' to people. Advising someone that they do not fit with the organisation can be positive in that almost certainly the individual will already be aware of this, as will the individual's colleagues. Although painful, and potentially troublesome to the individual in the short term, this type of action is appropriate for the sake of all, and usually in the longer term to the benefit of the individual affected.

'No' to unacceptable behaviour in the work place is positive; saying 'no' to people who discriminate on the basis of sex, race, religion or age is positive. Although this is also the law in most western societies, it is nevertheless incumbent on senior management and boards to ensure that this type of behaviour is the norm, that no discrimination of any form is acceptable anywhere within the organisation.

When I was a head-hunter back in the late 1990s I was frequently asked, totally off-the-record, if I could ensure that the short list contained people between the ages of 45-55; preferably male; etc... even though strict rules about discrimination had already been legislated and passed into law. In all cases I said 'No, I'm not able to do that. You have mandated me to find the best candidates for the vacant role. We have agreed the roles' key requirements and based on these I will find the best candidate be they a 29 year old woman, or a 69 year old gay man, I'm not interested in age, gender, ethnicity or anything else only their competence and cultural fit with the organisation.' And you know what, I never lost a mandate!

'No' to poor performers is positive; poor performance in any form of endeavour should not be acceptable. That is not to say everyone has to be a star, but everyone should be performing to their best ability. Accepting poor performance just drags everyone down. It is relevant here to refer back to my early point about 'complaining' as this is also about poor performance. If there is bad service, if there is poor delivery, if there is unacceptable behaviour it is important to alert those in leadership roles so the poor performance can be addressed and corrected.

'No' to mediocrity is positive; building on the above theme, organisations should never accept mediocrity. Mediocrity is under-performance, and as such will ensure that those who are

able will leave and find more stimulating and satisfying environments to work in. Mediocrity is a vicious circle that will lead to ever poorer performance and failure. Remember successful high performers want to be in successful high performing environments and will not stay long in environments that tolerate poor performers, poor quality of work and poor work ethics. There are plenty of roles for people who simply don't want to be in highly charged environments; environments in which there is a need to set the highest standards, environments that are more forgiving, perhaps less demanding.

'No' to unacceptable mandates/assignments: Many professional service firms would be better off if they took a much more discretionary approach to the clients and mandates they accepted to work on. There are of course some that already practice this, typically the firms at the top of their profession, but there are an awful lot to whom the principle driver is fees, and fees at almost any cost. There are unfortunately many examples of the past few years of very large very reputable organisations being implicated in very large and very unsavoury affairs, Enron, WorldCom, Tyco, Ahold, Parmalat, Health-South, Adecco, Mannesmann, etc. In many of these cases the outcome could have been very different had senior people taken a much more robust attitude, and a positive 'no' would have been of tremendous value.

Where would Arthur Andersen be had senior partners been more involved and more concerned about what was suitable for the firm as opposed to fees? How come that in the final days of the pre-credit crash euphoria Sports Direct was IPO'd with the support of some of the most respected lawyers, accountants and bankers, and the acceptance of the Stock Exchange, only to have broken virtually every corporate governance requirement? Fees, greed, and an inability by all those involved to say 'no'!

I have praised McKinsey many times throughout this book and yet even they have had their troubles, be it a client in South Africa that should have been refused after more thorough due diligence, or an ex-Global Managing Partner who got caught up in bribery allegations

- McKinsey has apologised for making 'several errors of judgment' in working alongside a company linked to South Africa's politically controversial Gupta family last year after conducting a four-month internal probe into the scandal.

- The cause of concern was the New York trial of Raj Rajaratnam, founder of the Galleon hedge fund group. He was accused of insider dealing, allegedly using tips passed to him by former McKinsey partner Anil Kumar, and the once-unimpeachable Rajat Gupta, who had served three successive three-year terms as global managing director of the Firm up to 2003.

Hindsight is all well and good. There is no way anyone could have known the future career path of a partner, even a global managing partner, who left in 2007 would be involved in 4 years later! But there is no doubt that someone senior should have said 'No' to the South African company, even in hindsight there were sufficient indicators that should have been taken into account!

On a somewhat different note, *'no' to unacceptable mandates/ assignments,* can equally be applied to non-executive chairman and directors. Whilst they sit on boards of substantial organisations, charge fees frequently in the 100s of thousands of pounds for non-executive chairmen, and +/- £100k for non-executive directors, it should be incumbent upon them to say 'no' to unacceptable risks, to unacceptable mergers, to unacceptable transactions. Where were the voices of these independent directors during the time of the global financial crisis of 2008/09?

What were the NEDs doing on the board of HBOS as it accumulated its toxic portfolio of assets and consistently rewarded the bankers who were leading the charge? Where were the independent directors arguing against the acquisition of HBOS by Lloyds TSB; where were the independent directors arguing against the acquisition of ABNAmro by RBS? Where were the independent directors arguing against subprime mortgages, securitisation, derivatives, the splicing and dicing of securitised products? Sir David Walker's review in the wake of the credit-crash/recession of 2008/09 has highlighted 5 key themes, one of which is concerned with 'Board Behaviour', and can be summarised as:

'...the most critical need is for an environment in which effective challenge of the executive is expected and achieved in the boardroom before decisions are taken on major risks and strategic issues...'

In other words an environment in which the non-executives can properly exercise their positive veto, their positive No; where they can effectively challenge and probe proposed executive action, where there is real 'Pursuit of Y' (Walker Review, Corporate Governance of UK Banking Industry, Nov 2009).

It is extraordinary how situations are condoned and even formally authorised. Take the appointment of Paul Flowers as Chairman of the Co-op Bank (July 2010), at that time wholly owned by the Co-op Group. A Methodist preacher with some modest banking background, Fowler was appointed to the Chairmanship which by definition meant approval by the bank's and Co-op Group's nominations committees; and of even greater significance approval by the UK's regulatory body, the FSA (the FSA approved his appointment but required the Co-op Bank to install two deputy chairmen with banking experience to advise him)…rather than saying 'No', this man is not suitable to Chair a major retail bank! The result was catastrophic for the whole of the Co-op Group:

- Eyebrows were raised when Flowers told lawmakers on parliament's Treasury Select Committee that the bank had £3 billion of assets on its balance sheet, when the true figure was £47 billion!

- This was a period when it racked up huge losses and faced a £1.5 billion capital shortfall.

- Flowers, the 63-year-old Methodist preacher with little banking experience, oversaw the Co-op bank's near collapse was caught on film allegedly arranging to buy cocaine and crystal meth.

- Group chairman Len Wardle quit with immediate effect for his part in appointing Flowers,

- The Co-op Group has since lost its majority stake in the bank to U.S. hedge funds that owned its debt.

What about all the non-executives directors on the board of both the bank and the group at that time? There is no evidence that any of them objected…said No! It would really have been a very 'positive no'!

'No' to unprofessional behaviour: The same goes here as above. The ability to say 'no' is critical in so many different circumstances. To say 'no' to colleagues, to say 'no' to incremental revenue opportunities, to say 'no' to larger potential profit share, because simply what is proposed is wrong and unacceptable. This is not just limited to professional firms, but to all environments, large or small corporates, quoted or unquoted companies, educational establishments, State-owned institutions etc. Examples of the

tolerance of unprofessional behaviour have emerged in the past in the armed forces, the police force, and even hospitals causing huge damage to their reputations, behaviour that could and should have been stopped. These were, without doubt, positive 'no' situations.

Another massive positive 'no' situation has been the 2008/09 scandal over MPs expenses in the United Kingdom, perhaps one of the very best examples of the importance of ensuring that someone is able to say *'no' to unprofessional behaviour.* During the global pandemic of 2020 there are many examples where people in positions of power and authority could have stood out and done the right thing, but failed. Chairman and boards of major organisations could have aligned themselves much more closely with the suffering of their employees, they could have demonstrated their sharing of the pay by taking significant cuts in their fees/salaries; by ensuring dividends were moderated; by being more prepared to say no to behaviour that was clearly inappropriate given the magnitude of the global crisis. The word…'unprecedented'… used with frequent repetition, required unprecedented actions form all in positions of responsibility and leadership which unfortunately were not seen with the degree of regularity that one could have hoped for!

'No' to unethical methods: A rapidly growing issue. An issue of increasing concern at the highest level in organizations and gaining airtime within the board room. An issue that is increasingly being linked with that other 'fashionable' issue of 'Corporate Social Responsibility' or CSR for short. According to Unilever's ex-Chairman and CEO, CSR is 'not just an act of kindness but a hard edged business issue which is now centre stage'. Unilever has implemented a 'zero tolerance' environment, and has made it clear that it will not tolerate bribery and corruption, it will

not give any executive a second chance if found to be involved in unethical behaviour - one strike and they are out! And that is exactly what happened. When it became known that Unilever's business in Bulgaria was involved in certain corrupt activities, the Chairman implemented zero-tolerance, and closed the business down. A very simple and very clear message. An excellent example of 'positive no' in action within one of the world's largest corporations. Ethics is also the key issue at play in many of the discussions concerning better corporate governance. Here again, there is plenty of room for positive 'no's.

'No' to environmental abuse: Taking sensible steps to protect our environment, to positively seek ways to improve energy efficiency, and to say 'no' to wastefulness and pollution wherever one may be exposed to them. In 2019/20 with the support of Deloitte, a new organisation, Chapter Zero, was established aimed at gaining the attention of the boards of major corporations in the UK and globally about the issues of global warming, and the immediate and urgent steps required to be taken. In particular to help non-executive directors engage with the potential risks and opportunities for businesses and take this discussion into their boardrooms. In other words to educate and support those with influence to in the boardrooms of major corporations to be able to stand-up and say no with knowledge and data.

'No' to bullying: At schools, at work, at home. Quite simply 'no'! For me this is 'no' in all circumstances. I mentored a senior executive in a major corporation and he recalled the bullying he endured during the previous three years under his past Chairman. It virtually destroyed him, his self-confidence, his ability to perform as a CEO. Fortunately this was rapidly recognised by the new Chairman who was prepared to give him time to 'heal' and support to recover. And my mentoring was one part of the

recovery programme. I stressed to him that if he either ever experiences bullying or comes across it ever again, he absolutely must call it out immediately and essentially 'punch the bully hard' on the first occasion. What bullies hate is being hit back!

'No' is such a simple little word with such enormous potential powers. It was Charles de Gaulle, post second world war President of France, who was frequently parodied for having refused to allow Britain to join what was then the European Common Market by saying simply '*Non!*' In turn it was Margaret Thatcher who came to be known as the 'Iron Lady' for saying consistently 'No' and meaning it. 'The Lady is not for turning', and she wasn't, 'no, no, no!'

In all the companies where I have worked and especially when I had responsibility over people, one of the first things I wanted them to learn was the ability to say 'no'. I wanted them to know that they had a voice and that I expected them to use it, without fear. I also implemented exactly the same culture around board tables. I wanted all my directors to know that I expected them to have views, I expected them to be vocal, that I respected divergent views, welcomed open constructive discussion and that I did not tolerate bullying under any circumstances.

The simple message of this chapter is that positive 'NO' is powerful.

Do it Right: Do it Now!: Everyone should learn when and how to use it

Do it Right: Do it Now!: It isn't difficult to use the positive 'no'!

Do it Right: Do it Now!: But it is immensely powerful, and could be of very real importance to you, your business, your environment, your life!

Do it Right: Do it Now!: Speak up when things are wrong

Do it Right: Do it Now!: Use your position of independence as a non-executive to question, to probe and to say NO when appropriate!

Do it Right: Do it Now!: To question waste, to drive for a net zero carbon emission environment!

Do it Right: Do it Now!: Call out the abusers, the bullies!

Do it Right: Do it Now!: +'NO' is OK!

Do it Right: Do it Now!

13: THE NO PAY GAIN

One of the most frequently analysed, discussed and evaluated issues of the last few decades has been how directors, executives, managers, and employees are generally compensated. One of the most heated topics of conversation is top executive pay; in annual reports, the page most frequently turned to is the page setting out the compensation structure of the board of directors. This is reflected in the amount of column inches dedicated in newspapers to this one topic and equally to the amount of research undertaken shining a light on the compensation in particular of the FTSE 100's CEOs and Boards.

- ...report from the CIPD and the High Pay Centre examines FTSE 100 CEO pay packages... looks at how CEO pay in the UK's largest firms has changed between the financial year to 2015 and the financial year to 2016. It finds that over this period, FTSE 100 CEO remuneration has fallen by 17%, from £5.4 million in 2015 to £4.5 million in 2016...it would still take the average UK full-time worker on a salary of £28,000 (median full-time earnings) 160 years to earn what an average FTSE 100 CEO is paid in just one year...(The Executive Pay Review – CIPD – 3rd August 2017)

- Why we need to shine a light on the FTSE 100's 1,397 fat cats. A new report shows they were paid a collective £2bn, with an average salary of more than £1.4m. We investors need to be told more about where our money is going, says James Moore (@JimMoore Journo Tuesday – Independent Premium - 20 August 2019)

- UK anger over executive pay saps support for capitalism,

> says think tank - 'Capitalism is at risk from a new gener-
> ation of populists seeking to harness public anger at
> the way the system works,' says Global Future (Olesya
> Dmitracova Economics and Business Editor @dmitra-
> cova - 30 August 2019 – Independent)

There is and has been continuous outrage at the compensation of FTSE 100's CEOs which I have found totally illogical. Illogical that the FTSE 100 CEOs should attract such attention when in reality they represent a miniscule sample of leaders of British business. Their compensation is completely irrelevant to what's going on in British business; and in reality most of these CEOs are leading businesses where the majority of their revenue and profit is generated from outside the UK. It is the reward of the 1000s of CEOs running the many 1000s of SMEs that really matter. CEO compensation of SMEs is virtually never surveyed or examined in any detail. Yet it is exactly these CEOs who are leading the businesses that make up the largest part of UK's economy. Strange that! In reality these CEOs are not 'Fat Cats'; they are the first to take cuts when the going gets tough; they are compensated on a much more modest basis with fewer perks and more aligned with the businesses they lead.

There are many ways in which people can be rewarded. The most obvious and often the most tangible is cash – 'Loads of money', as famously depicted by Harry Enfield in the late '80s Channel 4 television programme and later in the West-End play, 'Money'. But non-financial rewards are also of significant importance and occa- sionally can have an even more important impact than pure cash.

There are well-established consultancies that have well-developed 'compensation' practices, advising large and small companies alike on how to structure salary levels, incentive schemes, executive share option schemes (ESOPS), long term incentive plans (LTIPs) and short term bonus arrangements. The 'HAY' point structure is well established and used by many organisations. There is little value in my delving into this well-developed and well-served area, except perhaps for one little observation:

- *KEEP IT SIMPLE!!*

The tendency is to complicate. The tendency is to *grossly* over-complicate.

DON'T COMPLICATE

Fewer than half of the UK's largest companies have sales incentive plans that are perceived to be effective. Many incentive plans are too complex to explain to staff, have the wrong mix of rewards and are badly targeted. If the subject matter is relatively complex, advisers tend to complicate it further, rather than simplify it. If something can be made complex, it will be; if something can be made to *sound* complex, it will be; if something can be made to *appear* to be complex, it will be.

In the world of executive compensation combining elements of finance and law, can you imagine the extraordinary contracts that these well-intentioned experts have been able to dream up? The rationale is frequently to ensure that everyone is properly protected. What a load of garbage! Complexities lead to confusion, lead to the need to unravel as and when the time comes that the substance of the contracts is dealt with.

Simplicity has huge merit in gaining buy-in by all and hence through simplicity gaining the desired motivational impact. Clearly complex schemes that are difficult to understand may ultimately deliver financial benefits to the recipients, but often fail to achieve either retention or motivational benefits, as the recipients simply don't understand the details but don't want to appear not to understand the details and so have never questioned the details. Hence their value is dramatically reduced.

> *Do it Right: Do it Now!*: keep compensation structures as simple as possible
>
> *Do it Right: Do it Now!*: remember that the UK's economy is driven by the 1000s of SMEs not the actions of FTSE 100 companies!

THE WHYS

Why are so many senior executives immune from the impact their compensation systems have on the rest of their organisations?

Why is there this insane focus on the compensation of FTSE 100 CEOs?

Why is the compensation of the 1000s of leaders of SMEs not surveyed, analysed and evaluated?

Why do advisers like to complicate compensation structures to such an extent that no one understands how they work and what they're worth?

Why has top executive pay as a multiple of average pay in the UK been allowed to get to the size it is?

Why are remuneration committees not better able to moderate executive compensation packages?

Why are boards of directors not prepared to take more control in terms of compensation structures?

However, this chapter is not about the size and composition of top executive compensation packages. This chapter is about how to really reward those who have made significant contributions to a company's performance, in a non-cash manner – 'the no pay gain'!

REAL REWARD

My intention here is to focus on non-monetary rewards. Without doubt one of the most valuable, yet one of the least used, forms of reward has no monetary value at all - this is simply the words **'thank you,'** to acknowledge a job well done. There are infinite opportunities to thank individuals for their contribution; there are no budgetary constraints on the number of times people can be thanked, nor does it devalue through overuse, as long as it is said sincerely.

A new salesperson in one of the companies I chaired signed up their first sales contract, and a good one at that. The Sales Director called to advise me of this new employee's achievement. I was on the phone within minutes to congratulate and thank the new employee for an excellent result. The employee was amazed that the chairman had called and was enthused to have got the call. There is no monetary value to this but real and immediate value by the recipient!

I have made a point throughout my career to give special attention to my secretary/personal assistant, to the receptionists, the telephone operators and caretakers, and extend genuine gratitude for their contributions, to acknowledge their input into making the business run smoothly. I have said thank you to my secretary numerous times, have surprised her with flowers or chocolates or a small gifts from business trips, all to demonstrate that I really do care and do value the support provided. I have done likewise with receptionists and telephone operators and have gone to find the caretaker to shake hands and express my personal thanks.

These people are often the invisible assets of an organization, without whose positive attitudes and contributions life would be a lot less bearable. And the reality is that their contribution is often very visible to customers and clients, for example, in the speed and quality of answering calls, in the cleanliness of the building, and in the perceived effectiveness of the whole organisation!

Back in the late 70s during my time at McKinsey the caretaker was a young guy called Nicky. He was one of the world's truly outstanding human beings. Always smiling, always ready to help, nothing was ever a burden. He was the first one in, and the last one out. If a toilet was blocked, he was there to unblock it; if there was a special function on in the evening he was there helping to take the guests' coats and/or serve the drinks. When the office got together for regular update sessions the office manager would frequently take time out to express thanks to Nicky for his untiring contribution, and correctly so. On these occasions this delightful man would glow with pride - it meant more to him to be recognized, and thanked by his colleagues, than to be awarded an honour in the Queen's list!

During the time that my brother and I were building IDOM we would frequently call to acknowledge an action or an achievement by one of our colleagues. It meant a lot to them, and a lot to us. At times we would travel for many hours, and many thousands of miles, just to be able to shake an individual by the hand, put our arms around their shoulders and express our gratitude, to have breakfast, lunch or dinner with a member of our staff, and to give them some quality time on a one to one basis.

We also implemented a culture that really celebrated success, whether it was the success of the individual, the success of the team, the success of the office, or the success of the whole company. Whenever and wherever there was an opportunity to celebrate we did just that, be it in the form of getting people together for a glass of wine, awarding the use of a Porsche for six-months, gifting a one ounce gold bar, or taking the whole company on an annual outing. And the results spoke for themselves…great team spirit, great loyalty, great commitment, great sense of belonging, great delivery of service to our clients.

I had lunch with John Neill, CEO of the Unipart Group of Companies. My lasting impression of this encounter was not the discussion we had over lunch, although that too was interesting, but the walk to and from John's office. Walking along the corridors John acknowledged every single person we passed by, 'Hi, Jim, how's your wife?', 'Well done Mary, great achievement by your team the other day', 'Hi, Danny, heard that you've signed up for an evening course, great idea, let me know how you get on'…etc. A truly amazing experience. John knows his employees, invests time to get to know them, and clearly acknowledges them and their achievements, whatever they may be.

Leadership is leading from the front. Leaders can reward massively by what they do and say. It's tough to reward, to acknowledge achievement, if you don't know your people! And although pay is important, John's ability to connect with his employees, to acknowledge them as individuals, is something that money simply cannot buy.

THE INVISIBLE LEADER

Contrast the above with an earlier experience I had when I joined a major UK-quoted company in 1980. As already mentioned I set about getting to know the company and physically visiting every plant, wherever we had operations. It became apparent to me reasonably quickly as I travelled around from plant to plant that being visited by a main board director, was a rare event. How rare? I began to think. How much do these people who are genuinely at the sharp end know about their company? So rather than just asking about the business and the processes, I wove in questions about senior management, the company as a whole, the holding company etc. Amazingly enough - or not, as it turned out - only a tiny number of people had a clue about anything outside their immediate orbit, including in many cases who the company's CEO was.

When I fed this fact back to the CEO, he was somewhat surprised, but then said: 'So what, why should any of this matter?' I bet that there are no ships where the crew doesn't know who the Captain is, no army where the soldiers don't know who their General is! What sort of leadership can anyone provide if they are unknown to those they are responsible for leading?

This was an environment in which no one ever said thanks, in which there was little or nothing outside the formal annual pay review procedure usually formally negotiated, and nothing was ever done on a spontaneous basis. The senior executives kept very much to themselves! But the CEO was profoundly wrong, it really does matter and can make a real difference especially when there is a need for the workforce's engagement and involvement!

- ### BE THERE, BE IN TOUCH

When I was CEO of Valin Pollen I implemented a number of innovations in what was already an excellent place to work. I held regular lunches with a cross-section of people from the office, from most junior to most senior. I organized a regular monthly get-together where I, or someone else, spoke for a few minutes to praise specific individuals for specific achievements or to highlight an issue and I walked the corridors often with no agenda, just to bump into people on a random basis, and would frequently walk to see someone rather than get my PA to arrange for them to come to my office. This all had an impact. Although somewhat sceptical to start with, I was told that people actually wanted to be mentioned at the monthly get-together. I had to do some of these things with care, attention and forethought. Some could happen randomly, but I thought about my actions and planned accordingly.

We celebrated success with champagne. We celebrated success by sending the winning team who had worked long hours into the night to get the pitch together on a long week-end, all expenses paid! We celebrated a good year by a massive party at the Savoy for everyone; and a bad year by an even more massive party also at the Savoy, also for everyone! And the results spoke for themselves.

The phoenix of Valin Pollen (the VPI Group plc unfortunately went bust in 1991 due to a poor acquisition in the US) is a firm that started life in the depths of the early 90s recession as 'Fishburn Hedges Boys and Williams', re-named Fishburn Hedges after a couple of years. This small communications consultancy grew rapidly, based very much on the principles and values of Valin Pollen, refined and accentuated even further. By the late 90s Fishburn Hedges was recognised as one of London's leading corporate communications consultancies and was taken over by the large advertising group Abbot Mead Vickers (AMV) which had by then also been taken over, and became part of the global communications empire, Omnicom Group.

Nevertheless, Fishburn Hedges was left very much untouched and continued its people practices unimpeded by whatever may have been the norm within the much larger Omnicom Group.

Fishburn Hedges established the most fabulous internal culture in which there was recognition and reward, there was fun time and time to celebrate, there was party time and time to share news. A week-end trip to France, a crate of wine or champagne, picking up the tab for a night out for two, none of which costs a fortune, were tokens of appreciation that went perfectly with the words 'thank you'.

The performance of the company was wholly commensurate, achieving more each year. More new wins, more profitability, more productivity, more creativity. Fishburn Hedges was formally recognized as one of the best places to work in the UK in a *Financial Times* award. Fishburn Hedges went on to be one of the most consistently nominated 'Best Place to Work' company.

Of course, people must be paid in an honest and fair way too. People need decent salaries and should have decent bonuses to aspire to. No amount of 'thank you' is sufficient if the ultimate recognition in terms of pay is missing or inadequate. But it certainly helps in every other respect. It also makes hard times easier, and the likelihood that people will go with you, will be supportive, when you really need them to.

As with all the previous chapters nothing said above is difficult. Nothing outlined above is complex or expensive. And yet actually implementing the actions referred to above is still very much the exception. They are all about an attitude of mind that demonstrates a caring and concerned environment. They are all amazingly easy to implement, to ensure that they are pursued systematically and spontaneously, but they have to be introduced and actioned from the top. The company leader has to be seen, has to be seen to care, to be committed, only then will it begin to flow through the organization and over time penetrate sufficiently deeply that it actually becomes part of the company's DNA.

During the COVID 19 crisis of 2020 the Government stepped in to provide financial support to businesses including a measure called 'furlough' where the Government paid up to 80% (up to a maximum of £2,500/month) of those employees compensation who were put on temporary leave (English dictionary definition of furlough. n. 1. a. A leave of absence or vacation, especially one granted to a member of the armed forces. b. A usually temporary layoff from work…) …during which time they received the payment but were not allowed to work. Companies were allowed to maintain communication with furloughed employees. At the height of the crisis, Nick Robeson, Senior Partner/CEO of Boyden UK & Ireland, sent a crate of wine to all the employees (active or furloughed) with a simple note 'thank you from Lisa and myself for your understanding, tolerance and contribution'…a powerful 'thank you' in troubled times!!

As ever there are a few actionable ideas to leave you with:

Do it Right: Do it Now!: Say thank you

Do it Right: Do it Now!: You cannot thank anyone too often – thank you never devalues from over-use

Do it Right: Do it Now!: Remember the back-office staff

Do it Right: Do it Now!: Whom can I acknowledge today?

Do it Right: Do it Now!: Be informed

Do it Right: Do it Now!: Know your people

Do it Right: Do it Now!: Keep formal reward structures as simple as possible

Do it Right: Do it Now!: Introduce random and informal rewards

Do it Right: Do it Now!: Celebrate success, a huge motivator for all

Do it Right: Do it Now!: Surprise by the little things, it needn't cost a fortune

Do it Right: Do it Now!: Be consistently spontaneous

Do it Right: Do it Now!: This is very much top down

Do it Right: Do it Now!: Do the unexpected, do it randomly, do it frequently

Do it Right: Do it Now!: Surprise and delight

Do it Right: Do it Now!: And keep it simple!!!

Do it Right: Do it Now!

As the saying goes 'money talks, bullshit walks' but saying thanks and doing some of the above is only bullshit if in every other way the company behaves in a manner likely to undermine its people and make their lives a misery. There has to be sincerity and internal consistency, not just an ulterior motive.

14:. 'PEOPLE – THE ESSENTIAL INGREDIENT FOR SUCCESS.'... MY CONCLUDING 'BITZ & PIECES!

In the past thirteen chapters I have tried to dramatize the overwhelming importance of ensuring that action is taken to *Do it Right: Do it Now!* especially with a people centric approach to management and leadership. I have consistently raised issues under the 'why' heading and have endeavoured to provide certain simple actionable suggestions.

But as I have been writing, more and more topics have come to mind that are suitable for treatment. In this final chapter I have therefore aimed to collect this growing number of topics not yet treated under the previous thirteen chapter headings, for a relatively brief but focused treatment or just to elaborate and add an extra dimension to topics I may have already covered in the past thirteen chapters. This is just to whet the appetite, to raise a few more simple issues, to suggest some more simple actions and in a number of cases to repeat and re-emphasise the message, and to continue to ask 'why?'.

LISTENING

Refer to previous sections on interviewing. But just for the record, listening in my view is a significantly undervalued, underemphasized, under-taught skill and attribute. How many times have you been in meetings when you simply do not hear what is being said, not because the volume is too low, but because you have switched off internally. Listening, really listening, is critical to understanding. It is really difficult to 'half' listen... you may hear the words, but they rarely penetrate the brain.

It is so very easy to become distracted. If you're distracted, it's almost certain that you'll have stopped listening. If you've stopped listening, you've stopped taking in what is being said.

I get seriously upset by people in meetings playing with their Smartphones or other devices, scanning e-mails and answering text messages or worse actually speaking on their phones. Not only is this a clear indication that they have stopped listening but also it is the height of discourtesy.

Some years ago, I was invited to make a brief presentation to the board of a company. As I was making my presentation, I noticed that the company's chairman was focused on his e-mails on his smartphone. I noticed him repeating this action throughout the rest of the board meeting. I knew then that this chairman was totally disengaged with what was happening and seriously removed from his executive team and the business I was not the least surprised when I learned that he was replaced a few months later.

Let your body signal that you are listening, nod, show an expression on your face that you understand or that you don't understand, physically engage. I have been to conferences when, especially after lunch in the early afternoon, it gets very difficult to keep your eyes open unless there is an absolutely outstanding speaker, and even then it can be demanding. I recall being at a conference where the speaker was a highly regarded management guru. As he started to speak after lunch, a chap in one of the front rows nodded-off. He called down from the stage to the person sitting next to the now slightly snoring delegate, and suggested that he should wake him up… to which came the reply, 'you put him to sleep, you wake him up'! At least he was awake and listening.

Many decades ago I came across a pamphlet produced by a then major listed company, Sperry Corporation, with the strap line, 'We understand how important it is to listen...' it included 10 Keys to Effective Listening namely... 1) Find areas of interest; 2) Judge content, not delivery; 3) Hold your fire; 4) Listen for ideas; 5) Be flexible; 6) Work at listening; 7) Resist distractions; 8) Exercise your mind; 9) Keep your mind open; and 10) Recognise that thought is faster than speech! It also contained the wonderful fact that we learn 1st to listen; 2nd to speak, 3rd to read and 4th to write! Ain't that the truth!!!

> *Do it Right: Do it Now!*: Never get distracted by phones/e-mails/other activities when in a meeting with other people
>
> *Do it Right: Do it Now!*: Engage fully with those you are listening to
>
> *Do it Right: Do it Now!*: Let the person you are listening to know that you are engaged by your body language
>
> *Do it Right: Do it Now!*

LEADING FROM THE FRONT

By definition people look-up to their leaders, well initially in any case. People expect to be led by them, expect to be provided with clear guidance, expect to be set their 'compass' by them.

I say 'well initially' because just as it takes years and years for organisations to establish their reputations it takes but a nano-second to destroy it, so leaders arrive with a certain established 'halo'/reputation and a certain expectation by the people within the organisation they are appointed to. There's the well-known first 100 days during which new leaders are expected to establish their own way of doing things and it is often this same first 100 days during which the people within the organisation either reaffirm their support for the new leader, or begin to question whether this is a person they are happy to be led by?

Leaders need to lead from the front… just as within the armed forces the Generals, the Brigadiers, the Majors, the Captains need to lead from the front and not just set strategy and plans to be carried out by the troops. What corporate leaders do matters. What they say matters. How they behave matters. And there's no better example than in a crisis.

The global COVID 19 pandemic that stormed the world in the 1st half 2020 is the greatest crisis of my life time, with two behaviours that magnify the quality of leaders - their identification with reality, their care for the people within their organisation…

- *Arne Sorenson*, president and chief executive officer of Marriott International, Inc: made a clear statement that we're all in this together – 'I will not be taking any salary for the balance of 2020 and my executive team will be taking a 50% cut in pay.' Clear leadership from the front… needs nothing more.

- *Stelios Haji-Ioannou*, the founder of EasyJet and the largest shareholder with 34% decided to take £60m dividends from the airline as the pandemic was raging and the airline's future was clearly going to be in difficulty with its entire fleet grounded. Clearly it's all about me and let's not worry about others.

Arne Sorenson is without doubt leading from the front and providing the sort of example others will remember for a long time. (Arne Sorenson, led Marriott International's transformation into the world's largest hotel chain, unfortunately died of cancer at the age of 62 in late 2020).

Stelios Haji-Ioannou is a clear example of what not to do even if you are no longer in the executive seat! How can £60m of dividends be extracted from a company which is facing a massive hit on its cash flow, and all the resulting implications on its entire workforce! And then to justify it by stating that the dividend was in respect of the past year! Dividends are always in respect of the previous year but paid from current cash.

> *'At times such as these, it is important that a company's leadership team is front-and-centre, ensuring they guide their people through the difficult period by maintaining a sense of fairness, commitment and optimism. To do so, they must ensure that they are not seen as protecting self-interest over the interests of employees, shareholders and the broader community.'*
>
> BRINK: NISHANT MAHAJAN - HEAD OF EXECUTIVE REMUNERATION ASEAN/GROWTH MARKETS LEADER AT MERCER SINGAPORE - 11TH MAY 2020

Leaders matter and especially so when the going gets tough. Great leaders are relatively rare, but they shine in times of adversity, as did Arne Sorenson…and no doubt numerous others who have done the right thing.

Do it Right: Do it Now!: Leaders need to have a well-timed moral compass.

Do it Right: Do it Now!: Leadership means leading from the front, doing as you say and saying as you do!

> *Do it Right: Do it Now!:* Especially when the going is tough, leaders should take the pain and be seen to be taking the pain
>
> *Do it Right: Do it Now!*

BORED BOARD

I have had the privilege of sitting on many boards both as an executive and as non-executive director. I have also been entrusted with the Chairmanship of a number of boards. As a consequence, there are some observations that may be helpful to ensure that anyone taking part in a board meeting is never bored!

It is vital that all board meetings (indeed all meetings) have a well-structured agenda, meaning an agenda that clearly stipulates when and where the board meeting will take place, what time it will commence and what topics will be considered. Brevity is a real advantage. Absolutely insist that relevant papers are circulated at minimum 48hrs in advance (but preferably 3 days in advance) to be able to be read/studied properly.

Keep the agenda focused and short. The topics should be 60%-70% forward looking and 30% – 40% retrospective, rear-view, in other words checking the performance of the business, month and year to date etc. But the board's key role is to plan the forward development of the business, the forward financial requirements, the forward resourcing requirements both of people and equipment and the strategy. To ensure that this can be undertaken in a knowledgeable manner, the board needs to have relevant information - financial, market, market share, competition, competitive positioning, product and product development, relative strengths and weaknesses… etc.

It is therefore valuable from time to time to invite non-board members to present their part of the business and their area of expertise. This also provides board members with a little insight into the other executives.

The manner in which a board is chaired is critical. The chair is there to chair, not to monopolise. The chair is there to ensure that the meeting is kept on track, that a certain momentum is maintained, that EVERY board member has suitable airtime and EVERY board member knows that they have a voice, that there is effective challenge, probing and debate of the executives, that there is no bullying by anyone, or excessively domineering voices, that it is as collegiate and participative as possible.

The chair is there to ensure that the minutes are properly recorded, that actions from previous minutes have been actioned, and that the board meeting is not allowed to drift on for hours and hours. And the Chair is there to ensure that there is the right mix of skills and competences and diversity around the board table. It is the Chair's responsibility to ensure that the people around the board table can add real value to the business, and diversity helps enormously.

Keep it brief, keep it to the point, keep it relevant, keep it focussed, but if possible have some fun along the way too!

Do it Right: Do it Now!: Ensure relevant board papers are circulated well in advance to be able to be properly studied.

Do it Right: Do it Now!: Ensure all board members have a voice.

Do it Right: Do it Now!: Keep to the point, be relevant and brief

Do it Right: Do it Now!: Get the right people around the board table and ensure good diversity of talent

Do it Right: Do it Now!

BUILDING LOYALTY/EXCEEDING EXPECTATIONS

Not by bullying, not by buying, not by threatening, but by winning trust and confidence.

There are organisations that are able to achieve this and benefit massively by it. This is about much more than money, this is about the very culture of the organization and the way people are treated from day one, how they are valued from day one. It can be done and in reality it is not so difficult. It takes the will of the owner, the top management. 'Innocent', the fruit smoothie drink company, comes to mind, as do Apple, Google, Unipart, Fishburn Hedges, Steel Business Briefing, Richer Sounds, Cripps, Deloitte, and many other small and larger organisations that understand the importance of ensuring that all the people employed by them are treated fairly and with dignity.

Sunday Times, 18th July 2010 Appointment section, page 2, 'Companies need to offer a little something extra to retain their top talent – and it doesn't have to be money... Opportunities to have a voice and to influence an organisation help to ensure senior talent is developed and retained.' (James Ashton)

Indeed, this has come of age. For a number of years *The Sunday Times* has constructed the 100 Best Companies to Work For and Fortune does exactly the same in the United States. The companies so recognised gain substantial benefits, especially in being able to attract and retain the best talent to their organisations. They also benefit in attracting media coverage, which is effectively free promotion, and increasing the likelihood of winning business in competitive situations. Buyers like to buy from acknowledged leaders. Maintaining this status becomes part of the organisation's strategic objective.

Creating the right environment that enables people to grow, that allows them to take responsibility, that trains, develops, stretches and at the same time that knows how to celebrate success and how to ensure that there is clarity of communication throughout the business may sound challenging, but in reality is not so difficult. This is exactly what Venquis has excelled in... and it shows and is magnified during the pandemic crisis when it just continued to perform despite the massive issues around it... because it energised, communicated, embraced and rewarded its staff.

So why do so few seem to practice these easy steps? Because the alternative is even easier! It is easier not to think, not to communicate, not to reward, not to train and develop, not to assess and provide feedback, and it may also be cheaper - in the short term. So for the majority the easy option will do. Ugh!

Do it Right: Do it Now!: Focus on what makes your people go the extra mile, and implement accordingly

Do it Right: Do it Now!: Avoid the easy option of doing nothing!

Do it Right: Do it Now!: But ensure authenticity!

Do it Right: Do it Now!

RESPECT

For others and for diversity in the workplace. In 1980 I joined a FTSE 100 mining and finance house called Consolidated Goldfields, essentially a holding company which had at that time a charismatic CEO called Rudolph Agnew (now Sir Rudolph Agnew), a larger than life, Gitanes and cigar-smoking character. He is one of the few people I have come across who was able to be utterly ruthless with subordinates, make them feel about 2 inches tall, totally destroy arguments unless they were thoroughly thought through and fully substantiated, and yet make the subordinate feel that he just had a 'royal audience', and leave his office almost backing out backwards saying 'thank you, thank you'! I have no idea how he did it. Good or bad, the man possessed an ability to connect with people.

I became very aware of this when I was an executive director of Amey Roadstone, wholly owned by Consolidated Goldfields. As mentioned earlier I toured all the various operational sites and casually enquired of various members of the workforce if they could name the business's CEO. The most frequently mentioned name was that of Rudolph Agnew, who had been CEO of Amey Roadstone many years earlier and had passed the role on to his successor, who was totally unknown.

At the time I, too, was touched by Rudolph Agnew's charisma. But in reality, most people do not like being beaten up and made to feel inadequate, especially in public. In reality this was verging on being bullied. The net result tends to be avoidance and withdrawal, which is not ideal in a business environment, not ideal when one is trying to get the best solutions, solutions that may at times be risky, unusual, even unorthodox. I believe in being courteous to others and showing them respect regardless of where they may be in the hierarchy.

This reminds me of an anecdote...

An all-powerful CEO calls in one of his analysts and requests a detailed report on a certain topic. The analyst asks by when the report is required. 'Well, just tell me how long you need' came the response. 'Probably three days would be sufficient' replied the analyst. 'So be it... let me have the report in three days' time'.

Exactly three days later, a beautifully bound report is waiting on the CEO's desk. At the end of that day the CEO calls the analyst... 'Thanks for the report. Tell me is this the best you can do?' The analyst feeling somewhat apprehensive suggests that he could do a much better job if he could have another two days to work on it. The CEO agrees to the extension and again two days later the revised report is on his desk. Another conversation takes place as before, and the analyst again states that he could really do an outstanding finishing job if he could have just another 24hrs. The CEO is agreeable to this extension and in 24hrs time the report is back on the CEO's desk. At the end of the day the CEO calls the analyst for a third time to ask whether this is really the best he can do? The analyst now loses it and says 'Damn it, yes this is the best I can do, why is there something missing?' The CEO replies... 'No. Now I'll sit down to read it!'

Perhaps a more subtle way of being demanding, yet at the same time showing some respect for the individual!

Similarly diversity needs to be respected, diversity in every sense of the word from religion and race to sex and disability. A close friend had a business marketing and distributing corporate gizmos, i.e. a vast range of 'corporate gifts', the pens, the golf balls, the tee-shirts, the wallets etc., with a company logo. In his factory warehouse and office there were people of many different races, people with different types of disabilities, men and women, people of different ethnicity. As long as they were able to undertake the job they were hired for, Tony Cohen, the business's owner, was happy. And as a consequence, he had a loyal workforce, many of whom often did go the extra mile when required. In fact Tony went the extra mile and specifically hired the disabled and the underprivileged as long as they were able to undertake the tasks required.

At McKinsey, despite what many may think, there has always been, and there is today, an extraordinary degree of tolerance and acceptance of diversity. It is positively one of the great advantages of any organisation that can effectively integrate a wide and diverse group of people.

Given the hard work culture of most professional service firms and the demanding hours, it may seem that being a practising and observing Jew would be totally incompatible. And yet the culture is able to live with people going home at sunset on Friday evenings and not being contactable again until sunset Saturday evening. McKinsey has had an Indian as its global Managing Director, it has had a Brit, a Canadian, and in 2020 has a Scot who earned his stripes in the Far East.

The global McKinsey team is a real potpourri of all people, race, disability, religion and sexual orientation. In fact way back in the mid-70s when I was in my first year and received my first invitation to a black-tie function for the professional staff the invitation was addressed to 'John Dembitz, plus husband/wife or functional equivalent', that was in 1975! Pretty progressive even then! Diversity enriches all our lives and without doubt makes every organisation a better place to work in and better at what it does.

It would be inappropriate to leave topic of 'diversity' without reference to the role of women in business. I have an absolute belief in women taking their rightful place in business, in any and every type of business, and at all levels. There should be no glass ceiling. And I believe that women, each and every one, should be treated equally in terms of pay, reward and opportunity. Indeed an ISS (International Shareholder Services) study has shown that women have been breaking through the barrier far faster than others, with 45% of new Russell 3,000 board seats being occupied by women.

This is clearly not happening for Blacks, Hispanics, Asians, as the statistics remain worryingly poor with the following data highlighted in the *Financial Times* 14th June, 2020 in an article by Mamta Badkar and Andrew Edgecliffe-Johnson 'US boardrooms pressed to end racial divide' ... of the 5,670 board seats in Fortune 500 companies 83.9% (4,758) were taken by White people; 8.6% (486) by Black people; 3.8%(213) by Hispanic people; 3.7%(209) by Asian people; and 0.1% (4) by other people.

This is probably repeated in the UK and Europe. There has been progress for women, more is still needed, but much much more is needed to address the glaring imbalance faced by others.

Nevertheless, I do *not* believe in positive discrimination, either for women, or minorities of any description, or for the disabled. All barriers must be removed but artificial stimulants should not be introduced to prefer one group over another. Positive discrimination would undermine the notions of merit and level playing fields. (This has happened in South Africa, with all businesses being required to appoint Blacks to their boards. The results were not positive.)

And lastly, whilst on the topic of diversity, in my mind, despite the frequent references to global organisations, an organisation only becomes truly global if it has a truly global board of directors. Most organisations labelled global would fail this test, as to me, just because a business operates on a global basis, it does not qualify as global if it is essentially controlled locally.

HSBC would qualify, as it has a multinational board (its unitary board is composed of 14 members of whom 5 are UK; 3 Chinese; 3 US; 1 French; 1 Mexican; and 1 Dutch – 9 men to 5 women), but Deutsche Bank would not, as its board is composed very substantially of Germans (it's Supervisory Board has 20 members of whom 14 are German; 4 US; 1 Austrian; and 1 Spanish – 14 men to 6 women).

> *Do it Right: Do it Now!*: Create a fair and respectful environment in which people of all ethnicity/gender/ disability/sexuality can grow and develop based on their competence
>
> *Do it Right: Do it Now!*: Respect your colleagues, be demanding but never ever bully anyone!
>
> *Do it Right: Do it Now!*: If you say you are global, then let your board be global, too
>
> *Do it Right: Do it Now!*

COMMON SENSE
Use it!

Much of this book can be described as common sense and yet much of what is contained in this book is not applied in many organisations and by many managers and senior executives. As I have said repeatedly this is not rocket science, it is not so difficult.

We really should rely more on our common sense than on trying to adopt complex processes and procedures, many of which are doomed to failure.

Think back to the early 80s and the Taurus project that the London Stock Exchange initiated. The objective was to develop a wholly electronic, paperless, trading system from scratch, dedicated to the requirements of the Exchange's members. A massive project with massive complexities and a suitably massive budget. No one at that time gave any thought to taking an existing system and modifying it, tailoring it, to the specific needs of the Exchange - no, a proprietary system had to be developed. Ten years later, and many millions of pounds later, the project was abandoned, with the Exchange having to write off the whole development budget.

Where was common sense then? Does common sense not suggest that taking something that is up and running and tailoring it to your specific needs is much more likely to deliver the goods? This is exactly what has led SAP to becoming a world leading enterprise software vendor; what has led to many banking packages gaining massive markets around the world. This is exactly what led to the success and rapid growth of IDOM, and its eventual successful exit to Deloitte in Central and Eastern Europe.

Does common sense not suggest that when shareholders see the value of their investments decline, when pension funds see the value of their portfolios shrink, is not a good time for senior executives to go for inflation-busting, performance-unlinked, salary and bonus increases? Does common sense not suggest that when the Government has to bail out much of the banking sector using taxpayers' money, this is not the time to negotiate multi-million pound packages, irrespective of whether it goes with the 'role'; and this is not the time to agree to massive pay-offs to departing executives, with unbelievably large pensions? (The reality of what transpired right in the eye of the global financial storm of 2008 as portrayed in *Too Big To Fail* by Andrew Ross Sorkin, published by Penguin, beggars belief). It took public pressure for a small concession to have been made begrudgingly…

> …former Royal Bank of Scotland chief executive Sir Fred Goodwin bowed to public anger by agreeing to give up more than £200,000 a year of his controversial pension… Goodwin was originally awarded £703,000 a year when he retired,… (or was made to retire).

Does common sense not suggest that if you are already earning a multi-million dollar package it may not be appropriate to use the corporate jet for personal vacations? Even an executive with the reputation of Jack Welch came under serious criticism and lost a lot of the allure he had gained from his years as Chairman and CEO of GE when his retirement package was revealed in his divorce proceeding. And does common sense not suggest that expenses, irrespective of whether in business or in government, or indeed in any other endeavour, should only be incurred if they can be simply and honestly accounted for to whomever one is accountable to, be it a client, customer, taxpayer, boss.

Let them eat cake!

Does common sense not suggest that in 2009, a year after the dramatic and calamitous collapse of Lehman Brothers, this was not a great time for bankers to be suggesting that their bonus culture needs to be retained?

> '*Leading bankers have defended their bonus culture as they square up to regulators who want tough controls on pay*'.
>
> PHILIP ALDRICK, *DAILY TELEGRAPH*, 09-09-09*)*

But there was a voice in the wilderness. HSBC's Executive Chairman, Stephen Green, was prepared to speak up against the madness of excessive bonuses and the reality that 'some parts of our industry have become overblown, and certain products and services failed the test of usefulness, suitability and transparency'. So refreshing!

Does common sense not suggest that we can all learn from history? Does common sense not suggest that we *should* all learn from history?

Does common sense not suggest that we are all imperfect, that we all make mistakes, and as such we should all learn from our mistakes? Here is the sign-off on Esther Dyson's e-mails…

'Esther Dyson – Always make new mistakes!'

…Esther being one of the nicest, most pragmatic and smartest investors I have ever known, and a recognised global expert on investment in new technology. What a great lesson.

Common sense suggests that during a global pandemic when millions of people around the world are losing their jobs; millions are exposed to infection from a virus with deadly consequences; when most of the world is in lockdown - is not the time to 'profiteer' from anything!

Do It Right: Do It Now!: Retain perspective, retain common sense!

Do It Right: Do It Now!: Do unto others as you would like to them to do to you – in other words apply basic common sense to your actions/decisions

Do It Right: Do It Now!

CREATING AN OPEN AND RISK-FREE CULTURE

The upside is vast, the downside is very limited!

The energy and creativity that comes with open and risk free environments can generate significant benefits, not only in terms of calculable statistics such as man-hours lost in sickness and absenteeism, but often in much more subtle manifestations, such as the general atmosphere, the preparedness of colleagues to support and help each other, and the willingness of staff to align their situations with that of the business. The flow of ideas can help to retain and accentuate competitive advantages. The attitude of employees can help win and retain customers or clients, it can increase the speed with which the reputation of the company is built, and spread and the ease with which the company will be able to recruit and retain staff. This is not theory, this is reality.

At IDOM this is exactly what we did consciously and deliberately, and it worked. At Semco this is exactly what Ricardo Semler created, and it worked (A detailed explanation is provided in Ricardo Semler's book, *MAVERICK*, published by Tabletun Inc 1993). This is what has fuelled the growth of Google and Facebook, Pret A Manger, and Innocent.

And what of the downside? There isn't one. This works and is risk free. Creating an open and risk free environment can only help and support the development of a business. It encourages everyone to have a sense of ownership of the business and their contribution to it. It is predicated on the belief that everyone has the ability to contribute; that everyone has the ability to see ways to improve; that everyone can identify issues.

Regrettably many companies are the exact opposite. Employees are there to do a specific bit of work; are never asked for their input, contribution, thoughts; rebuked if they make suggestions;

basically told to shut-up and mind their own business – what a total waste of talent! I experienced this at a very early age when I was working in a men's retail shop. The owner of the shop had zero interest in anything I could have contributed and on the one occasion when I tried to suggest something he pointedly told me to not interfere, it was his business and he would do as he wanted!

Do it Right: Do it Now!: Try it, take steps to create a risk free environment, and see the benefits accrue

Do it Right: Do it Now!: recognise that every single employee could have potential to contribute, create the right environment, and some will!

Do it Right: Do it Now!: Be prepared for the odd exceptional contribution that can have a material impact; be prepared for some that may not, but remain supportive and enthusiastic

Do it Right: Do it Now!

ALIGNING ASPIRATIONS WITH REALITY

This has already been discussed in previous chapters and sections above. In a nutshell this is all about managing expectations. Get it right and you will have a bunch of happy bunnies in the form of stakeholders. Get it wrong and you will have rapid disenchantment, frustration, anxiety, and distrust. The implications here are manifold, not just for employees, but for all shareholders, suppliers, customers, banks and other professional advisers, tax authorities and regulators alike. I recall an article in *The Sunday Times* about Sir Philip Green and how he built his Arcadia Group, a retail company that included Topshop, Topman, Wallis, Evans, Burton, Miss Selfridge, Dorothy Perkins Outfit, and. BHS… clearly before his reputation got sullied by the demise of BHS and subsequent issues… *The Sunday Times* article made specific reference to the fact that he always delivered. More specifically whenever he borrowed to fund a deal, he always ensured that the debt was properly serviced and repaid on or ahead of schedule. This record of 100% reliability facilitated his ability to undertake ever larger deals, which grew his Arcadia Group (which went into receivership at the end of 2020!).

Someone else I got to know well built a multi-billion-pound fortune again by ensuring that he always, always, delivered. He was involved in the commercial property market and after a decade of success in the early 90s he decided to go for broke. It was a time of major disruption in the commercial property world with a major crash in commercial property valuations. This was the time he decided to buy major 'trophy' buildings as long as his rental yields were at least 10 basis points (0.10%) ahead of his borrowing costs. And the banks were happy to back him because of his impeccable track record. These properties' valuations grew rapidly as demand for properties in the West-End and City of London returned, his rental yields improved and his wealth grew exponentially!

As chairman I have stressed the absolute importance of this to my executive teams. Some took to it with little resistance, others thought that their entrepreneurialism, their charm, their ability to have gained commitment in the past, would enable them to continue to do so even if they failed to deliver on promises. This is a delusion! Despite raising this issue with them frequently, unfortunately they only learned when doors were slammed in their faces!

Meeting and exceeding expectations helps to build credibility over time. Delivering on promises and commitments should be the norm. Unfortunately, this is rarely the case... and under-delivery is frequently the norm especially in employee-related issues such as performance assessments, salary reviews, bonus computations, and training. But remembering that people are the essential ingredient for success, should facilitate this alignment with reality, as all stakeholders are people, and as such have an extraordinary ability to both remember and act accordingly.

> *Do it Right: Do it Now!*: Only promise what you know you can deliver
>
> *Do it Right: Do it Now!*: Remember reputations take long to establish but can be destroyed in a nano second
>
> *Do it Right: Do it Now!*: People are essential to success... so always manage their expectations and always deliver accordingly
>
> *Do it Right: Do it Now!*: Over delivery = happiness; under-delivery = misery!
>
> *Do it Right: Do it Now!*: Under promise and over deliver
>
> *Do it Right: Do it Now!*

PURSUIT OF THE BEST, 'NO' TO MEDIOCRITY

There should never be room for complacency and mediocrity. When this state is reached it is the beginning of the end. Mediocrity leads to the tolerance of under-performance, which leads to a loss of competitiveness, to a loss of productivity, to higher prices, lower revenues, declining profits, weaker cash flows and ultimately the death of the business. Mediocrity leads to losing the best and most able who will vote by their feet and seek more challenging environments to work in. Mediocrity will make it impossible to hire the best, the brightest, to drive your business forward.

Always strive for excellence in everything you do, from the very beginning. And above all always try to recruit the best for your business almost with a 'whatever it costs/ whatever it takes' attitude. The best will attract the best and will drive the business forward to ever higher levels.

I am not suggesting that you should do what GE did under Jack Welch and actively cull the bottom 20% on an annual basis, but I am suggesting that you should aim high, and aim to keep standards high by not tolerating under-performers for long. Pursuit of the best does not mean that you have to ensure first class travel, and deluxe hotels, and offices in the most expensive part of town, furnished with the most expensive furniture and equipment. If having a good address is important, then have one. If having the best telecommunications equipment, then get it. Pursuit of the best means what is best for your business, what is relevant for your business.

Many years ago, I was involved with one of the UK's leading natural resource research/information businesses. The founder/ CEO of this business became seriously upset that the data he sold to management consulting organisations at a given price was re-packaged by them with the addition of other value-added bits of information, at many times the price he had sold at. He decided that he wanted to explore establishing his own management consulting business. I undertook a small but detailed analysis and came up with a set of recommendations. These included the recommendation to hire a few highly trained and experienced management consultants, preferably those trained by reputable firms. So far, so good. I then indicated that the amount he would need to invest per consultant would be in the region of £250k, requiring a minimum investment of £500k for 2 consultants, plus a budget of another few hundred thousand pounds for junior consultants, support staff etc. He totally lost it, thought I was out of my mind and canned the whole project. He simply could not recognise the price of excellence.

Above everything else, it means having the best resources for the requirements of your specific business, in line with the business's capabilities and an overwhelming intolerance of mediocrity and under-performance in everything that impacts on your business. What matters is the people you employ, the way the company is presented on the web, the internal quality controls to ensure that everything that has external visibility is 100% consistent and reflects well on the business, and the way you deal with your employees, your customers and your suppliers.

Half measures are not possible. You cannot have a business that professes to deliver excellence to its customers but treats it suppliers and staff badly.

But this can only be done if you recognise that (1) bringing in the best talent may mean better than you; (2) recruiting best talent has a price to it; (3) managing talented people can be highly demanding; (4) you will need to measure performance on a consistent and regular basis; (5) you must have the systems and procedures in place to be able to measure performance, i.e. you know the key performance indicators relevant for your business; (6) retaining the best is the sum of all of the above plus more. It all sounds so easy but regrettably may be aspired to by many, but achieved by the very few. Even those who aspire often cannot reconcile what it takes to make it happen.

Do it Right: Do it Now!: Reject mediocrity, go for the best

Do it Right: Do it Now!: Recruit the best, retain the best

Do it Right: Do it Now!: Aim for excellence in everything

Do it Right: Do it Now!

TRAINING

Human Capital, the very term suggests investment. If this is true, then by definition investment in people should be an ongoing activity that is relentlessly being undertaken by organisations keen on maintaining competitiveness. It should be synonymous with sustainable competitive advantage, as nothing else can achieve this oft-quoted strategic objective. Yet sadly, training is frequently viewed not as a strategic investment, but as discretionary expenditure, a cost that can be turned on and off with the prevailing economic and market circumstances.

Having been Chairman of a long-established training company, TACK International Limited, I saw at first-hand how incredibly variable expenditure on training was. In strong growth years expenditure expands. In slow growth years, expenditure declines. Classic example were the 3 years from 2006-2008, when revenues grew sharply, and the forward order book continued to grow through to the last quarter of 2008 (remember the height of the credit crunch, the collapse of global banking and the onset of recession all took hold in the second half of 2008). All of a sudden by November 2008 TACK's order book fell off the proverbial cliff and continued at a significantly reduced level for the duration of the recession caused by the Global Financial Crisis.

Yet expenditure on training should be counter-cyclical. In weak years, the need to train and improve is arguably even more important than in years of strong demand and healthy growth. Almost like advertising expenditure, the need is for a degree of consistency, with the volume and intensity being turned up to secure future growth and future competitive advantage during downturns, easing back slightly during upturns.

But it simply is not like that. Expenditure on training is turned on and off along with the underlying prevailing economic growth or contraction. However, the best companies do train their employees consistently. The best companies do strive to develop exceptional training capabilities enhancing their reputations for the training they offer their staff. These reputations in turn help to differentiate them in the recruitment market, which makes it easier for them to recruit the best and often to retain the best...

> *'...Vodafone has put into place a five-year global-learning programme for high-potential staff, including overseas placements and an MBA...'*
>
> *THE TIMES* 15TH JANUARY 2004

This makes them much more appealing to new recruits, giving them the pick of the best, establishing inbuilt and sustainable competitive advantage.

Some companies are now waking up to the demand for, and appropriateness of, 'lifelong learning', i.e. training that does not stop after graduate level entry, or first line management. Training can, and should, continue throughout one's career, changing shape and emphasis, but always remaining challenging and stimulating. The business schools are busy developing executive education, life-long learning programmes, top management forums, etc., all aimed at this evolving and growing market.

And yet I wonder to what extent is lifelong training actually practised outside of a narrow band of professional service organisations? CPD – 'continuous professional development' – is a core component of most professional service businesses, including of course all medical practitioners. In my own case I regularly attend seminars and presentations on a wide range of contemporary and board related issues from 5G to Blockchain; from executive reward to audit issues; from the economy to global trade; from leadership to Brexit! This way I can stay relevant and reasonably up to date.

In reality even though I am often the oldest around the board table, I am more in tune with current day issues, current day developments, than my board colleagues, both executive and non-executive. I re-call raising Blockchain and its potential application with one of the boards I sat on. The then CEO's eyes glazed over and he immediately rejected the idea as something only relevant to crooks and fraudsters – when in fact Blockchain was entirely relevant to the business and could have propelled the business competitively!

I also wonder to what extent employees are sent on to training programmes in a planned and structured manner to develop their skills expertise and competence, based on clearly defined developmental requirements? Senior executives may well be encouraged to participate in executive education courses run by leading business schools, Harvard, London, Insead etc. as a badge of recognition, almost as an additional component of their executive reward package. But I doubt whether many organisations are prepared to invest in their up-and-coming talent to the same extent. And yet it is exactly this group, this group of early twenty- to late-thirty-year-olds who would benefit the most.

Before leaving this section on training, I do wish to air one key hobby horse of mine. I was on the Global Advisory Council of the London Business School and have been associated with

London Business School one way or another for over 45 years. I graduated with my MBA from there in 1975. I have been on various alumni committees and advisory boards for many years and in 1976 started the very first Alumni newsletter. I have tried to convince the school's leaders that they are missing the opportunity of offering courses in probably the single most important skill that everyone needs, that of sales and selling. On January 8, 2008, the *FT* journalist Michael Skapinker wrote *'Why business ignores the business schools',* and in response I wrote the following brief letter, which was published in the Letters to the Editor section *'Why not give selling a priority in business curriculum?'*

> And why do business schools ignore business? As chairman of the oldest established sales training business, TACK International (60 years), I have been trying to persuade business schools that they should include sales training in their MBA curriculum. Response, zero! Reason: not an academic subject.
> And yet everyone in business knows selling is a key requirement, selling products, services, ideas, even oneself!
>
> *FINANCIAL TIMES*, 15TH JANUARY 2008)

I do wish to labour this point about the critical importance of being able to sell. I refer to sales competence as 'evergreen'. Like an evergreen tree it is green irrespective of season, so with sales, irrespective of what is happening in an economy (growing, recessionary, inflationary, flat, etc.), irrespective of what stage of development a business is at (start-up, early stage, growth, mature, decline, etc.), irrespective of the nature of a business (consumer, manufacturing, professional service, b2c, b2b, private, public, charity, third-sector etc.), being able to generate revenue is critical. Without revenue there is no business! No matter how brilliant the manufacturing process, how exceptional the IP, how beautiful the design, how extraordinary the team of people, if you can't sell it, if you can't generate cash flow, you do not have a business. No ifs, no buts!

GEOX only became a business when its founder Mario Moretti Polegato decided to do it himself...

> *'...was almost 25 years ago when Mario Moretti Polegato, founder and chairman of GEOX, came up with the revolutionary idea of piercing the rubber soles of his shoes, allowing his feet to breathe during a trip under the hot sun of Reno, in Nevada. So, a normal rubber sole at the same time as guaranteeing extraordinary performance in terms of breathability and water resistance.'*

When he got back to Italy, Moretti Polegato decided to develop his idea in a small footwear company belonging to his family, a new technology was born, which he immediately patented. After pitching his invention to well-established footwear companies without success and having passed a market test with a range of kids' shoes, Moretti Polegato began manufacturing his GEOX shoes independently. He improved and perfected the initial patent and went on to extend the range of products to include not just children's shoes, but men's and women's too...' (GEOX Annual Report 2019)

So after unsuccessfully pitching his invention to several established footwear manufacturers, in 1995 he created an independent shoe company, and was able to *sell* his creation directly to the end consumers. Today he is one of the largest shoe manufacturers and retailers in the world, with net revenues in access of €805m in 2019; not a bad achievement in 24 years!

Despite being a brilliant engineer, James Dyson only came to the world's attention when he created a revolutionary vacuum cleaner *and* was able to sell the finished product to retailers who were prepared to stock it. In the May 2020 'Rich List' published by The Sunday Times, James Dyson was positioned as the UK's richest individual with a fortune of £16.2.billion, and that was after blowing £500m on the aborted development of an electric car!

The Smart car, despite being created by the designers of the Swatch and Daimler Benz, only took off when it was taken over by Mercedes and *sold* effectively around the world. David Cameron, Prime Minister (Conservative) and Nick Clegg, Deputy Prime Minister (Liberal Democrat) could only really make progress with their coalition government for the UK in May 2010, when they were able to *sell* the idea to their supporters. Barack Obama had to *sell* himself to the electorate of the United States to be elected President and to do so he had to *sell* effectively and convincingly the notion that 'change' is possible, and then as President he had to *sell* his healthcare reforms to both legislative houses. And in turn Trump had to *sell* his core idea of 'America First'... which he did and became the 45th President of the United States. Almost every day of the week in the Financial Times there are articles about company 'x' selling a subsidiary; or company 'y' being bought by a private equity firm; or company 'z' acquiring another business. On each and every occasion there was a need to 'sell'.

As I have mentioned, I used to be on the Global Advisory Council of the London Business School. As such I was invited to the School's annual key event called 'The Global Leadership Summit' a one day event with some of the world's leading business and economics related speakers. This event was followed by a drinks and canapés event for 'socialising and networking', usually fully attended by global business leaders, some politicians, economist and business gurus...so all in all a pretty good collection of influential people.

Also invited to attend the 'after party' was that year's graduating

MBA class. I recall wandering around the event chatting with people I have known for some while as well as new people, establishing in some cases new contacts. At one point I saw a group of about 8 people chatting together, so I approached the group and quickly established that they were all from the graduating MBA class. I then asked whether they had all secured jobs to go to on graduation? Of the 8, 3 said they had, the remaining 5 were still looking. I looked at them and said 'What the fuck are you doing talking to each other when you have within a few meters some of the most influential people imaginable? This is your opportunity to sell yourselves, establish contact, and maybe even secure a job!'

I am asked from time to time to give talks on being a non-executive… which I am happy to do. Nearly every time the first question I am posed is, 'How do you get your appointments?' At that point I lift one of my legs and point to the sole of the shoe, in other word 'I network, and when you think you've networked enough is probably the time to network some more.' It is a relentless activity if this is what you want to do. In other words, I sell, I sell myself.

Irrespective of who you are, selling is a key and core competence!

So let me emphasise… never forget the basics. Training in basics should be like one of the core levels in Maslow's hierarchy of needs, food and shelter. Basics is very much core skills focused, selling skills, writing skills, presentation skills, negotiating skills, interviewing skills, listening skills, and analytical skills. Business schools have unfortunately largely forgotten, or rather have never acknowledged, the importance of these basic skills, (with the exception of analytical skills) as they are not perceived as academic enough, which is a great pity and a huge omission in my mind.

Do it Right: Do it Now!: Training should be retained as a key requirement, irrespective of prevailing economic circumstances. It really is as simple as that

Do it Right: Do it Now!: Never forget the basics, they are forever important, selling skills, writing skills, interviewing skills, listening skills

Do it Right: Do it Now!: Remember if you can't sell you haven't got a business, no matter how brilliant you may be, for without selling there is no business

Do it Right: Do it Now!

I do not want to leave this section without explaining that my views on training (and the importance of dealing with all people related issues efficiently) have not just suddenly emerged... they have developed over many years. When I was CEO of Valin Pollen I wrote an article that was featured in PR WEEK December 3-9 1987 in which I stressed that 'because of the lack of training, our industry (PR) has traditionally been low pay and low reward' and went on to say 'that we must all do much more to invest in our most important assets... Selection of people, training and development, and tougher, more selective promotion, are undoubtedly the right steps which is why at Valin Pollen we have been investing substantial resources in our own in-house training and development programmes'...so I very much did as I am suggesting in these pages!

AGEISM AND OTHER 'ISMS'!
To my way of thinking, age is not a determinant of anything. It is the competence of the individual, their drive, motivation, energy

and enthusiasm, their experience and expertise, that determines whether they are suitable for specific positions or not. I do not subscribe to 'isms' of any sort, but I would argue that ageism is alive and well in the UK of the 21st century. As a consequence, UK PLC is missing out on the talent and expertise of a vast number of people deemed to be too old and also the drive and ambition of an equally vast number of people deemed to be too young! Is that crazy or what?

'Ageism is an increasing issue in the workplace. A third of workers over 50 experience age discrimination at work, CIPD research shows.' (The Times 15th January 2004)

Although laws have come into force aimed at eradicating discrimination based on age (as well as gender, sexual orientation, and disabilities) the reality is that it is still prevalent throughout the economy. It is tough for the over 50s or under 30s, and tougher still for the over 60s and under 25s.

If you are over 50 it gets harder to be considered for major new and challenging positions and if you are under 30 it is equally hard to be considered for senior and Board level appointments. There are not enough people standing up and shouting that this is crazy, especially at a time when there is so much debate about the lack of qualified executives. And this is at a time when so many boards are crying out for able non-executive directors and when diversity is needed more and more… and diversity could be supported by having a greater age range as well.

There are too few professional recruiters and search consultants who are prepared to debate their clients' mandate. There are too few who are prepared to ignore their clients' specifications and just focus on finding the best person for the job irrespective of age, and then debate the issue with their clients. I have, and

I can honestly state that not one client has ever criticised my actions or penalised me subsequently. Quite the opposite, they have accepted my advice, they have made appointments of people outside the unwritten age range, and they have come back for more.

A heading in the Saturday edition of the Daily Telegraph, 15th August 2009 'Children can prod us into action'...

> *'It was Tony Blair's kids, he would confess, who got him interested in global warming. The key green influence in Bill Clinton's White House was not Al Gore, but Clinton's daughter Chelsea. And children of Chinese leadership, active in university green clubs, have made it increasingly environmentally aware.'*

So if these children can have an influence with global implications, young people could impact on businesses without having to wait until their early 40s!

After all, at 43 David Cameron was the youngest Prime Minister of Britain since Lord Liverpool in 1812! And Simon Wolfson of Next plc, a FTSE quoted high street fashion retailer, was appointed Chief Executive at the age of 34 and is still very much in position and has been ennobled to Lord Wolfson, despite the average tenure for FTSE 100 CEOs in the UK being just 5.5years!

In a digital world we should be much more open to the insights, observations, expertise of those under 30... and often even under 20, as they are a generation who have grown up with technology; the generation who learnt how to use an iPhone/iPad from watching their parents and then just doing it instinctive!

With the onset of the Coronavirus pandemic, COVID 19, and the ensuing lock-down, there has been a massive shift to all things digital. Videoconferencing has had to totally replace face to face communications, with even Parliament allowing for the first time ever video-conference participation by members of the house, and electronic voting! All forms of video communications have exploded with growth, be they Zoom or Microsoft Teams et al. Webinars are prolific, with a recurring theme... pivot to digital! Those businesses which are agile and have pivoted fast have done well. And this is where youth can have a major impact. in agility, speed and pivot.

> *Do It Right: Do It Now!:* Age is irrelevant. The only criteria should be competence and drive
>
> *Do It Right: Do It Now!:* Deliberately reject any form of 'ism', any form of discrimination
>
> *Do It Right: Do It Now!:* Beware of unconscious biases... they exist, they are there, and they can have a materially negative impact!
>
> *Do It Right: Do It Now!*

REVIEW/FEEDBACK

There are many different approaches, methodologies processes and procedures for undertaking and providing feedback, but in its simplest form feedback is just providing simple, clear and honest communication to an employee about his/her performance of the tasks expected. Some companies provide no feedback to employees at all, which is an appalling situation, one in which it is difficult to see how employees can ever hope to improve their performance.

Possibly an even worse situation is one where there is consistent failure to perform, where an evaluation is set up to take place but gets cancelled at the last moment, where an appraisal discussion is scheduled to take place but fails to materialise, where the appraiser very clearly places greater importance on everything other than the provision of honest feedback to the employee. This is not fiction; this is very much reality. This unfortunately is the reality of many employees' lives. Just think of the message this is sending and the damage such inaction is creating! Little wonder then that the FT's Lucy Kellaway (July 12th 2010) was suggesting that appraisals should be done away with altogether.

This alone can contribute to the best, the most able, very quickly concluding that this is not the type of company they wish to be a part of, and leave! Talent is mobile. Raising expectations and not delivering is very poor, especially when it is in relation to people's lives.

There are companies where there are regular performance reviews, but they are considered by all to be part of the annual calendar of events, like budgets, that have to be done, but that no one really takes seriously, nothing happens as a consequence, and there are no expectations. They are a massive waste of time, money, and above all, opportunity. These certainly should be 'done away with'.

There are companies where the whole process is about ticking boxes. Forms have been designed, ratings established and boxes need to be filled in. This is process over content. This is another massive waste of time, money, and above all, opportunity. And theses should also be 'done away with'.

There are companies where feedback is provided in an open and honest environment, where feedback is treated seriously by everyone from top to bottom, where there are established processes, but they are there to facilitate understanding and analysis that leads to dialogue and discussion, that in turn leads to agreed actions by both the appraiser and the subject. This is value added. These should certainly NOT be 'done away with'.

There are companies where this whole process is taken seriously and under-performers are identified, corrective action is designed and subsequently if there is no material change, alternative actions are planned and discussed in a structured manner. It can, and in some companies does happen like this. Feedback has huge benefits to all concerned. This is value added.

Actually making an appraisal system work is not that difficult. But there are certain basics that have to be properly implemented: (1) there has to be clear commitment to the appraisal/feedback process, top to bottom, but very clearly the leadership has to come from the top; (2) has to be all inclusive, i.e. everyone is involved, and everyone is appraised; (3) the appraisers are properly trained to appraise; (4) the timetable is agreed and respected by everyone; (5) feedback is provided, comments are noted; and (6) clear actions are agreed, implemented and monitored.

It is vital that it is seen to be inclusive of everyone. It is vital that everyone understands that appraisals are taken seriously by everyone. The importance of appraisals is real, and not just gestures. One significant way of demonstrating the importance of appraisals is to ensure that in all managers' appraisals the effectiveness and timeliness of undertaking appraisals is one of the criteria of the assessment of their own performance. This builds internal consistency into the process.

There are numerous methodologies available, there are certain companies that specialise in helping their clients define and implement feedback processes and procedures. A well-known methodology and one increasingly favoured by many is the 360 degree feedback. This aims to provide feedback by superiors from above, subordinates from below, peer group colleagues from the side and occasionally even reaching out to customers and suppliers, i.e. a total perspective.

> *Do it Right: Do it Now!*: I really don't care what form it takes as long as it happens regularly, is taken seriously, is undertaken professionally, is honest and open, is based on actual rather than hearsay, is substantiated with examples and leads to action
>
> *Do it Right: Do it Now!*: Never raise expectations and then fail to deliver
>
> *Do it Right: Do it Now!*: It does not need to be sophisticated…it just needs to be honest and as simple as providing regular feedback with linked actions
>
> *Do it Right: Do it Now!*

PROMOTING EARLY TO CREATE STRETCH

The day has arrived, you've been called in by your boss and given a promotion. Congratulations. So what has changed apart from your job title? Too often the answer is nothing! This is a great pity, and a great missed opportunity. I have seen people being promoted with no change in their daily jobs, no increase in their responsibilities, virtually no change in their remuneration, just a new title and perhaps a better car entitlement. What madness! And if the bosses then complain that those promoted are not behaving any more differently from the way they did in the past, why should they?

There is essentially a high degree of risk-aversion in many corporations, both large and small. Even entrepreneurial businesses, especially where the founder is still directly involved and running the show, are risk averse. They avoid the risk of allowing the relatively young their head, of promoting early, of promoting deliberately to stretch, deliberately to maximise the energy and drive that comes from youth.

There are of course exceptions, and nepotism comes to mind, when the young are promoted way ahead of their experience because they are the children of the owner. There is nearly always a qualifying explanation that the offspring has gained relevant experience elsewhere and has the right experience and expertise for the role, that in other words, the promotion was entirely on merit. It is interesting to note that in the very same organisations no one else has ever been promoted to such senior roles at such a young age. Strange… News International comes to mind, amongst the larger organisations, as does Arcelor Mittal, the world is packed with examples from smaller entrepreneurial businesses, to large global organisations.

I was engaged to provide board level support to an organisation that was in its 4th generation. The founder (1st generation) of the business had passed away; his son, in his mid-80s was Chairman (2nd generation); the Chairman's two nephews (3rd generation) were shareholders and executive directors and fully engaged with the business; and their children, 4th generation, were also working in the business. The problems were (a) the nephews (brothers) actually hated each other and made it absolutely clear to all that they had no intention to be supportive of each other in any way; (b) 4th generation came into the business as a right, not because they had earned the right; they had little education; and yet they felt totally 'entitled' which greatly demotivated everyone else and

(c) the business was living off its past, no one was selling! This was nepotism that was damaging the business and also damaging the individuals involved as they had no motivation to improve.

I am not suggesting that it is wrong for families to pass on their business from one generation to another. Many large global businesses started in exactly such a manner, Marks & Spencer, P&G, Ford Motor Company, C&A, and Nestle to name a few that started as entrepreneurial businesses, passed to second and third generations, and then moved into the public domain as quoted companies with rapidly decreasing family involvement. However, what I am suggesting is that it is wrong not to recognise that there may well be significant talent elsewhere within the organisation that warrants early promotion and development, too. Competence is not exclusive to family membership and the blood line.

I strongly believe in the very real benefit of promoting early, promoting into tough and challenging environments, promoting to stretch the individual to the maximum. Promote and acknowledge that the promotion is a significant move, that the promotion represents a significant change and delivers a significantly different compensation package. Actions speak louder than words in these types of situations.

It is really staggering how able, well-educated and highly motivated people can grow rapidly in challenging new roles. The most successful organisations do exactly that. They cherry pick their stars for the future and place them in ever more demanding roles with ever greater responsibilities. They stretch and train and develop their stars, their leaders of tomorrow.

I have experienced an environment in which every promotion was very carefully planned. Those earmarked for promotion were trained for their next level of tasks and responsibilities so that they arrived developed and ready.

It can be done, and like so much else it is not so difficult either, all it takes is a little bit of forethought and close attention to know your people so you can select the stars!

Even in a non-executive capacity one of the things I try to do is get to know as many people in the organisations I'm engaged with as possible. Certainly all of the senior team and where possible others in the organisation too. In SMEs employing 30 to 100 people this is not an impossible task, in larger organisations it gets tougher. And even as a non-executive I have come across real talent and have done my best to facilitate their growth and development. In fact I have been able to be supportive guiding certain individuals as their careers have developed and remained in touch even as they reached the C-Suite!

Do it Right: Do it Now!: Know your people

Do it Right: Do it Now!: Pick your stars and manage them forward, always a little bit ahead of their expectations

Do it Right: Do it Now!: Stretch, train and develop your stars

Do it Right: Do it Now!: Beware of nepotism, it's all about talent, competencies, drive and ability

Do it Right: Do it Now!

FIRING

Never easy but unfortunately sometimes necessary. There is a logical linkage with the 'Relentless pursuit of the best, low tolerance of under-performance' section above, in the sense that removing under-performers will automatically require that certain individuals are requested to leave, i.e. are fired. There is also a close linkage with the section above concerning 'Respect' because the manner in which firing is undertaken is critical. It can be done in a manner which minimizes the pain and maximises acceptability. There is a link with the chapter, *Do it Right: Do it Now!* for delaying is harmful, prolongs the agony for all, especially if it is blatantly clear to all that an individual does not fit.

There is a link with the chapter on the 'Positive No', as by definition a firing is a form of no, meaning 'No, you do not have a job with us any longer. No, your career is not going to progress further with us and would be better served elsewhere'.

There is a direct link with the section above on 'Feedback' as this is where, if it is undertaken professionally, expectations can be managed. And through a well-managed exit process, really valuable feedback can be both provided and received through the exit interview.

But what is real is that firing another human being is never easy, nor pleasant irrespective of the overwhelming rationale that may exist. I have heard many times the statement 'In the end you will come to thank me for this decision', but frankly I have never ever known anyone who has been fired turning up months or years later and thanking their then boss for firing them! No one ever wants to be fired, although there are times when the redundancy package on offer is perceived to be highly attractive and a good reason to go.

So some of the key considerations are worth repeating. Always remember that firing an individual has a major impact on that individual's livelihood, self-confidence and ego. Ensure you have the facts and rationale for the decision, that all legal requirements and all contractual requirements have been fully met, and that the process is undertaken with tact and sensitivity. And if possible be overly generous and be supportive (unless the firing is for due cause!).

And wherever possible try not to forget to undertake an 'exit interview', as this could be an immensely valuable source of insight.

During the course of the past few years we have heard horror stories about people being fired by text messages, e-mails and voice-mails. This is just plain wrong! There are some organisations that ensure that every single individual who leaves them does so with as much of a positive feeling as possible, regardless of the circumstances (unless being fired for reasons of improper behaviour or illegal activities). This is an extraordinary achievement, but one that demonstrates that even in adversity, it is possible to do things right.

In the digital world there are increasingly fewer secrets, but more 'fake news'. So ensuring that your organisation's reputation is protected is important. Any ex-employee can place stuff on, for example, Glassdoor (https://www.glassdoor.co.uk/Reviews) about the company just left and seek vengeance for being poorly treated! And there are many other sites from Facebook to LinkedIn where positive or negative noise can be created. So doing it right matters.

Do it Right: Do it Now!: Always remember that even in adversity it is not only possible, but advisable, to do things right.

Do it Right: Do it Now!: If someone is wrong, make the call and exit the individual

Do it Right: Do it Now!: But when exiting do it legally right, morally right and be generous

Do it Right: Do it Now!

From time to time there are exceptional circumstances when it is necessary to make major changes in the number of people employed by the business. These are extremely painful situations and whilst it is impossible to undertake on an individual basis, they should still be done with as much care and concern for the employees' wellbeing as possible. In the unprecedented COVID world of 2020, business after business has been forced to make major redundancies, especially once the Government's furlough support safety net was removed. For examples one airline after the other has been forced to make huge reductions in their workforce making tens of thousands of people redundant. They have to do so according to the letter of the law. They need to do so with care and clear communications to all involved. They simply cannot do it individually even though every life matters!

RETAINING REALITY

With seniority there frequently comes a growing sense of self-worth. There is absolutely nothing wrong with that. But it is not unusual for some to allow seniority, especially in ever larger organisations, to have an unfortunate effect on their attitude to others around them whom they may have known for many years, and in turn on their own self-importance. That is most regrettable.

An acquaintance I have known since the mid-70s and I were young consultants in the same firm. He has had a stunning career, and I would estimate that he must have been one of the world's leading executives, with entry to any boardroom, any politician, including the White House and 10 Downing Street. As Executive Chairman of HSBC Group, Stephen Green was absolutely at the top of the pile. And yet he retained an extraordinary degree of both humility and modesty. He occupied a relatively modest corner office at the top of HSBC's Canary Wharf head office, with no deliberate show of excess or power. When I asked to meet him, he responded to my e-mail within 24hrs, personally, and we agreed a date and time to meet. Exactly on time he came to greet me and ushered me into his office. Note, he did not keep me waiting; he came to meet me not one of his assistants; 'a relatively modest' office! One of the world's truly outstanding human beings.

On the other hand, there have been other ex-colleagues who have also had very successful careers, but who have taken a different route. I recall walking into the office of another highly successful ex-colleague, also Chairman of a major bank, whose wall was adorned with photographs of him with the leading statesmen, Presidents, Prime Ministers, Royalty and celebrities he has met. What message was that trying to communicate? On arrival I was sent to the top floor of the building, met by an assistant, asked to wait. I was kept waiting for some 30 mins past the agreed time of our meeting. I was then shown in by an assistant while certain 'important' stuff was being completed by him at his desk. Note: glory wall announcing 'look whom I have met'; being kept waiting indicative of my time is much more important than yours; shown in by an assistant, because I can!

I have found Private Equity executives particularly poor at treating people well - unless they want something! If they want something and they think you can be helpful, they will be all over you. But otherwise forget it, you will be treated like a totally disposable object. I recall being called by a head-hunter acting for a PE firm who had an 'urgent need' for a Chairman for a company they were in the process of trying to acquire. From my first call I was invited to meet with teams of up to 4 people at least 4 times in a brief two-week period. They 'biked' a manila envelope of confidential data and documents to me to read and review. They made time to meet and discuss and review at times running into hours… i.e. they wanted stuff from me. And then the music stopped… total radio silence! I called; e-mailed; left messages… zero. Not even a thank you for your time. Just zero! I found out via another route that the deal had collapsed so they immediately dumped it and focussed on the next deal. All of which is fine except their behaviour to me. Irrespective how pressurised a world these PE guys may live in, it's good to retain reality that they are dealing with people!

The reality is that when all the corporate 'clothing' is removed, there is very little difference between us all. When the chauffeur-driven car is no more, when the diary secretary, and the PA/EA and the expense account are all history and the corner office is occupied by someone else, we are remembered by what we have contributed, what we have created, by what we have achieved and done. This is particularly true of Members of Parliament and in particular members of the cabinet who have certain privileges for the duration of their appointment but lose it all as soon as they are out of office.

Power, position and status are an explosive cocktail that are for many both irresistible, and once tasted, very hard to relinquish. Why do so many Prime Ministers hang on to power for too long and considerably after they have essentially passed their sell-by date? Why do so many entrepreneurs insist on retaining direct executive control when they should have passed the baton to someone else? It takes an enormous amount of self-control, honesty, and humility to be able to hand-over control without being forced to do so by external circumstances. But retaining a sense of reality throughout one's life helps all the way through.

Truly GREAT people can achieve the impossible! Nelson Rolihlahla Mandela was a South African anti-apartheid revolutionary, political leader, and philanthropist who served as President of South Africa from 1994 to 1999. He was the country's first black head of state and the first elected in a fully representative democratic election. And the first to step down and hand-over power after only 5 years!

> *Do it Right: Do it Now!*: Retain a sense of reality irrespective of the seniority of office reached
>
> *Do it Right: Do it Now!*: Retain a sense of humility irrespective of the seniority of office reached
>
> *Do it Right: Do it Now!*: Treat others as you would like others to treat you
>
> *Do it Right: Do it Now!*

INTERNAL COMMUNICATION

Let me address what is something very near and dear to me. Virtually everything in the previous pages is linked to this, one way or another. I have consistently argued the importance of internal communications in all the companies I have been involved with, I have consulted many organisations on their internal communications, and I have advised on improving and strengthening internal communications. Everyone working in any organisation has the right to know what is going on. They should all receive the company's annual and interim reports, the CEO should regularly communicate with his employees, depending on the company size, by whatever means is most suitable, which today could include webinars, podcasts, YouTube, CD, e-mail, video, newsletter, social media, staff newspaper, face to face, and by walking around.

For all business schools their MBA programme is their flagship. I was chatting to a graduate of London Business School about his two years (2004-06) at the school and asked what he thought of the Dean of the time. To my amazements he said that the Dean had never come to any of their classes and that the Dean was totally invisible to all the MBAs during their two years at the school. How appalling! Unfortunately, it is not that unusual for the CEO to be invisible to most of the people within the organisation. (I repeated my enquiry about London Business School Deans a few years later this with a graduate of the class 2012-14 who absolutely raved about the school's then dean, Sir Andrew Likierman (Dean from 2009-2017) who 'was everywhere, even came to support the school's rugby team, but genuinely was visible and engaged with the whole school and the people within it!' What an extraordinary difference.

All managers have a responsibility to communicate with their staff, to keep them abreast of what is going on, on 'how we are doing', on how the Group is doing, on joiners and leavers, on competition, on the market.

There is no justification for the mushroom style of management, i.e. keeping everyone in the dark and just keep shovelling shit on top of them! It simply does not work. We live in a world of communications. Organisations invest vast sums of money in communications. We employ specialists to help us communicate with defined target audiences that are deemed to be important, such as investors, shareholders, banks, providers of debt finance and rating agencies, so we should place the same, if not more, emphasis on the way we communicate with the people that ensure we have something to communicate to others about externally. Our employees.

I have frequently emphasised the importance of real communications - not e-mails or memos, but real face to face communications, of the type where you deliberately get out of the lift the floor above or below and walk the corridors to be seen, to make contact, to stop and chat for a few moments. It may be communication with a random selection of employees invited to a sandwich lunch, or communications by picking up the phone and congratulating an individual on a specific achievement/deal/contract/sale/task... or just to say 'thank you'. The power of those two words should never ever be underestimated.

Let me close by quoting Terry Lundgren, ex-Chairman, President and CEO of Macy's in the United States... 'The only way to address uncertainty is to communicate and communicate. And when you think you have just about got to everybody, then communicate once more.'

If people are the essential ingredient for success than make sure you communicate!

Do it Right: Do it Now!: It's good to talk. Talk openly, talk engagingly and listen!

Do it Right: Do it Now!: Treat your people as adults, share information with them

Do it Right: Do it Now!

TRUST

I have made reference to how reputations take a lifetime to establish but can be destroyed in a nano-second. And so it is with 'trust'… which also takes a huge amount of time and effort to establish but can also be destroyed rapidly. Rachel Botsman in an article in the Financial Times, 10th February 2020 titled 'Businesses can't build trust, people have to give it' provides a fabulous insight into the topic of trust and the issues many current major organisations are facing… including some of the very largest tech companies such as Facebook and Google with issues of privacy, data security, and of course 'fake news'! Rachel Botsman goes on to say 'money is the currency of transactions; trust is the currency of interactions' and provides Five ways for leaders to earn trust…

- **Competence:** Be up front about what you can do, but more important what you can't do.

- **Reliability:** Work on being consistent in your behaviours from day to day, especially when you are under pressure.

- **Empathy:** Take time to genuinely listen and understand other people's interests and needs as well as your own.

- **Integrity:** Develop an astute awareness of how closely your words align with your actions.

- **Honesty:** Communicate openly with people about your intentions and motives.

The absolute key word in the above is that leaders need to 'EARN' trust. This is not something that can be achieved by edict; it cannot be commanded; it does not come with position and status…it must be earned by leaders and by the companies they run!

Do it Right: Do it Now!

AUTHOR'S BACKGROUND... IN GREATER DETAIL

This book has been in the making for the past 60+ years since I first earned some money. It was 1958, a warm spring day at the Farnborough air show. I was 8 years old and bored.

We had arrived in London a year earlier in October 1957 from Budapest, Hungary, from where my family had emigrated after the Hungarian revolution of 1956.

I was bored. I neither knew much about aircraft nor was I terribly interested in them after the initial excitement of seeing them buzz over our heads had passed.   My parents had bought me a bottle of Coca Cola. I had consumed it with gusto, it being still a new experience (there had been no Coca Cola in Hungary in the 1950s), and I was about to throw it away in the assortment of bins around the grounds at that time. But hang on a moment, I remembered that you could get 3d (threepence, about 1.2p) back on each bottle returned. (Threepence was a lot of money to an eight year old in 1958). So I decided to collect the bottles people were just throwing away and return them. I disappeared and did exactly that. By the end of the day I had made more money than it had cost my parents to take us all to the show. And I got a real sense of achievement and a buzz from making money.

During the next 10 years I had an assortment of vacation jobs from being a lorry 'driver's mate', to working in a warehouse at Christmas time supplying booze to the corporate sector. I had worked as a 'Saturday boy' in a menswear shop and during one school holiday worked in the shop during the week as well. In many of these odd jobs I learned that initiative paid, despite the fact that it was not expected, especially from someone of my age or a 'casual labourer'. But initiative could also backfire.

While working as a shop assistant on Saturdays was OK because it was fairly busy, the weekdays were a nightmare. There were only so many times a day one could spray the glass top of the counter, or only so many times the clothes hanging on rails needed to be straightened. I was bored out of my mind, until one day when a salesman walked through the door. The shop owner took him to one side and was clearly having a detailed discussion with him but left him for some time while he went to do something in his office. I therefore took the initiative and started to chat to this man. After all, we were both just standing there doing nothing. As the conversation unfolded I asked the cost price of various garments. When the owner returned he overheard the salesman explaining his prices to me. After the salesman had left the owner went absolutely ballistic with me, that I had no right to talk to the salesman, had no right to ask questions, had no right to find out about cost prices etc. I wondered why he was so excited. Was it because I had inadvertently discovered that he was applying a 500% mark-up? In retrospect he was, of course, totally right. I had no right to stick my nose into his business.

As a 'driver's mate' my job was to help load and unload the truck. 'Thornett's Transport Limited' was in a side alley not far from where we were living at that time, close to Hendon Way, London. I was a tall, lanky, 16 year old. On my first day I was allocated to a truck with a rather large rotund driver, beer gut over-hanging a wide belt, his usual mate, relatively short, very muscular, tattooed and mean-looking, with me being the 'mate's mate'. We were assigned to go to a warehouse, meet the warehouse's owner, clear out the warehouse, transport the contents to a new warehouse and unload into the new premises. So off we went, six-foot-two 16 stone driver, six-foot 10 stone mate's mate (me), and five-foot-six rock hard and tattooed driver's mate.

When we arrived we were met by the owner who gave very clear instructions as to exactly what he wanted us to do, so we got on with it. During the course of the morning the owner gave us some further instructions and chatted with us when we took the inevitable tea break. When the loading was completed he suggested that I should go with him in his car, as the cabin was clearly a bit tight for the three of us. Along the way he explained to me that he would not have time to stay to supervise the unloading. He gave me written instructions as to where he wanted everything to go in the new premises, and asked if I would ensure that it was all unloaded accordingly. I suggested that he should ask the driver to do this. He said 'I can tell who uses their brain, and who uses their muscle. I want you to do this because I know you'll do it well' and he pushed a five-pound note into my pocket at the same time (a fortune!). And that is what happened. I ensured that everything went exactly where the owner wanted it to go as we unloaded. On the way back to the depot, sitting in between 16 stones 'rock' and the tattooed 'hard place', the driver said 'Good bloke, gave us a fiver tip before he left, but as a casual you don't share in the tips'. I didn't argue!

I was employed by Gresham Life Assurance Society Limited, in 1969. I was 19 and this was my first formal job for a six-month period prior to going to University. I can still re-call the feeling of slight apprehension as I walked through the doors on that first day. What would work be like? What would I be doing? What would the people that I'd be working with be like? Would I be able to perform adequately? Would they remember that I had been hired? And of course they did, and of course I had a desk to go to, and of course the people were a mixture of the good, the invisible, and the nasty.

I remember very clearly that there was no induction programme, there was no formal, thought-through welcome. I was met by someone from Personnel who gave me a file containing basic personnel policy matters, my week's ration of Luncheon Vouchers, walked me to my department, the Loans Administration Department, and handed me over to the department's head. And that was it. And in retrospect that was probably well above par for the late 1960s.

The department head, a greyish man in his mid-fifties, wore a three piece suit, very much in the style of the City in those days. The suit had probably been worn day in day out for years as it had a certain sheen to it, trousers lacking a razor edged crease, but nevertheless it was a three piece suit, and the standard issue brogue shoes were polished and buffed to a high sheen. He sat at the front of all the loans administrators, had to be addressed by his surname as Mr..., no first names in those days, clearly felt superior to everyone else in his section, and yet was hugely deferential to his bosses, all of whom he addressed only as 'Sir'. 'Excuse me Sir, may I raise a point concerning Mrs. Smith's policy... ...Yes Sir, I'll take care of that...' And so on and so forth. I think you've got the picture. A formal, structured, and inflexible environment.

I don't think he had ever come across anyone like me. Not that I had any training to be a loans administrator, but getting to understand what transpired to be a relatively simple process was not hugely difficult. Asking questions however appeared to be an innovation! And I asked a lot of questions given that there was no formal training. Asking the questions enabled me to rapidly get to understand the loans administration process and specifically what was expected from me.

After six months I was not sad to leave the job to take-up my place at University as it had become incredibly repetitive and boring. The idea of spending one's life paper pushing from 9-5 filled me with total horror. It was, however, reality for many people, the vast majority of whom had learned to accept robot-like working lives, the classic 9-5 existence.

But looking back, I had had an interesting time and started to learn about working life. And amazingly enough, I was able to make what at that time was considered to be a lasting contribution. But it took a minor war and the benefit of naivety to achieve it.

I noted down the instructions I was given as I was taught what to do to be a loans administrator. Whenever I didn't understand why a certain process was the way it was I asked. My questioning really bothered the head of the department and often times he responded by saying, 'For goodness sake just do it, it's been done this way for years, you really don't need to know why'. In the pub after work, chatting with other colleagues they would share their frustrations and boredom and yet none of them thought it worth their while to question anything, they just did as they were told. Some of them would explain certain processes and procedures and why they were the way they were. This allowed me to build a really good understanding of the whole process, warts and all!

As I was approaching the end of my six months I decided to document the loans administration department's process. In my own time, evenings and weekends, I documented what each member of the team did, how the process flowed, the various checks and balances and the authorisation procedure, so that when new people joined the department they would be able to pick up this simple document and rapidly understand both the process and their role within it. I also highlighted areas where the process could be simplified and duplication removed, thereby speeding up our ability to respond to loan requests by our policy holders, our customers. This was a minor revolution, but one that the department head begrudgingly accepted, then embraced with vigour once he added certain bits to it, made numerous corrections and effectively turned it into his own document for change! It was eventually implemented.

Without knowing, at the age of 19, with no business experience, I had completed my first consulting assignment. Without knowing, I had arrived at insights by applying 'why-why'!

I had learned of the very real resistance to change, of the expectation that young people should do as they are told and not question, of the acceptance of the status quo by the vast majority of employees, many of whom could have make significant improvements to the benefit of their employers. I had learned that however hard it was, keeping my mouth shut was not an option that I could comfortably live with.

Above all I had learned that there was an enormous amount to be learned, often just by observing, that asking 'why' was perhaps the most profound question any one could ask, a question one must continue to ask forever, and that by asking why, by understanding why, simple improvements become evident, i.e. the 'How'.

After having completed my job at Gresham Life Assurance Society Limited I went off for a short vacation to the South of France, before starting my life as an undergraduate at Manchester University. Whilst in the South of France I came across pizza restaurants for the first time. These were restaurants that had a simple menu consisting of a range of different types of pizzas, simple salads, a short wine list, a selection of other soft-drinks, and limited desserts. They were light and airy, pleasant to the eye, clean and simple, with a price list that was relatively easy on the pocket, even the pocket of a student to be. I ate in an assortment of pizza restaurants during my stay. On returning to the UK I contacted an uncle of mine, whom I knew had stacks of money and suggested that I would forget about going to university if he were prepared to back me financially to start up a pizza restaurant in London. Remember pizza restaurants were a total novelty at that time, with only Pizza Express being around with perhaps just one or two restaurants in London…

We chatted through the idea, after which he figuratively patted me on my head saying, 'You really don't understand the English culture yet. Pizza is not a dish the English would warm to, they like their fish and chips, their steak and kidney pies, they have little culinary imagination. So go off to university, because this idea of establishing a pizza restaurant will not catch on'. Very shortly afterwards Pizza Express started to expand at some pace and during the course of the next couple of decades swept throughout the UK! It was a good idea, it was the right time, but I was lacking the inner strength to ignore the advice of someone I thought was a successful business man, I failed to have belief in my own entrepreneurial ability and above all I simply lacked the experience needed to start a business from scratch with zero funding. So instead I went off to university. I failed to ask 'why not?', a question I have regretted asking ever since.

But life is full of 'if onlys'. And frankly there is little point in looking backwards and harping on about the 'if onlys'. Learn from those experiences and move on.

So these were the experiences during my early formative years. The experiences that followed played an even bigger role in formulating many of the ideas and concepts contained in this book.

I was rejected by Rolls-Royce for consideration of a university scholarship because I was not born in the UK. Given the business of the company at that time (1967), given that the cold war was at its peak and given that not only was I not born in the UK but was born behind the Iron Curtain, in Hungary, many would have said, 'fair enough'. I didn't. I protested that my place of birth was beyond my control, that we were naturalised citizens and that I posed no security threat. To my utter amazement I was invited for a day long selection session in Derby. I was amazed when the letter offering me a place on the Rolls-Royce Scholarship scheme came through the letter box. Months later I was utterly gutted when my whole world collapsed having failed to get the required 'A' level grades to take up my place at university. Out went my scholarship, my place in a hall of residence and of course my opportunity to start my selected course at university. After licking my wounds I decided, with huge encouragement and moral support of my parents, to re-take my 'A' levels in the following January, and have another go. This time I got the grades, I got my place at university for the next academic year, I got my place in hall of residence but without the Rolls-Royce Scholarship!

I studied Management Sciences at Manchester University, Institute of Science and Technology, or UMIST, for short. This was one of the first undergraduate business courses in the UK. What a great place to have spent three years in the late 60s, early 70s.

During my three years at university I gained more confidence in asking why and generally questioning the status quo. Everyone was required to write a dissertation as part of the final year's assessment. I wanted to explore the slowly emerging trade between Britain and Eastern Europe, and Hungary in particular. 'But no one undertakes international research for an undergraduate dissertation' was the initial response from my faculty supervisor. 'Why not?' was my response. Is the topic relevant, I was asked? Yes. Would it satisfy the requirement for a dissertation? Yes. So why not? Just because something of this nature had not been done in the past, surely does not mean that it can't be done! 'OK do it, but don't blame me if you screw up' were the encouraging final words by my supervisor.

I made a list of all the major UK companies that were trading with Hungary and constructed a questionnaire that I sent to all of them. I got a fantastic response. Next I visited Budapest, and interviewed all the key buyers in all the major central purchasing agencies, the 'Impexs' (import-export agencies), in particular, on the subject of how they perceived the performance of British exporters in relation to their principal competitors, i.e. exporters from other Western European countries. I then assembled the findings which I sprinkled with some insights from various articles and books that I had read along the way on the subject of exporting to add a more academic feel to my completed dissertation. (At this time countries within the Soviet bloc referred to a 'Comecon' could only trade with other countries via state-owned import-export agencies that represented all the various businesses, also state owned, within their border. So there were agricultural impexs, technical product impexs, consumer product impexs; medical product impexs... etc.)

On completion, I wrote to all the British companies that had taken part in the survey and offered them copies of my findings (i.e. my dissertation) for a small fee of £25.00. I sold a good number of copies of the document, I received some very kind comments, but I also received a couple of irate letters questioning my cheek of offering to sell a product that they had helped to produce by responding to my original questionnaire. On balance the responses were positive and the money helped to pay for the cost of the undertaking. What's more important is that I was awarded a 1ˢᵗ class grade for my work, AND created a precedent that I know has been emulated many, many, times since.

Another fantastic result of my dissertation project was securing my first job after graduation. On graduating with a B.Sc. Hons. (2.1) degree I joined an international marketing organisation, Morganite International, that was part of a long established quoted industrial concern, Morgan Crucible. They had participated in my dissertation research project. They had been a willing purchaser of my finished product and they had approached me to explore whether I'd be interested in joining. I was clearly flattered and above all they were prepared to let me undertake a real job fast. They were prepared to let me loose on potential customers after a brief initial period of product training, customers in Hungary (because I spoke Hungarian) and Romania (because I spoke French, and the second language at that time in Romania was French).

Three months after graduating I was flying regularly to Budapest and Bucharest, staying in international hotels, renting cars, had an expense account and most importantly I had true responsibility for selling the company's products. It was great experience, experience I could not possibly have got had I gone along the usual path and joined a standard graduate training programme, irrespective of how well structured it may have been, or how well known and respected the organisation that may have offered it.

Selling was hugely challenging, and rewarding, an extraordinary experience at such an early stage in my career. But I wanted more than to be a 'travelling salesman' aka 'international marketing executive'. So I started to chat with a few people outside of work about alternatives. Many people simply couldn't understand why I was even thinking about doing anything different. The job was good, the pay was good, the company was well respected, and at a young age you were being given both responsibility and an expense account! There were others who advised staying put for a while longer, 'hang around for another couple of years and then apply to Business School', which was a relatively new form of postgraduate education, imported from the US.

Why hang around for a couple of years? I decided to apply to business school immediately. Although business schools were looking for people with at least three years' experience I managed to 'sell' my year with Morganite International as easily the equivalent given what I had done, given my responsibilities and achievements. I took the then equivalent of GMAT, the Princeton Test, and made my application to London Business School and to my delight was accepted. I am sure I was accepted in no small measure due to the influence of Charles Handy, at that time in charge of the master's programme (MBA), who had interviewed me as part of the admissions process, and who was prepared to take a risk with this 23 year old, oddball!

It was a two years master's programme and I also had the extraordinary privilege of being selected for the school's embryonic International Exchange Programme in our second year. This gave us the opportunity to spend one term at HEC, (École des Hautes Études Commerciales), just outside Paris and a term at New York University, Graduate School of Business Administration, now called 'Stern', before returning for the final term and graduation.

None of this would have been possible at the age of 23-25 had I just gone along with the flow. None of this would have been possible had I not asked 'why?' None of this would have been possible had it not been for the vision and even more questioning mind of Charles Handy. None of this would have been possible had I not been prepared to 'sell' myself!

It was Charles whose welcome lecture to the class of 1973 told us to be proud of our achievements to date, to recognize the fact that gaining admission into the London Business School meant that we were part of a tiny elite, that we were 'Eagles' who would fly out of the school in two years' time and go on to achieve great things. He shared with us his vision for us and the school, his hopes for the coming two years, his desire for us to be as questioning and demanding of the faculty as they would be of us. It was a wonderfully uplifting and memorable experience and an experience every member of the class of '73 remembers to this day! On this point I think it is worth sharing an e-mail from one of my London Business School class mates:

All Eagles of '75

I keep getting Notices of the 2020 virtual Reunion - our 45th. So here's looking forward to our 50th when we can actually be together. I remember fondly all of Diana's and my 2 years amongst the brightest group of people I have ever spent time with - before or since.

In a very C-19 reality I wish everyone all the very best

Stay well

WALTER and DIANA

How amazing is this some 45 years after graduating with our MBAs!

So two years later was decision time, but this time about where to go after graduating with a Master's degree in business, (an MBA), and this time gaining the recognition and distinction of prospective employers. I had flirted with the idea of merchant banking (the term investment banking had not yet become part of the vernacular) or management consulting. I had undertaken a quasi-consulting project during one of the vacations and thoroughly enjoyed it. Also I felt consulting would continue to keep all my options open. I applied to a bank and a consulting firm. I decided to aim high and go for the best in respect of both options. I was hugely fortunate in being invited for an interview by both. I was even more fortunate in receiving offers from both. The consulting firm that invited me to join was McKinsey and Company Inc., already a firm with an immense reputation. And again, it was the courage and conviction of one man that facilitated my entry into such a prestigious firm at the ridiculously young age of 25, Brigadier Harry Langstaff. Yes, I had to be interviewed by many, yes I had to jump through numerous hoops, but had it not been for Harry's belief at the beginning of the process that I was a suitable candidate, none of the following would have been possible.

My career from then on continued in an unorthodox pattern. I left McKinsey in 1980, despite being on track for partnership, because I was hungry for real executive responsibility. I was dying to get my hands on the tiller, to have direct control over an organisation. In simple terms I wanted to do, rather than consult. I was fortunate to be invited by my last client to join them in an executive capacity - in fact, I was invited to join the Board of a company employing 12,000 people, with revenues of £500,000,000, a big number in 1980.

A few years later I had a brief taste of merchant banking because I was invited to do so, it seemed like the right thing to do at the time and would satisfy a leftover desire to explore this business. But I had to accept a backward step in status as directors and associate directors in a merchant bank had signing rights and never having worked in banking before they were, quite rightly, not about to give me signing rights. OK, so be it. Within six months I was promoted to associate director and within another six months to a fully blown executive director of the bank.

Wow! But hang on a moment... I was *one* executive director from a list of some 25 without any defined responsibilities. So I went and met with the CEO, Victor Blank (now Sir) and asked if I might have something for which I and I alone could have real responsibility. 'What do you have in mind?' he asked. This clearly was not part of the text for promotion to the Board. 'Well it seems to me that no one has responsibility for the bank's marketing and communications, would you allow me to take responsibility for this, and get the marketing and communications department to report to me? I will of course continue with my revenue work in corporate finance, but it would be great to have functional management over this part of the bank.' And so it came to be. And so I was allowed to drive change in what was a long established institution... drive a new approach to marketing the merchant bank and our range of services, a new approach to both internal and external communications, and the implementation of a new logo for the bank!

A head-hunter's call took me to become Managing Director of Valin Pollen, a rapidly growing corporate and financial communications business from PR to advertising, from design to corporate identity, from annual reports to corporate videos etc. I spent five years with Valin Pollen and loved every moment except the last couple of months. Here I really could put into practice many of the things that I believed in passionately... and just how important some of these were to the people I worked with only came to me a decade after I had left. Between 1985 and 1989 I was first

MD, then CEO and finally Chairman of this wonderful company called Valin Pollen Limited. Unfortunately the VPI Group went bust in 1991, but that's another story.

In 2001, ten years after its collapse, a reunion was held for all the people who could be contacted who had worked at Valin Pollen. Almost 100 turned up for what was a terrific evening at the Savoy Hotel, in London. This in itself, the fact that 10 years after the company's demise so many willingly agreed to put their hand in their pocket for a re-union, speaks volumes about the type of culture that had been created. During the course of the evening one of my ex-colleagues came up to me and said 'I've never really had a chance to thank you. You probably have no idea what an important impact you've had on my life, what a role model you provided.' 'How kind of you but I haven't got a clue what you're talking about' I replied. 'Well,' he said, 'we all knew that you were highly focused, worked incredibly hard, but we all also knew that come 5.30pm on a Friday evening there was no way anyone would be able to meet with you, book you into a meeting, or get anything into your diary irrespective of the subject matter. We all knew that on Friday evenings you wanted to be at home, on that one night, in time to eat with your family, and everyone really respected that. The fact that you put your family first, and stuck to it, was admired and I have learned from that and have endeavoured to put it into practice myself'. Wow, that brought tears to my eyes, probably one of the best things ever said to me!

It was extraordinarily rewarding to get that feedback!

After Valin Pollen I linked up with my brother and tried something truly entrepreneurial. A fantastic experience with lots of learning, much of which is contained in the pages of this book. The company we built, IDOM, was a success and was sold to Deloitte and Touche. After helping with the integration of our small entrepreneurial firm with the much larger, more bureau-cratic, Deloitte, I left with a strong desire to spend more time in London. During the IDOM years I once calculated that on average I made eight flights every week, and on average I was abroad Sunday evening through to Friday evening, every week over a four year period! I then agreed to become a partner in one of the world's largest and most international executive search firms, but became rapidly disillusioned with it, and especially its culture. This book's chapters contain much of the learning from this less positive experience too.

Following that experience I decided never to work for anyone else again. Over the past twenty+ years I have built-up a portfolio of non-executive roles with diverse ownership structures, family, PE, Hedge Fund, private founder, AiM listed... all can be categorised as SMEs... I have mainly been appointed to be non-executive chair, a role I thoroughly enjoy. There are very few things that are more satisfying in business than to be able to have an impact on the destiny of an organisation and the people within it. That is exactly what being non-executive chair facilitates. My learning has not stopped and much of what is contained in this book's chapters will have benefited from, or will have been influenced by, the past twenty+ years too.

The vast majority of the material for this book, sometimes knowingly, sometimes totally subconsciously, has come from the companies where I have worked during this past 49 years or so. As they say, you start life as a blank sheet of white paper, upon which experience writes. I feel that my blank sheet of paper has been extensively written on and it is time for me to pass some of this on and share it with a wider audience.

A simple theme has been a constant throughout my working life, and one that now permeates this book, which is to question, not to accept the status quo. It is therefore clear that to ask the questions what, how, when, where and why are all simple, but immensely powerful nevertheless!

I have also written an earlier version of this book called '*It's the People! What really drives great management and leadership.*' and '*The 2x2 Manager*' a book about the use of 2x2 matrices to support problem solving especially in SME businesses.

I live in Wimbledon, UK, with my wife, Alexandra, and have two adult children, a daughter in-law, a son-in-law, and four grandchildren, the absolute apples of my eyes!

SUMMARY OF *DO IT RIGHT: DO IT NOW!* CHAPTER BY CHAPTER

1. THE HUMAN CAPITAL EQUATION

Do It Right: Do It Now!: Ask the questions

Do It Right: Do It Now!: Keep asking the questions

Do It Right: Do It Now!: The only assets that have legs and can walk are people. Treat them fairly, with dignity and respect and the payback is immediate

Do It Right: Do It Now!: Treat ALL employees with respect, not just the executive team

Do It Right: Do It Now!: Talk with as many of your employees as possible, get them to talk to you, invite them to talk with you randomly and frequently

Do It Right: Do It Now!: Treat people as AAA assets day one, and always

Do It Right: Do It Now!

2. PASSIONATE ABOUT PASSION

Do It Right: Do It Now!: Help the next generation to do better in their pursuit of careers; give them options that were perhaps not available to you; facilitate them to think outside the box

Do It Right: Do It Now!: Give the simple advice to 'follow your dream' early – if not straight after school/college/ university then it may be too late

Do It Right: Do It Now!: Combining a real desire to do something with true ability has a better chance of success than just following what seems to be the right thing to do

Do It Right: Do It Now!: Passion, plus ability, plus determination, plus tenacity makes a powerful combination

Do It Right: Do It Now!: Passion is not a 'here today, gone tomorrow' thing; it can be with you throughout your life and grow in substance and intensity

Do It Right: Do It Now!: Passion is a key driver of entrepreneurial activity

Do It Right: Do It Now!: Economic growth and passion are closely linked

Do It Right: Do It Now!: Passion can to be released in the corporate world; passion should be released in the corporate world

Do It Right: Do It Now!: Be an inspirational leader by fuelling passion within your organisation

Do It Right: Do It Now!: Passion enhances creativity and adds value

Do it Right: Do it Now!

3. FINDING GREAT PEOPLE

Do it Right: Do it Now!: Consider the suitability of your personal network

Do it Right: Do it Now!: Know the available talent pool, the existing internal resources

Do it Right: Do it Now!: Respect the individual, in terms of courtesy, timeliness, honesty

Do it Right: Do it Now!: Always respond, irrespective how many there may be to respond to, or how poor the application may have been

Do it Right: Do it Now!!: Respond in a timely manner

Do it Right: Do it Now!: Always be on time; never keep candidates (or anyone else) waiting

Do it Right: Do it Now!: Learn to listen: we were born with two ears and one mouth and should use them in that proportion

Do it Right: Do it Now!: Move HR from process to value added

Do it Right: Do it Now!: Select external professional service providers based on need and demonstrable expertise

Do it Right: Do it Now!: If you use professional firms use them as professional advisers, not as body-shops

Do it Right: Do it Now!: Value independence in advisers

Do it Right: Do it Now!: Never forget that all applicants are also your customers, potential future competitors, regulators, tax inspectors, advisers etc.

Do it Right: Do it Now!

4. KEEPING TALENTED PEOPLE

Do it Right: Do it Now!: Treat all people right, right from the start

Do it Right: Do it Now!: Graduates/young people have a lot to give: harness their energy and enthusiasm

Do it Right: Do it Now!: Really care about everyone in your business, not superficially but in words and deeds

Do it Right: Do it Now!: Be honest

Do it Right: Do it Now!: Know the skills, the talents and the competencies of your people

Do it Right: Do it Now!: Invest in training and development

Do it Right: Do it Now!: Do not treat training and development as a discretionary expenditure

Do it Right: Do it Now!: Better to exceed expectations, so manage expectations with great care

Do it Right: Do it Now!: Keep the best, remove the worst

Do it Right: Do it Now!: Reward generously, but not too generously

Do it Right: Do it Now!: Surprise and delight, rather than short-change and disappoint

Do it Right: Do it Now!: Pre-empt, rather than wait to be pushed to action

Do it Right: Do it Now!: Pre-empt, rather than be reactive by which time it's too late

Do it Right: Do it Now!: Make your team want to stay, you

don't need to tie them down Do it *Do it Right: Do it Now!*: Complex contractual arrangements are good for the lawyers only, keep it relatively simple

Do it Right: Do it Now!: One size does not fit all

Do it Right: Do it Now!: Stretch, promote to stretch not to fill a hole

Do it Right: Do it Now!: Days of slavery are over

Do it Right: Do it Now!: No bullying of any sort; no micro-management

Do it Right: Do it Now!

5. THE FEEL GOOD INTERVIEW

Do it Right: Do it Now!: Always do your homework well in advance

Do it Right: Do it Now!: Don't ask candidates to 'run me through your CV'

Do it Right: Do it Now!: Know the purpose of the interview

Do it Right: Do it Now!: Know how to probe, ask probing questions, ask open questions

Do it Right: Do it Now!: Stay awake and alert

Do it Right: Do it Now!: Listen, listen actively

Do it Right: Do it Now!: Understand that the environment has an impact

Do it Right: Do it Now!: Understand how you come across as an interviewer

Do it Right: Do it Now!: Take time between multiple interviews

Do it Right: Do it Now!: Keep notes

Do it Right: Do it Now!: Set the scene; set the tone

Do it Right: Do it Now!: Maintain a high level of energy

Do it Right: Do it Now!: Be on time, never keep an interviewee waiting

Do it Right: Do it Now!: Take control, but don't dominate… be generous with 'airtime'

Do it Right: Do it Now!: Don't hog the conversation

Do it Right: Do it Now!: Always give airtime to the interviewee, especially at the end

Do it Right: Do it Now!: Silence is golden

Do it Right: Do it Now!

6. DAY ONE

Do it Right: Do it Now!: Has there been communication with the new employee about what time to arrive on day one, whom to ask for etc.

Do it Right: Do it Now!: Has there been internal communication to advise everyone about the new recruit (including the building's security), where he/she will be located, what he/she will be doing, who she/he will be reporting to and providing a mini bio to all within the organisation

Do it Right: Do it Now!: Has anyone been asked to mentor/buddy the new recruit for the first few days/weeks

Do it Right: Do it Now!: Has an induction programme been created suitable to the recruit's requirements

Do it Right: Do it Now!: Has a desk/office been set up, has an e-mail address been allocated, is there a computer ready and setup, has a mobile phone been allocated and set up, have business cards been printed (why wait until someone arrives before getting this sorted, there is usually ample time to get this done well in time to ensure that the new employee has her/his business cards ready for day one), is there a starter pack of required stationery/stuff, is there an internal telephone list and internal floor plan

Do it Right: Do it Now!: Who will be taking the new recruit to lunch days one, two, three, four and five

Do it Right: Do it Now!: Who will be the most senior person to welcome the new employee

Do it Right: Do it Now!: When will the chairman/senior partner/MD/CEO/divisional director, or whoever is the most senior executive, welcome the new recruit

Do it Right: Do it Now!: Is there time scheduled for a debrief with the new employee at the end of week 1 or week 2

Do it Right: Do it Now!: Has the new employee been guided about how to portray his appointment on LinkedIn

Do it Right: Do it Now!

7. INSPIRING FROM THE START

Do it Right: Do it Now!: Hire the best for your organization, but then recognize that you've hired talent and handle it accordingly

Do it Right: Do it Now!: Foster an open environment in which to ask is good, to question is better, to challenge is best

Do it Right: Do it Now!: Making mistakes is okay, it's part of the learning process

Do it Right: Do it Now!: Pressure is better than leisure, you'd be amazed how much the young can cope with

Do it Right: Do it Now!: Provide excellence and you'll get excellence back

Do it Right: Do it Now!: Manage expectations; not everything can be challenging all the time

Do it Right: Do it Now!: Foster contagious enthusiasm, a high yielding harvest

Do it Right: Do it Now!: Harness their energy, capture their spirit

Do it Right: Do it Now!: And positively discourage mediocrity

Do it Right: Do it Now!

8. THE POSITIVE EXIT

Do it Right: Do it Now!: Don't get mad, people come and they go

Do it Right: Do it Now!: The days of slavery are over

Do it Right: Do it Now!: Treat those exiting with the same degree of professionalism and courtesy as those joining

Do it Right: Do it Now!: Treatment of outgoing employees is visible to all and can impact on overall morale

Do it Right: Do it Now!: Exit interviews are valuable, can and do provide insights

Do it Right: Do it Now!: Your past employees can be valuable assets

Do it Right: Do it Now!: They can have a direct impact on revenues

Do it Right: Do it Now!: Don't turn them into liabilities, into enemies

Do it Right: Do it Now!: Turn ex-employees into assets, ambassadors

Do it Right: Do it Now!: Remember there are likely be more ex-employees than employees!

Do it Right: Do it Now!: Avoid litigation if at all possible; it sours the relationship, costs a lot of money

Do it Right: Do it Now!

9. PURSUIT OF Y

Do it Right: Do it Now!: question

Do it Right: Do it Now!: question everything

Do it Right: Do it Now!: question the status quo

Do it Right: Do it Now!: question the established wisdom

Do it Right: Do it Now!: nothing is ever set in tablets of stone forever!

Do it Right: Do it Now!: zero tolerance for corruption

Do it Right: Do it Now!: think profit, people, planet; think zero carbon; think ESG

Do it Right: Do it Now!

10. DO IT RIGHT: DO IT NOW!

Do it Right: Do it Now!: Always question

Why are things the way they are

Do it Right: Do it Now!: Challenge the status quo

Why should we spend more time analysing the past then preparing for the future

Do it Right: Do it Now!: Because the alternative is unacceptable

Why is the unacceptable wrong

Do it Right: Do it Now!

11. THE 3 'CS' – COMMUNICATE, COMMUNICATE, COMMUNICATE!

Do it Right: Do it Now!: Get out of the office, meet those at the sharp end, meet the customers

Do it Right: Do it Now!: Walk to other people's office rather than getting them to come to you

Do it Right: Do it Now!: Get a random group to meet with you over a sandwich lunch from time to time

Do it Right: Do it Now!: MBWA

Do it Right: Do it Now!: There is no substitution for direct contact, for direct feedback, for direct dialogue

Do it Right: Do it Now!: PUtFP

Do it Right: Do it Now!: Call to congratulate on a job well done

Do it Right: Do it Now!: Talk to your employees as you are walking around

Do it Right: Do it Now!: Meet with your employees, let them talk to you, listen to what they have to say - some of it could be 'gold-dust'

Do it Right: Do it Now!

12. POSITIVE 'NO'

Do it Right: Do it Now!: Everyone should learn when and how to use it

Do it Right: Do it Now!: It isn't difficult to use, the positive 'no'

Do it Right: Do it Now!: But it is immensely powerful, and could be of very real importance to you, your business, your environment, your life

Do it Right: Do it Now!: Speak up when things are wrong

Do it Right: Do it Now!: Use your position of independence as a non-executive to question, to probe and to say NO when appropriate

Do it Right: Do it Now!: To question waste, to drive for a net zero carbon emission environment

Do it Right: Do it Now!: Call out the abusers, the bullies

Do it Right: Do it Now!: + 'NO' is OK

Do it Right: Do it Now!

13. THE NO PAY GAIN

Do it Right: Do it Now!: Say thank you.

Do it Right: Do it Now!: You cannot thank anyone too often – thank you never devalues from over-use

Do it Right: Do it Now!: Remember the back-office staff

Do it Right: Do it Now!: Think - whom can I acknowledge today

Do it Right: Do it Now!: Be informed

Do it Right: Do it Now!: Know your people

Do it Right: Do it Now!: Keep formal reward structures as simple as possible

Do it Right: Do it Now!: Introduce random and informal rewards

Do it Right: Do it Now!: Celebrate success, a huge motivator for all

Do it Right: Do it Now!: Surprise by the little things, it needn't cost a fortune

Do it Right: Do it Now!: Be consistently spontaneous

Do it Right: Do it Now!: This is very much top down

Do it Right: Do it Now!: Do the unexpected, do it randomly, do it frequently

Do it Right: Do it Now!: Surprise and delight

Do it Right: Do it Now!: And keep it simple

Do it Right: Do it Now!

14. IT'S ALL ABOUT THE PEOPLE – MY CONCLUDING 'BITZ & PIECES!

LISTENING

Do it Right: Do it Now!: Never get distracted by phones/e-mails/other activities when in a meeting with other people

Do it Right: Do it Now!: Engage fully with those you are listening to

Do it Right: Do it Now!: Let the person you are listening to know that you are engaged by your body language

LEADING FROM THE FRONT

Do it Right: Do it Now!: Leaders need to have a well-timed moral compass

Do it Right: Do it Now!: Leadership means leading from the front, doing as you say, and saying as you do

Do it Right: Do it Now!: Especially when the going is tough, leaders should take the pain and be seen to be taking the pain.

BORED BOARD

Do it Right: Do it Now!: Ensure relevant board papers are circulated well in advance to be able to be properly studied

Do it Right: Do it Now!: Ensure all board members have a voice

Do it Right: Do it Now!: Keep to the point, be relevant and brief

Do it Right: Do it Now!: Get the right people around the board table and ensure good diversity of talent

BUILDING LOYALTY/EXCEEDING EXPECTATIONS

Do it Right: Do it Now!: Focus on what makes your people go the extra mile and implement accordingly

Do it Right: Do it Now!: Avoid the easy option of doing nothing

Do it Right: Do it Now!: But ensure authenticity

RESPECT

Do it Right: Do it Now!: Create a fair and respectful environment in which people of all ethnicity/gender/disability/sexuality can grow and develop based on their competence

Do it Right: Do it Now!: Respect your colleagues, be demanding but never ever bully anyone!

Do it Right: Do it Now!: If you say you are global, then let your board be global, too

COMMON SENSE

Do it Right: Do it Now!: Retain perspective, retain common sense

Do it Right: Do it Now!: Do unto others as you would like to them to do to you – in other words apply basic common sense to your actions/decisions

CREATING OPEN/RISK FREE CULTURE

Do it Right: Do it Now!: Try it, take steps to create a risk free environment, and see the benefits accrue

Do it Right: Do it Now!: Recognise that every single employee could have potential to contribute, create the right environment and some will!

Do it Right: Do it Now!: Be prepared for the odd exceptional contribution that can have a material impact; be prepared for some that may not, but remain supportive and enthusiastic

ALIGNING ASPIRATIONS WITH REALITY

Do it Right: Do it Now!: Only promise what you know you can deliver

Do it Right: Do it Now!: Remember reputations take long to establish but can be destroyed in a nano second

Do it Right: Do it Now!: People are essential to success… so always manage their expectations and always deliver accordingly

Do it Right: Do it Now!: Over delivery = happiness; under-delivery = misery

Do it Right: Do it Now!: Under promise and over deliver

PURSUIT OF THE BEST, NO TO MEDIOCRITY

Do it Right: Do it Now!: Reject mediocrity, go for the best

Do it Right: Do it Now!: Recruit the best, retain the best

Do it Right: Do it Now!: Aim for excellence in everything

TRAINING

Do it Right: Do it Now!: Training should be retained as a key requirement, irrespective of prevailing economic circumstances. It really is as simple as that

Do it Right: Do it Now!: Never forget the basics, they are forever important, selling skills, writing skills, interviewing skills, listening skills

Do it Right: Do it Now!: Remember if you can't sell you haven't got a business, no matter how brilliant you may be, for without selling there is no business

AGEISM

Do it Right: Do it Now!: Age is irrelevant. The only criteria should be competence and drive

Do it Right: Do it Now!: Deliberately reject any form of 'ism', any form of discrimination

Do it Right: Do it Now!: Beware of unconscious biases… they exist, they are there, and they can have a materially negative impact!

REVIEW AND FEEDBACK

Do it Right: Do it Now!: I really don't care what form it takes as long as it happens regularly, is taken seriously, is undertaken professionally, is honest and open, is based on actual rather than hearsay, is substantiated with examples and leads to action

Do it Right: Do it Now!: Never raise expectations and then fail to deliver

Do it Right: Do it Now!: It does not need to be sophisticated… it just needs to be honest and as simple as providing regular feedback with linked actions.

PROMOTING EARLY TO CREATE STRETCH

Do it Right: Do it Now!: Know your people

Do it Right: Do it Now!: Pick your stars and manage them forward, always a little bit ahead of their expectations

Do it Right: Do it Now!: Stretch, train and develop your stars

Do it Right: Do it Now!: Beware of nepotism, it's all about talent, competencies, drive and ability

FIRING

Do it Right: Do it Now!: Always remember that even in adversity it is not only possible, but advisable, to do things right

Do it Right: Do it Now!: If someone is wrong, make the call and exit the individual

Do it Right: Do it Now!: But when exiting, do it legally right; morally right; and be generous.

RETAINING REALITY

Do it Right: Do it Now!: Retain a sense of reality irrespective of the seniority of office reached

Do it Right: Do it Now!: Retain a sense of humility irrespective of the seniority of office reached

Do it Right: Do it Now!: Treat others as you would like others to treat you

INTERNAL COMMUNICATION

Do it Right: Do it Now!: It's good to talk. Talk openly, talk engagingly and listen!

Do it Right: Do it Now!: Treat your people as adults, share information with them

TRUST

Do it Right: Do it Now!